JEWISH LUCK

A True Story of
Friendship, Deception, and
Risky Business

by
Leslie Levine Adler and Meryll Levine Page

*Vera and Alisa saying their good-byes in St. Petersburg at
Pulkovo Airport, September 2011*

© 2013. Not for publication or photocopying.

Disclaimer
Jewish Luck is a non-fiction work based on actual events as recounted by our sources. Some scenes have been dramatized. For protection, the names of Vera and some of her family members, Russian associates, and businesses have been changed. The name of the American businessman whom she represented has also been changed. Names of several of Alisa's friends and acquaintances have been changed. The authors take responsibility for opinions and statements about the Soviet and Russian governments that are not attributed to our characters.

Jewish Luck
A True Story of Friendship, Deception, and Risky Business
Published by Salt Mine Books

Map of the Jewish Pale of Settlement from: Routledge Atlas of Jewish History, Sixth Edition. Gilbert, Sir Martin. Copyright 1995. Routledge, London. page 72. Reproduced by permission of Taylor & Francis Books UK.

Photographs provided by characters and authors.

Cover design by Cathy Spengler.

Book design by Patti Frazee.

ISBN: 978-0-9897356-5-0 (softcover)
      978-0-9897356-6-7 (ebook)

Library of Congress Control Number: 2013946376

Manufactured in the United States of America

JEWISH LUCK

A True Story of
Friendship, Deception, and
Risky Business

Dedicated to the memory of

Our dad—our favorite storyteller
George M. Levine ל״ז

and

Extraordinary friends
Natasha Garbuz Rechtman ל״ז
Lori Rosen ל״ז
Sandi Rosenberg Soffer ל״ז

Contents

Vera's Family Tree

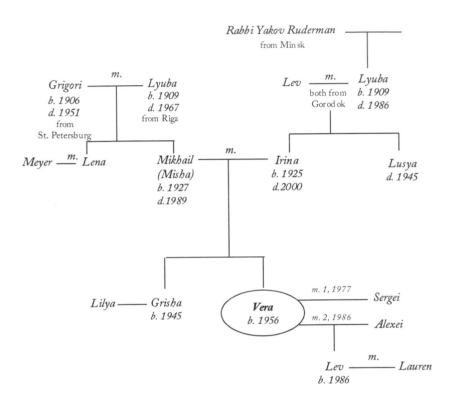

Rabbi Yakov Ruderman
from Minsk

Grigori — *m.* — Lyuba
b. 1906   b. 1909
d. 1951   d. 1967
from   from Riga
St. Petersburg

Lev — *m.* — Lyuba
both from   b. 1909
Gorodok   d. 1986

Meyer — *m.* — Lena

Mikhail — *m.* — Irina
(Misha)   b. 1925
b. 1927   d. 2000
d. 1989

Lusya
d. 1945

Lilya — Grisha
b. 1945

Vera
b. 1956

m. 1, 1977 — Sergei

m. 2, 1986 — Alexei

Lev — *m.* — Lauren
b. 1986

xii

Alla/Alisa's Family Tree

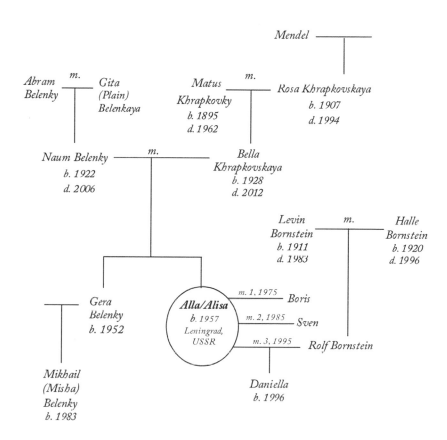

Mendel

Abram Belenky — *m.* — Gita (Plain) Belenkaya

Matus Khrapkovky
b. 1895
d. 1962
— *m.* —
Rosa Khrapkovskaya
b. 1907
d. 1994

Naum Belenky
b. 1922
d. 2006
— *m.* —
Bella Khrapkovskaya
b. 1928
d. 2012

Levin Bornstein
b. 1911
d. 1983
— *m.* —
Halle Bornstein
b. 1920
d. 1996

Gera Belenky
b. 1952

Alla/Alisa
b. 1957
Leningrad,
USSR

m. 1, 1975 Boris

m. 2, 1985 Sven

m. 3, 1995 Rolf Bornstein

Mikhail (Misha) Belenky
b. 1983

Daniella
b. 1996

"For seven decades of the twentieth century, the Soviet Union followed the path mapped out by Lenin. It became a military superpower feared by the rest of the world, and it built a mighty technological, industrial military and scientific economy. But it failed to make its people either happy or free." *

This is the story of two women who were determined to be both.

*Dimitri Antonovich Volkogonov, *Autopsy of an Empire: The Seven Leaders Who Built the Soviet Union* (New York: Free Press, 1998) p. xvii.

1

Vera and Alisa: Pirate Island

July 2010

To run away is not glorious but very healthy.
—Russian proverb

*O*y, *Sdrastvy.* ("hello!") The Russian exclamation rang through the Grand Cayman airport, sliced through the tinny sound of the small calypso band, and pierced the hot, humid air, fragrant with expensive colognes. The rolled "r's" and guttural sounds of Russian seemed out of place in this steamy airport where lilting Caribbean accents meshed with English and romance languages.

Nearly six thousand miles from their birthland and propelled light years beyond their Soviet girlhood dreams, the two women, now in their early fifties, dashed across the miniature concourse into each other's arms. With the distance between them closed, they sang out *nakonyetz* ("at last"). Now they felt complete. Moving apart but still holding hands, each eyed the other with affection and began the assessment ritual. *Is she healthy? Is she happy? Has she gained or lost weight? Is she the soft or the hard Vera? Is she the closed or open Alisa?* From the intensity of their greeting, eavesdroppers might assume this reunion followed years of separation. They would be wrong. Just a few months ago, they had met in Stockholm, Alisa's home, but every reunion was significant for these old friends.

One look at Vera, and Alisa knew—the soft Vera was back. It wasn't just the casual designer clothes, a far cry from the hard power style Vera favored in St. Petersburg. It was the natural and happy expression, no doubt in anticipation of her son's wedding and the arrival of her friends. Vera's black hair was hanging loose to her shoulders and framed her heart-shaped face. She was smiling the relaxed, sweet smile that Alisa had known since their youth. *Svezhaya* ("fresh") was the word that leapt to mind when Alisa stepped back.

Vera gazed at her friend Alisa and found the longed-for openness in her full gap-toothed smile. Even after the overnight flight from Tel Aviv, Alisa's lively curls and whimsical style disguised her fatigue. Alisa was animated, fully here, not "underground."

Alisa's luggage was laden with Israeli purchases from her recent family vacation, including a gift from Vera's Aunt Lena. Knowing Lena's Russian mafia connections, Alisa had sweated through the security lines in Israel. Alisa's husband and daughter were on their way home to Stockholm as she was arriving on this Caribbean island to join Vera for the wedding.

Vera sensed her friend's fatigue, linked her arm with Alisa's, and directed her out of the tropical heat to the cool luxury of the Lexus driven by Vera's husband, Alexei. Alexei was looking relaxed and handsome, perhaps less Soviet? Alisa's conclusion—*this place must suit him.* She thought happily—*there is no Russia in the air.*

Upornaya (so stubborn). Time and time again, Alisa pleaded with Vera to "leave that horrible country." Alisa had not been surprised that her pleas were tossed aside like worn-out shoes. She was just as stubborn as Vera, never backing down from an argument. In the Caymans, Vera would certainly be safe, but Alisa wondered whether she would feel a sense of belonging to this Caribbean island. As Aunt Lena confided to her in Israel, "Shouldn't a person want to wake up in the morning and care about the local news they are reading?"

How did Vera and Alexei choose this "pirate island"

renowned for tax shelters, jewelry stores, diving, and friendly stingrays? Alisa couldn't make sense of it. For her part, Vera couldn't understand her friend's obsession with Israel and Jewishness.

To Alisa's question of "Why the Caymans?" Vera would answer "Why not?" Israel is too small with too many Russians. Not to mention, she doesn't feel Jewish. The Caymans is a place where ethnic identity doesn't matter. Vera had no need to seek out a community of like-minded people. Besides, Alexei likes his "bubble," his solitary existence with only Vera invited inside.

First on the itinerary—drive Alisa straight to Vera and Alexei's home to rest. However, curiosity trumped fatigue. Wide-eyed as she approached the newly renovated one-story villa, Alisa blinked in a double take at the large plaque on the coral stucco, engraved with the word "VeraLex." *So, their merged business persona was now their identity.* As Alisa stepped into the house, she squinted at the unexpected light flooding the interior. Shining through the French doors were the dazzling blues of the pool, the sky, and the inlet, underscoring how far she and Vera were from the dark days of their Communist upbringing.

Light and airiness. Vera had created this environment with intention. In her new home in a new world, she purged the old Russian heaviness and drabness. Vera had selected ocean and sand colors with a burgundy accent. The walls, decorated with abstract art, announced the modern spirit of this home. A small yacht christened *VeraLex* was visible beyond the pool, anchored in the narrow waterway. Alisa appreciated the design but missed any hint of Vera's roots.

"Vera, it's beautiful, but I don't see anything from your history here." Alisa was used to speaking her mind.

"This is who I am now." The ever-evolving Vera was relieved to have the chance to leave behind unwanted baggage. Vera was not sentimental.

Who was she to judge? Alisa reminded herself that she had reinvented herself from the Alla that existed thirty-five years ago. She now lived in Stockholm's exclusive enclave of Bauhaus architecture. Like Vera, she wanted her home to proclaim her freedom, and her two-story penthouse commanded a view of the forests and sea beyond the white expanse of apartment buildings. Unlike Vera, she had not merged with her husband. The top floor, which reflected his modernist sensibilities, contrasted with the main floor, which Alisa had carefully curated, selecting memorabilia from Leningrad and Bauhaus-crafted furniture, culled over time.

Alisa's view from the balcony of her Stockholm apartment.

After dinner, Alisa unpacked the gift she had thoughtfully selected from a Jaffa craftsman.[1] She wondered how Vera and Alexei would receive the handmade mezuzah fashioned like a tree.[2] She had told her husband, Rolf, "If my best friend has decided to build a new home, she needs to grow some roots, like a tree."

Alisa ceremoniously handed the present to Vera. Hugging Alisa, Vera thanked her for the beautiful artifact and reminded her that she is not Jewish. Alisa rolled her eyes. Vera tossed her head back and forth and examined Alisa again. Those large glasses gave Alisa the bookish, serious look that reminded Vera of an older and wiser sister. Alisa had always served as Vera's moral beacon, flashing the lights at Vera to alert her whenever she was off course. But the glasses couldn't hide the mischievous teenager and young adult that Alisa had been, and Vera remembered her, too. It was not a one-way relationship. Vera had counseled Alisa plenty of times when she was in trouble even though Alisa may have deposited those old memories into a vault. Nevertheless, both women had navigated their lives successfully and were at a comfortable distance from their starting point in Soviet Russia.

While they were reminiscing, Alexei unobtrusively nailed the mezuzah to the doorpost. Vera and Alisa both stared in surprise and smiled at each other when Alexei showed them his work. Vera appreciated Alexei's gesture on behalf of Alisa, but it did not mean this was a Jewish home. Alisa had hoped to recite the blessing with Vera and Alexei as they affixed the mezuzah. Alisa's smile masked her disappointment. And so a conversation that began in Russia in September 1974 continues. Tomorrow, they would focus on the wedding plans for Lev and Lauren.

For Vera, Alisa's arrival ignited the elation that expanded as she gathered her friends together at her new home over the next day. Only a few people were coming from Russia, no business connections—only family friends and relatives. It would be good for Alexei to converse in Russian with others. It was not simple work for Vera to be his interpreter because his obscure and unpredictable ideas could not easily be translated. Her brother Grisha should be here, too, but his family had arranged her niece's marriage in St. Petersburg for the same weekend. Vera winced at the insult.

Although no members of her extended family would witness Lev's wedding, her Minneapolis friends would stand in as close relations. RD and Lars were ensconced at the hotel. Leslie and her family would arrive later today. Vera often replayed the key acts comprising the drama of her life. Due to a chance meeting with Leslie and Lars in Leningrad on an overcast day thirty-five years earlier, Vera met RD Zimmerman. RD led her to business success; her success led to threats from the Russian mafia; then, RD helped her with decisions that enabled her to maintain her sanity. She sent Lev to safety at a Minnesota boarding school, and eventually Vera and Alexei sought their own sanctuary in the Cayman Islands. That's the short version, of course. Jewish luck would not be Jewish luck if it were that simple.

Alisa's voice interrupted the reflection, "How can I help with logistics?"

"Oy." Vera ticked off the list of tasks: "Get the bride to the hairdresser, follow up with that foolish wedding planner who can't be trusted, check on the banquet room and the menus at the Ritz-Carlton."

Alisa nodded. Later, there would be time for her to talk to Vera about her own life. They had set aside the day following the wedding as their own. "Time to rest," Vera said as she put her arm around Alisa and led her into the deluxe guest quarters.

Vera directed the wedding photographer to capture
the moment that she brought Leslie and Alisa together.
Leslie's husband Harry photographed the trio as they posed.
From left to right: Vera, Leslie, and Alisa.

Notes

1. Jaffa is the name of an ancient port city south of Tel Aviv. Today it is famous for its artisans.

2. A mezuzah is a small parchment scroll, inscribed with Deuteronomy 6:4–9 and 11:13–21, enclosed in a decorative case. Cases are traditionally affixed to the entries and inner doors of Jewish homes. The blessing recited is short and simple—"Praised are You, O Lord our God who has commanded us to affix the mezuzah."

2

Leslie: Takeoff from
Michigan to Leningrad

June 12–18, 1976

*It doesn't matter where we're going as long as we're
on our way.*

—Grandma Rae Levine

At the age of twenty, I flitted carelessly through the world,
never fully appreciating the role that history and luck
played to give me wings. I was completing my junior year at
the University of Michigan, majoring in Russian Area Studies.
I had never worried about a quota blocking me from college
admission. Here in the United States, quotas limited my
parents' generation but not mine.[1] Nor had I devised a grand
plan for the future. I was simply following a passionate interest.

This passion latched itself onto a brochure that
advertised a study program at Leningrad State University for
the summer of 1976. Finally, I'd have an authentic reason to
speak Russian. To see the Soviet Union firsthand was still an
unusual experience for someone raised during the Cold War.

I wish I could say that I was politically savvy, that what most weighed on my mind were the recent Helsinki Accords,[2] which granted the Soviet Union recognition of its expanded borders in exchange for human rights guarantees. I wish I could say that I jumped at this trip in order to aid Soviet refuseniks, Soviet Jews who were denied the right to emigrate to Israel. I'd be lying. I simply chose to go out of a sense of personal adventure.

The dynamics of our family also served me well. We all have checklists in our lives. Mine consisted of the things I didn't have to worry about. I was the youngest. My sister Meryll had fulfilled the academic achievement role nicely. Breaking the gender barrier, she enrolled in the first coeducational class at Yale. So I didn't need to be brilliant or apply to an Ivy League school. Check. Furthermore, she rebelled against our family's somewhat assimilated Jewish practices by keeping kosher and observing Shabbat from the moment she stepped past our threshold bound for New Haven. I could check becoming an observant Jew off my list. My brother Chuck, studying at Kellogg School of Business, was headed off to fame and fortune. I could check "wealthy" off the list. Both of my siblings married by age twenty. Check. My role was to be unpredictable, spontaneous, and impractical, setting forth on new adventures fully financed by my parents, who were left scratching their heads, wondering how they could have acquiesced.

Months earlier, when I proposed this trip to the Soviet Union to my father, I imagined I could see wheels turning in Dad's head. Like Tevye from *A Fiddler on the Roof*, he was weighing both sides. On the one hand, how could he allow his daughter to travel to this communist country, the land where his parents were born and that he associated with brutality? On the other hand, how could he say "no" to his daughter if it would further her education? Most Americans at that time believed that the Russians were our enemies. "Know your enemy," I argued.

Dad's mother, Grandma Rae, was not so easily swayed. Seated in her kitchen, her office for serious discussions, she said, "Why would you want to go to the country we escaped from?"

"That's why," I tried to explain. "Because I have the freedom to come and go as a US citizen."

To my grandmother, such curiosity was a risk and a luxury. In short, it was nonsense.

"Better to stay with family. America is the best country in the world."

She waved her hand vigorously as if to wipe away the past in Russia.

"There's nothing to see."

A rare shadow crossed her face. I knew better than to say more. She signaled the end of this conversation by offering me poppy seed cookies.

As summer approached, it was time for final goodbyes in Ohio. I doubted my dad would get a good night's sleep while I was gone. I tried not to meet his gaze as his blue eyes fixed on me, as if committing my face to memory. I knew he was silently praying for my safe return. He wrapped his arms around me in the way he often did that always made me feel protected and loved. My mom was more optimistic about my chances for a safe return but was sure that given my absentmindedness, my belongings would be strewn about the world. She itemized a final checklist for me—passport, visa, cash, Traveler's cheques, aspirin, address book. She had already packed the suitcase and double-checked the supplies of pens, contact lens solution, feminine hygiene products, and soap.

Over the past months I had been too busy to mentally prepare myself for Russia. Fortunately, a three-day orientation program was set up in Paris precisely for this reason. Few Americans had personal knowledge of the Soviet Union. The group leaders enthusiastically assured us that if we learned the following lessons, we would have the best possible experience.

1. The Soviet state has told its citizens to be wary of foreigners from capitalist countries.

2. In a communist country, individuals such as ourselves, with American dollars, have access to goods that regular citizens cannot purchase such as cognac, sardines, and American cigarettes.

3. It is illegal to give, sell, or barter those products in the Soviet Union.

4. We are of enough interest that the KGB may send lackies to follow us.

5. Despite intimidation and possible arrest, some Soviet citizens will be interested in getting to know us because they are so hungry for an exchange of ideas or for access to Western goods, such as jeans.

6. It's worth trying to find these Soviet citizens because we'll have a more interesting experience if we do.

7. Be back by curfew because the bridges are raised at 1:00 a.m. to enable boats to pass, and there is no other route to the dormitory.

These were lessons I understood. Here are the rules, and here are the risks. You may want to break the rules but understand the possible danger and, if you do choose to break the rules, you could have quite an adventure. This was my way of life. However, this wasn't a game. The risks were far greater for Russians, who were obliged to report any Westerner who came to their house or whom they met privately. By socializing with Westerners, they risked their jobs, their places in university, or their membership in the Communist Party.

The midwestern group gathered. I had an opportunity to check out my fellow travelers and figure out who among them would become my friends. I edged over to eavesdrop on the conversation dominated by a handsome, blond-haired young man with a moustache, a tennis player's build, a raspy voice, and a deep, contagious laugh. He combined the looks of the popular guy, who could attract all the pretty girls, with a personality that was inviting, warm, self-deprecating, and inclusive. He quickly became the group's heart and soul. Although RD Zimmerman had grown up in privilege on Chicago's North Shore, summered at Lake Geneva, and attended boarding school, he possessed an old Russian soul. He had a deeper knowledge of Russia than the rest of us. RD was an aspiring writer, and Russia was his passion. Though we had all studied Russian history, it seemed as if only RD had experienced it personally. When visiting any landmark, he hypnotized us with his spellbinding narrations that seemed like recollections of a past life in tsarist Russia. Later all these images and "recollections" would form an opus of his historical novels: *The Kitchen Boy*, *The Romanov Bride*, and *Rasputin's Daughter*.[3]

Positioned a bit outside the center of the group was Lars Peterssen, a young man who looked every part of his Danish name. Six feet tall, his broad shoulders and strong neck were definite assets for his college swimming career. His small, rectangular, wire-rimmed glasses and the bushy, dark-blond moustache hiding his smile suggested shyness and modesty. It took me a day or two to approach Lars and begin a conversation with him. Lars, a physics major at Carleton College in Minnesota, began studying Russian in high school. Russia had fascinated him ever since. When I stood close to Lars, I could hear evidence of his dry wit muttered in one-liners under his breath. His humor was not for show, but to amuse himself. We attached ourselves to each other like an old married couple, constantly bickering but finding comfort and humor in our differences.

RD came from American aristocracy. His great-grandfather had been one of the richest men in the Midwest, an industrialist, a civic activist, and a philanthropist. A major street in downtown Chicago is named after him. Over the generations, the family was defeated by one enemy— alcoholism. RD understood quite a bit about nostalgia for a more glorious past.

Lars was a modest, bright young man, the descendant of many modest, bright people whose goals were to work hard, do well, and live simply. The Peterssens could have been residents of Garrison Keillor's Lake Wobegon except that they were firmly agnostic, not Lutheran. Lars came from a Danish-German heritage in which one did not aspire to be the "tallest poppy." His father earned a sufficient salary working for Sperry Rand on projects such as the landing equipment for the Boeing 747, the jetpacks for the spacewalk, and the Hubble Space telescope. Had the family lived in Russia, this type of work would have meant limitations on travel and heavy surveillance. It never dawned on him that although his father worked on sensitive projects that required security clearance, Lars was still permitted to travel to an "enemy country."

Lars was the least spoiled among us. His greatest need in Paris, aside from orientation, was to buy the cheapest pair of pants he could because his one pair of jeans had holes. Lars observed the Soviet Union through the lens of a scientist and future architect. He was attuned to the mechanisms, structures, and aesthetics in this society.

An evening of dancing and laughter with Lars and RD and other group members in our Leningrad dormitory.

My dad's parents arrived in the United States in 1905 and 1914 from the Jewish Pale of Settlement in Russia.[4] My dad and his brothers were first-generation Americans who served in the US military and attended college under the GI bill. Despite his hearing impairment, Dad earned an MBA from Harvard and became the president of a successful company. For my grandparents, this was proof that all things were possible in America. Dad loved nothing better than his daily walks through the pipe-fitting factory that originated in my great-uncle's garage. He greeted employees by name and asked about their families. "Business is about people," he would say.

I arrived on Russian soil, the first of my family to "return" and played out a fantasy of what my life might have been like if my grandparents had never left, that is, assuming our family had survived World War I, the Russian civil war, Stalin's purges, and World War II. Had I been born in the Soviet Union, I would have been limited and defined by my Jewish ethnicity, but now I was just an American student, not so different from RD and Lars, despite our disparate backgrounds.

We shared the same education and the same curiosity

about the question that three years of university study had failed to answer: "Why was the Soviet Union so peculiar?" During our trip as we realized how unresponsive the Soviet government was to the needs of its people, our daily question to each other became "What appalled you today about the Soviet Union?"

This question did not stem from naiveté. Russian was a third language for us. We all had knowledge of another culture or two. Russia was indeed a unique place. Winston Churchill recognized this when he spoke of Russia as "a riddle, wrapped in a mystery, inside an enigma."[5] We would soon find out that we were opening an infinite *matryushka*.[6]

Notes

1. During World War I, elite US colleges imposed quotas on Jewish admissions with the justification that Jews posed a social problem. Although there were no written guidelines, Jews were kept to approximately 10% of the student population at many prestigious colleges. Admissions officers accomplished this by asking for the mother's maiden name and a photo and then imposing geographical distribution. This continued through World War II as anti-Semitism in the United States increased (according to public opinion polls). Charles Silberman, *A Certain People: American Jews and their Lives Today* (New York: Summit Books, 1985), pp.52–57. Challenges to quotas began with the reports from President Truman's Commission on Higher Education from 1947–1949 but did not disappear in practice until the rise of the Civil Rights movement in the 1960s. Dan A. Oren, *Joining the Club: A History of Jews and Yale* (New Haven, CT: Yale University Press, 1985), pp.177–178.

2. The Helsinki Accords, signed in August 1975, were widely viewed as a major breakthrough in the Cold War.

3. These three historical novels were published under the pseudonym of Robert Alexander. RD wanted to move his surname to the beginning of the alphabet.

4. The Pale of Settlement was the area designated by Catherine the Great in the eighteenth century for Jewish permanent residency. It existed until the Russian Revolution, and at its height the Jewish population numbered five million. Within the Pale the tsarist governments imposed numerous restrictions and feigned ignorance when violence against Jews occurred.

5. Churchill broadcast this pronouncement on October 1, 1939, when the Soviet Union was not yet allied with Great Britain but had snatched the eastern half of Poland after Hitler's conquest of Poland in September. Despite their ideological differences, the Russians and Nazis had signed the Molotov-Ribbentrop Pact. Hitler calculated that a slice of Poland would keep the Russians out of the war until Germany had conquered western Europe.

Stalin saw an opportunity for expansion and a means to enlarge the buffer zone between Russia and Germany. To Westerners in 1939, the Nazi-Soviet cooperation was unexpected and inexplicable.

6.   *Matryushka* are popular Russian nesting dolls, originally from Japan.

3

Leslie: Landing

June 18, 1976

Ni shaga nazad.
No step back.

—Stalin

Russia was a place that did not operate on the principles of logic.

Lars and I sat together on the bus as we left the Leningrad airport for the forty-minute journey into the city. Nothing prepared us for the odd dystopia we saw outside our dirty window. We soon found ourselves on Moskovsky Prospekt, an empty eight-lane boulevard used for military parades, our bus, one of just a few vehicles. In tsarist times a narrower Moskovsky Prospekt led from St. Petersburg to Moscow. Now, it was lined with an odd mix of tsarist and Soviet monuments along the way.

Simply viewing the facade of Leningrad architecture would not reveal the soul of the city. The so-called Soviet style was imposing and overwhelming. Along both sides of Moskovsky Prospekt were the massive brown and gray blocks of Stalinist buildings, which dwarfed the people on the boulevard. "Monumental" is the favorite term of Soviet tour guides. We were told how for the first time, thanks to communism, ordinary workers were comfortably housed in these blocks of buildings in the 1930s near cultural centers, schools, and hospitals. As our bus moved closer to the city center, the Soviet-engineered buildings gave way to the Imperial style. The pastel facades of the once grand buildings of the 1800s were faded. Instead of housing noblemen, they now housed Grocery #6, Laundry #37, or School #53 on the street level, and, no doubt, communal apartments, on the levels above. With the cloud cover that is typical of Leningrad, the scenery resembled an inhabited moonscape.

Grocery Store #1, once an epicurean market that boasts chandeliers from tsarist days, displays pyramids of canned goods—possibly also a vestige of tsarist times.

Never had we considered that a world without advertising could be so bleak. The human figures we detected from our bus windows were dressed to match their surroundings. Clad in dark, shapeless overcoats meant for a colder season, their bodies were entirely enveloped. Ah, the outer shells of unpainted *matryushki*. They moved zombie-like through the streets without interacting, their faces devoid of expression. Everyone carried an umbrella and an *avoska* (mesh bag), just in case they found a line for oranges or toilet paper or another product in *defitsit*.[1] The only bright color the city had to offer were the pictures of the square-headed, bristly-haired Brezhnev and big red banners blasting the goals of the thirty-eighth Communist Congress.

Could this really be the city of Peter the Great? Could these same buildings be the beautiful Italianate architecture he had commissioned in the 1700s to create a city of imperial grandeur? The city, then called St. Petersburg, a city of canals and four hundred bridges was considered "The Venice of the North." Now the buildings looked dilapidated. Half of them had signs saying *na remont* (in repair), which, we learned, described a constant state, not a process. The *remont* consisted of leaving the facade up, with the building hiding an empty shell.

Our guide Olga interrupted our musings by telling us repeatedly, *Eto zdaniye silnoye razrusheno vo vremya voini* (this building or statue or memorial was terribly destroyed during the time of the Great Patriotic War). She would then tell us how Leningrad bravely survived the siege. The heroic tale of the citizens of Leningrad would be repeated to us time and time again. "Over six hundred thousand people died."[2] This city, besieged in September 1941, with supplies for no more than two months, held out against the Nazis until January 1944, when the Fascists finally retreated. This memory is burned not only into the mortar scars of Leningrad's monuments and buildings, but into the souls of all her survivors and their children.

The shrapnel damage from World War II scars many of the buildings and sculptures of Leningrad — a reminder of the Great Patriotic War. Behind is a building "in remont."

In contrast to the somber history, and despite the fact that sunlight was hidden under cloud cover, I caught my breath as we turned off Nevsky Prospekt and saw the brilliance of the golden cupolas of St. Isaac's Cathedral on the left and then the golden spire of the Admiralty directly in front of us. Of course, the navy, responsible for protecting Russia's westernmost harbor, was the backbone of Peter's Russia and deserved a prominent space. I felt a thrill as we passed the wide plaza to our right with the bluish-green buildings of the Winter Palace, accentuated with white and gold. We crossed a bridge onto Vasilevsky Island and traversed another over the Neva River to Petrogradskaya Storona. We were nearing the tall golden steeple of the Peter-Paul Cathedral within the fortress, the original part of the city. Our bus pulled up in front of a trapezoid-shaped, five-story building on Dobrolyubova Prospekt, Dormitory #6, our temporary home.

To our driver's shock, we thanked him and then climbed down and grabbed our luggage. We slowly filed past the *dezhurnaya*, the ever-present, bad-tempered, old woman, whose job would be to hold our keys and keep track of comings and goings. We smiled in greeting. She glared back. We would think of *dezhurnayas* as trolls. We climbed up the chipped stone stairs and noticed that the walls seemed not to have been painted since before the Great Patriotic War. Our barren dorm rooms had multiple cots, and our hall bathroom would provide us with hot water from 2:00–4:00 p.m.

The next day's walk to the university offered extraordinary views across the Neva River. Just as we turned the corner from our dorm, we passed an ironic piece of "Soviet marketing"—a celebration of the Communist Congress theme word "Quality" with the middle letter dangling in mid-air, looking like it desperately wanted to jump the fifteen feet to its demise.

*Dormitory #6, home for US students, once outfitted with
"bugs" and gruff "dezhurnayas," has recently been
converted to luxury condominiums.*

*The "Quality" sign—an example of Soviet propaganda coloring the
landscape. Notice the falling "c" in the second word which spells out
"quality," one of the catchphrases of the latest five year plan.*

Notes

1. In *defitsit:* This is the Russian descriptor for goods that were in short supply. Although Vera and Alisa speak fluent English, they still use this term when discussing a shortage of anything in Soviet times.

2. The death toll from the *blokada* was probably closer to 1.5 million (soldiers plus civilians). The Soviet Union routinely underreported the death toll and the grislier aspects of the siege. Most civilians died from the effects of malnutrition.

4

Leslie and Vera: A Chance Encounter

July 12–August 9,1976

Because I met you, I understood that I truly existed.
—Vera

Lars was always on the prowl for Russian art and took a fancy to icons, which he found in the oddest places. Icons scared me, which delighted him. On yet another overcast day, we stood on a corner, a block from Dormitory #6, about to embark on another senseless icon hunt when we started bickering about which bus to take. In back of us, on the opposite bank of the Neva River, stretched the majestic Winter Palace awaiting a ray of sun. In stark contrast—facing us—stood the imposing Soviet-era Yubilevnaya Sports Palace. Leningrad, a city of canals, was a tough place to navigate. Lars and I both studied the map, squabbling about which direction to take.

Out of nowhere, a little voice piped up in British English, asking in a musical tone, "May I help you?" The voice emerged from a friendly, heart-shaped face with inquisitive, laughing hazel eyes. She had slightly wavy, dark hair, fair skin, and looked familiar. There was no doubt from her plump figure, monochromatic clothes, and a little uncorrected gap between her teeth (not surgically repaired like mine) that she was Russian; yet, her polite manner, amused expression, and indifference to our jeans seemed unusual, to say the least.

Gracefully escorting us across the street, she made small talk that might be appropriate at tea with the British royal family. Fascinated by her Britishisms, we continued conversing as we retraced our steps past the dormitory to the correct bus stop. When it came time to separate, she introduced herself and made her apologies.

"I am Vera," she said in proper British English. "I studied English at a special school here in Leningrad. You are the first Americans with whom I am acquainted. I would love to see you again, but I am on my way to work at the Institute of Finance and Economics."

Suddenly her attention shifted to the necklace I was wearing. As if we were already intimate friends, she reached over and lifted the Star of David (Magen David) charm, saying, *Svoi chelovek* ("one of us").

Of course. Vera was Jewish. That accounted for the familiarity of her appearance to me. She looked like family. She hesitated, then wrote her number down. Now her English sounded more colloquial. "Here, call me later tonight, around eight?"

It was not an order. It was a question, and Lars and I nodded. Mission accomplished. We had befriended a real Russian citizen—this time, someone who wasn't simply "surfing" Nevsky Prospekt for American products to buy.

By the end of our first week, Lars, RD, and I had already found separate groups of people who sought us out for our music, clothes, and the knowledge we could provide about the outside world. Russians were in an opaque bubble. They couldn't see out. They were constantly barraged with the idea that they were part of a great Soviet society, which, one day, would lead the world on the glorious path of socialism. Our acquaintances, jaded by the propaganda and willing to risk arrest for access to Western ideas, scraped by or lived a double life. Vera was trying to do much better than merely scrape by and believed she could conquer the system.

Looking back, many of the most important decisions of

our lives evolve from mundane choices—to turn right or left, to approach a person or walk by, to sign on for a trip or forgo. Yet, the result of these simple choices can be life-changing. We call this luck, sometimes good and sometimes not.

Vera made a choice that afternoon to take a risk. She knew it was dangerous and illegal to be around Americans without contacting the KGB's First Department,[1] conveniently located in every institute and large workplace. Expulsion from an institute could be the price for fraternizing with a Westerner. In the Soviet Union, a permanent record was kept, where a black mark could severely limit educational and employment opportunities. Vera's daring to pursue this encounter was the first step on the journey that would transport her to the Cayman Islands years later.

I called Vera's home that evening from a public phone, and we arranged a meeting for the next evening. Through the Russian friends that I met the first full day in Leningrad, I had gained experience with the prerequisite etiquette. If you valued the friendship, you called at the designated time from a pay phone on the street. The person expecting your call would pick up the receiver directly, and conversations were kept short. It was taken for granted that our dorm rooms were bugged. Likewise, Russians assumed home and work phone lines were tapped.

At the appointed time, Vera stood waiting across the street from our dorm. We passed by the familiar scraggly park with its fenced-in playground. Here the *kvass* truck parked, and the ale made out of rye bread was poured out of a metal tank into glasses shared by the customers, old and young. After walking just a hundred yards or so, Vera turned into a courtyard. *So, Vera lived within three blocks of the dorm that housed American students. Why had she not met Americans before?*

She explained, "It isn't so simple. My father had a high position in the military, and it is risky for anyone to be seen with an American."

*The view from the courtyard where
a nosy neighbor on the third floor kept watch.*

We stood outside in Vera's courtyard for a briefing. With some embarrassment, she told us, "You will be meeting my grandmother tonight, Baba Lyuba. She was assigned to look after me while my parents are vacationing to make sure I do not get into trouble." Vera smiled. "Americans are not the kind of trouble she is worried about. Baba Lyuba is more concerned about my virtue, if you catch my meaning. She is excited and curious to meet you."

Since Lars and I had already visited several apartments, the darkness of the entry hall, the missing floor tiles, the paint peeling from the walls, and the musty odor did not faze us. As we entered, first through the metal door, and then the heavy wooden door of the apartment of Vera's family's, my eyes alighted on a spoiled Siamese cat sitting in the chair at the head of the table who did not rise to greet us.

"This is Roma. She is said to be the first Siamese cat in all of Russia or at least in Leningrad, given to us by a patient of Mama Irina's."

Baba Lyuba, with her elegant graying blond hair and the bone structure of an aged Princess Grace, dressed in a fashionable pantsuit, rose from her chair to extend her hands. She clasped my hands, then touched the Magen David charm around my neck and repeated Vera's words, *svoi chelovek*. She spoke Hebrew to me *Shalom aleikhem*. ("Welcome, how are you?")

We spoke in a mix of Hebrew, Yiddish, and Russian. I

had no idea why I brought a Jewish prayer book except that I knew they weren't available in Russia, and I offered my gift to her. She looked up at me with tears and said something to the effect of, "It's not enough that an American college student like you wears a Magen David, but you also have a *siddur*. Judaism must not be dead."

Vera silently observed the conversation, mouth agape.

It was only a matter of time before Baba Lyuba broached the subject of the *blokada*, the siege of Leningrad, bedrock of all Leningraders' memories. Through her conscientiousness and connections, Baba Lyuba had kept her diabetic daughter Lusya alive during the blockade. After the war, despite Lyuba's objections, a careless nurse injected too much insulin and Lusya died. Over the summer I heard this story so many times that it wearied me. Now that I have two insulin-dependent children in their twenties, I have chills recalling Lyuba's story. We embraced Lyuba that night and said our good-byes. She had met the official enemies—Americans—and we were family now.

As Vera walked us back to our dormitory, we debriefed. Vera announced she was absolutely stunned. She had no idea that her very modern grandmother was so sentimental about the Jewish religion. Hearing her grandmother speak Yiddish, refer to herself as a Jew, and receive a prayer book with gratitude was a complete shock. That night Vera witnessed the melting of the tough veneer of her grandmother who had grown up embracing Communist ideals. Thirty-five years later, Vera would learn from her brother that her grandfather attended synagogue weekly, and the couple often spoke Yiddish at home. That night, before we separated, we made plans for our next meeting.

Now began our dilemma. Both Lars and I had two sets of Russian friends who claimed our loyalty and wanted us to join them every night. To an American, nightly gatherings seemed too intense. Besides, why not just introduce everyone and bring them together? A bad idea. By nature, Russians do not trust each other. So Lars and I would divide our time, sensing Vera's jealousy and disapproval when we were with other friends.

During our next encounter, Vera told us Baba Lyuba had given us strong recommendations, and now her parents were eager to meet us as well. When we returned to her apartment, I knew this would be my Russian home. The impersonal gray of Leningrad's streets was sealed off. This was a refuge. I never noticed the darkness etched in Vera's memory of her apartment. Instead, from the evening we first met her parents, my memories of her home are suffused with the smells of blini and cabbage soup and the warmth of affection and conversation.

As Vera escorted us through the double doorway, we were greeted by a bear of a man. It shook our image of the Soviet officer to see her father dressed in military uniform, breaking into a broad smile of acceptance, stretching his arms out to embrace us like a long-lost uncle. Mama Irina was a bit more standoffish, perhaps because she was protective of her family or due to her responsibility as hostess. She was shuffling back and forth, bringing a remarkable supply of food for a Russian home. This meal represented hours of inventiveness. The table was laid, and the food was more luscious because of its scarcity. Russian black bread has never tasted as flavorful. Nor has an orange section been as juicy and delectable as when sharing one piece of fruit with several people. The blini, cabbage soup, and *pirozhki* tasted as wonderful as they smelled.

The family that was gathered around us at the table was complete except for Vera's brother. Whenever Grisha's name was mentioned, tension was palpable from the momentary hesitation and the tightening of Papa Misha's mouth. Mama Irina turned the conversation to Lars and me, inquiring about our parents. How surprised Irina was when she learned that my mother's *ank'et*[2] did not include work despite university graduation. Why did my maternal grandparents live in Florida far away from children and grandchildren? Why did Lars's grandmother live in the same city but not the same home? How young our grandparents looked to them as we shared photographs! Did we live with our parents? Where did we go to university?

Papa Misha was warming up to begin our education. In subsequent visits, he explained that he had recently lost his rank in the Communist Party because his sister had emigrated to Israel. While it was legal for a Jew to "reunite with family" in Israel, the remaining family in the Soviet Union was viewed with suspicion. More consequences might follow for Misha, including loss of his pension. With his position already compromised, he was willing to shed his Soviet persona and be himself.

The truth that I learned from Vera's family could not be found in a newspaper, history book, or on the street. I felt like their witness, their transmitter. This man, who spent his work life jamming the frequencies of Voice of America and the BBC, had absorbed all the information blocked to others. The first lesson began: "Nothing is as it appears to be." Throughout the summer he explained the true political and economic lessons I would need to know to understand the Soviet Union.

While Lars visited Vera from time to time that summer, Vera and I became inseparable. We found ourselves in each other. With family and then with her friends, Vera opened the iron door for me to people's heartfelt beliefs, usually strictly guarded. With this access I observed how Vera's sweet tone turned acerbic when describing the government. My knowledge of Russian was key to understanding the subtleties of conversation.

Bringing me along conferred status on Vera. I was introduced to the latest boyfriend candidate Ivar. After a quick assessment of me, he scanned for anyone walking close-by. Assured we were alone, Ivar decried the lack of creativity permitted in the Soviet Union. "We are robbed of our individuality from our early school years, left empty. If stifled when you're a child, what can you hope for?" Vera, referring to the ubiquitous Communist Party propaganda, pointedly added "Camps and nurseries shovel the same shit down our throats."

Ivar referred to the insulation of Soviet society. "When high school curricula are all identical, then there is no new knowledge to share with one another. The idea that it is illegal to talk to Westerners is even more bizarre in terms of limiting the universe of thought. I only hope that our children do not grow up with all this bullshit." Vera nodded rapidly continuing to look around for eavesdroppers.

Emigration was the one way to ensure freedom for their children, but it was generally only open to those "lucky" enough to be Jewish.[3] Israel was the ticket out. Many of their friends from ages fifteen to seventeen would have given anything to move to the West. They predicted that by thirty, the same people would be too afraid.

Being Jewish for Vera was fraught with ambivalence. Vera assumed that I would want to explore the Leningrad Grand Choral Synagogue. Arm in arm on a Saturday morning, we entered the grand door of this once-elegant cavernous building. We studied the faded interior, which echoed with the quiet prayer of about thirty elderly people that we counted from the sparsely occupied women's balcony. Above the voices, the *ḥazzan*[4] soulfully chanted words that few remembered how to read. As Vera curiously studied the architecture, I realized it was her first visit inside a synagogue. Just as the service concluded, she rushed me out, warning me that we were being watched.

Our next stop that day, on the other end of town, was Alexander Nevsky Lavra, the illustrious cemetery where beloved writers and musicians, such as Dostoevsky, Tchaikovsky, and Rimsky-Korsakov are buried. As Vera proudly conducted me on a tour, I noticed that she was far more connected to the glorious Russian cultural tradition than to the dying, Jewish religious community.

When we had a chance to talk alone, Vera and I did not limit ourselves to politics or history. We confided the details of our love lives to each other. They weren't so very different, and both of us approached them with an equal amount of angst and drama. Vera cautioned me strongly against falling too hard for my Russian boyfriend. He could just be looking for a ticket out of the country, she thought.

By the end of my time in Leningrad, melancholy shadowed me as I prepared to move out of the intensity of this life, where friendships and experiences had so much depth, through the invisible wall that would lead back to my life of freedom. I distributed my belongings to friends. I knew exactly what I wanted to give Vera.

Vera could have recognized me as *svoi chelovek* without the Star of David necklace. Later, I understood that it was my brazenness in displaying my Judaism on the outside of my clothing that amazed her. At the end of the summer, the Star of David graced Vera's neck, but was tucked carefully beneath her blouse. Vera embraced me tightly as we said goodbye and whispered through her tears, "Don't forget us."

Notes

1. *First Department* was the office of the KGB representative in each institute and workplace. Individuals were required to report any contact with citizens from Western countries.

2. An *ank'et* is an official résumé of a Soviet citizen and includes school and work history.

3. Soviet law stipulated that a family could emigrate to be reunited. Jews from outside the Soviet Union wrote invitations to their relatives or their putative relatives to enable Soviet Jews to leave legally. Israel has an open door immigration policy for Jews and helped facilitate the immigration process after Jews left the Soviet Union.

4. A *ḥazzan* (cantor) in a synagogue leads the chanting. By 1975, there were no longer seminaries or training available for Jewish clergy in the Soviet Union.

5

Leslie and Vera: Back in the USSR

Summer 1977

Za chem poidyosh, to i naidyosh.
What you look for, you will find.

—Russian proverb

Throughout my senior year at the University of Michigan, Lars, RD, and I kept in close contact. RD drove from Lansing to Ann Arbor for important occasions such as the premier of the *Star Wars* film. I had the honor of reading his first book, still unpublished, and witnessing his dream to be an author fulfilled over the next three decades to the nth degree—twenty-three books to date.

Before moving to Minneapolis after graduation, I kept my promise to Vera to return. Much had transpired in one year. I had left a fun-loving girlfriend and found a more serious and driven woman in her place. Was it due to her marriage? She had married an artist named Sergei, but her letters described the relationship with more resignation than passion. Vera's father had also aged over this year and was recovering from a serious heart attack. He was retired and on pension. Vera could see the change in her bigger-than-life father who had once been so purposeful and engaged. Now in ordinary street clothes, he paced the apartment as he brainstormed projects to which he could devote his energy. He apprenticed as a jeweler. He mastered this work but needed more activity to suit his extroverted nature. He was eventually offered the position of chief engineer of the dacha's (summer home) cooperative. Finally, he was in charge again and could do something useful for others.

I felt comfortable with Sergei and found him welcoming. Lanky, laid back, artistic, Sergei had jet black hair, dark, piercing eyes and a pale chiseled face. Despite towering over Vera with his six-foot-two frame, Vera led in this relationship and Sergei followed.

Vera had her worries. She was intent on finding work for Sergei that would exempt him from military service. This could be done *po blatu*, through connections, but involved a lot of details and logistics. Vera plotted out the daily goals and presented her plan to me. Sergei would talk to a contact of Vera's parents to secure a job as a lithographer. Perhaps, because of the importance of propaganda, this work would be considered essential and could replace military service. By 1977 even Papa Misha admitted there was no glory in military service. Vera's foresight prevented Sergei from the fate of so many of his peers two years later—deployment to Afghanistan.

Vera and I both might describe our friendship as wonderful, strange, and bittersweet. I could enter any university, any profession, and any workplace if I had the qualifications. I didn't have to rely on *blat*. I could travel freely between continents and choose my city of residence and my apartment. I could read anything I wanted and write scathing letters to the editor, argue politics, denounce the US president, all without fear of reprisals against me or my family. It was too much for Vera to imagine and added to the dissonance she already felt about her homeland. If not for the decisions of our grandparents, we said, "I could be you and you could be me."

As Vera watched her father's encounters with me that second summer and listened to his encouragement to delve into the deeper story underlying the communist system, she saw him regain some of his old vitality. He took joy in telling stories that would not be confined to the four walls of his home but would reach beyond the borders of the vast Soviet Union. I saw a direct line between father and daughter, with Vera taking up the mantle and moving even further to succeed within this crazy system.

Vera's home functioned like an information bureau. There were frequent requests for services to be arranged, from securing an abortion to obtaining a garage. Vera and Mama Irina were constantly responding to the needs of friends.

"Without friends," Vera said, "Sergei and I would be naked and hungry. This is how we survive. We all depend on our friends."

No wonder they were exhausted and needed to leave for the weekends. When we went to the dacha, I pretended to be Sergei's Estonian cousin. This deflected questions about my accent and hid my American nationality, which could put the family under suspicion.

After a trip packed like sardines on the *electrichka* (electric train), where each person was holding their *avoska* filled with delicacies for the weekend, we arrived at the station and then walked to the dacha. The green two-story wooden house was situated in a clearing near a lake. As soon as we arrived, a weight fell off everyone's shoulders. The mood became light and festive.

Family and guests shared stories, food, and vodka. Mama Irina begged me to eat more to the point where I burst into tears, pleading, "I can't." Then, there was the moment when Vera and I waded into the lake, and I said "Okay, let's swim." She replied forlornly, "I can't. I don't know how." Never did I think I would teach anyone else to swim, but that day I did, or at least—to float and dogpaddle.

The time came to leave Leningrad. I tearfully said my good-byes to Vera and her family. Vera had not released my arm the whole morning, patting and caressing my hand. Her expression, usually so lively and cheerful, was downcast. Sergei, who by this time related to me as a true cousin, warmly hugged me. I tightly embraced her parents, feeling their warmth for the last time. Even Vera's brother Grisha made a special effort to stop by his parents' apartment to say farewell. When Vera repeated the same words from the previous summer, "Don't forget us," I gave her my promise. I would never forget them, but I had no idea when I would return.

6

Meryll: Keeping the Iron Curtains Drawn

1953–1970

Vladimir Lenin, Joseph Stalin, Nikita Khrushchev, and Leonid Brezhnev are all traveling together in a railroad car. Unexpectedly, the train stops. Lenin suggests: "Perhaps, we should call a subbotnik (volunteer work day) so that workers and peasants can fix the problem." Stalin puts his head out of the window and shouts, "If the train does not start moving, the driver will be shot!" But the train doesn't start moving. Khrushchev then shouts, "Let's take the rails behind the train and use them to construct the tracks in the front." But it still doesn't move. Brezhnev then says, "Comrades, Comrades, let's draw the curtains, turn on the record player, and pretend we're moving!"

—Soviet joke

It's time for my boring afternoon nap in 1954. Tired of playing with dolls, I zoom across my double bed and reach for the heavy floral curtains, drawing them open and then closed, yelling, "The iron curtain is closed!" Somehow the Voice of America public service announcement implanted itself in my three-year-old brain. Although officially a child of the Cold War, I barely noticed the clash of the titans except for trips to my grandma Myrtle's basement, equipped for nuclear attacks; duck and cover exercises in school; and the laughter in response to antics like a Hebrew school classmate banging a desk with his shoe à la Khrushchev at the UN.

Little changed in my world after Eisenhower packed up and left the White House in 1961 and the Kennedy Democrats moved in, unlike in the Soviet Union where the great hope when one leader died and a new one assumed power was that life would improve. No matter who assumed leadership, for Jewish Russians like Vera and Alisa's parents, life remained a struggle.

Stalin's death in 1953 stunned the country. He had terrorized his people, and they dared not believe that it was over. Vera's brother is old enough to remember the tears in his classroom that morning before they were excused. Youngsters had been indoctrinated to view Stalin as their loving father. The millions of family members of those executed by him knew better. After much jockeying inside the Politburo,[1] Nikita Khrushchev emerged as the premier. He shocked the Communist Party and the rest of the world in 1956 when he denounced Stalin's crimes in a secret speech.[2] Russian Jews, especially, breathed a sigh of relief as the intense period of anti-Semitism culminating in the Doctors' Plot drew to a close.[3] From 1956 until 1961, along with the almost 170,000 other Jews in their city, Vera and Alisa's families experienced a liberalization of religious practice in Leningrad.

Khrushchev kept the Cold War front and center.[4] Soviet brainpower and industrial resources were invested in military hardware, the space race, and maintaining a *cordon sanitaire* in Eastern Europe,[5] with Soviet satellite countries arrayed to ward off encroaching capitalism. Education and culture were maidservants of the Cold War, serving first and foremost the interests of the State, which intended to cultivate scientists before historians and mathematicians ahead of writers. Culture and sports were considered exportable commodities to showcase Soviet preeminence. Although Stalin was gone, fear upheld the power structure. Stalin's dreaded secret police, the NKVD, was restructured and rebranded as the KGB with the dual role of monitoring external threats and internal threats within the Soviet Union, including a vigilant watch over their own citizens and foreign visitors.

When Khrushchev was ousted in 1964 after the Cuban missile crisis debacle, Leonid Brezhnev, his replacement, plodded along the same well-worn policy path trod by Khrushchev. He was less jolly looking, appearing more like a bushy-browed bear with indigestion. There was good reason for Brezhnev's distress. The Soviet Union was losing its prestige in the socialist world. China and Cuba challenged Soviet dominance.[6] In the European satellite countries, Russia was also losing its iron grip. This was most evident to the world in 1968 when Russian troops were sent to "restore law and order" in Prague. Brezhnev had to resolder the Iron Curtain. Internally, the Soviet Union's economic situation was dire. The country could not produce both "guns and butter." Food and consumer goods were sacrificed for nuclear armaments. Even in 1970, it was difficult to predict that the Soviet Union would ever alter its approach and begin a slow dance of détente.

Notes

1. Politburo: The Political Bureau of the Central Committee was the small executive committee of the Communist Party that wielded the real power in the Soviet Union.

2. In 1956 Nikita Khrushchev delivered his "secret speech" to a closed session of the Twentieth Party Congress. He denounced Stalin and his inner circle for crimes against the Soviet people. The speech was printed in the *New York Times* in its entirety (via Poland via *Mosad* via the CIA to the *New York Times* according to William Taubman) and slowly leaked to the Russian public. William Taubman, *Khrushchev: The Man and His Era* (New York: WW Norton, 2004), p. 285, 723n57. Today's historians estimate that from four to five million Russians were purged during the 1930s.

3. Doctors' Plot: From 1952–53 Stalin fabricated a conspiracy that Jewish doctors were attempting to poison him and other Communist leaders. The

familiar pattern established in the 1930s of accusations, arrests, show trials, sentencing, and anti-Semitic propaganda began anew. After Stalin died, the imprisoned doctors and other Jews who survived the mania were released.

4. Cold War: This term came into general use in 1947 and referred to the tension between the Soviet Union and the United States. It led to a high stakes nuclear arms race with each side assessing the strength of the other and attempting to forge ahead in the arms race. Although there was never an outright clash of arms between the two superpowers, there were proxy wars such as the Korean War and the Vietnam War when the United States and the Soviet Union allied with opposing sides. The tensest moment occurred during the 1962 Cuban missile crisis when it seemed the Cold War would turn hot.

5. *Cordon sanitaire* refers to buffer states. Since the time of Napoleon's invasion of Russia, the country feared its flat western plains would enable enemy forces to quickly reach the Russian agricultural heart and population centers. Following World War II and the devastating Nazi invasion, the Soviets determined to protect their country by creating a strip of friendly allies along its western border. For that reason, it was deemed essential by the Soviets that from Poland in the north to Yugoslavia in the south, each country was governed by a communist regime friendly to Moscow. The US and its allies interpreted the actions as Soviet aggression in Eastern Europe and assumed the Soviets would continue to press westward.

6. China was provoking firefights along the Chinese-Russian border, and Mao refused to be dominated by Khrushchev whom he disdained. Castro lost respect for the Russians after the missile crisis and began to deploy Cuban troops in conflicts like the Angolan fight for independence without clearance from the Soviets.

7

Vera and Alla: Long-Lost Sisters

August–September 1974

Skazhi kto tvoi druzya i ya skazhu kto ty.
"Tell me who your friends are, and I will tell you who you are."

—Russian proverb

From Vera's apartment on Zayachny Island to Alla's on Dekabristov Street in Leningrad, the same categorical imperative issued from their parents: "Get a university degree!" The Kremlin, however, erected a major roadblock to keep Jewish students out—a quota system.[1]

Both girls dreamed of their future careers. Vera envisioned herself as an interpreter, fusing her well-honed English language skills and her extroverted personality. Alla's love of animals drew her to biology. To realize these dreams, they would need to attend Leningrad State University. Despite the efforts of both parents to provide tutors and support, Leningrad State University remained outside their reach. As the time for university applications approached, the girls plotted their different strategies.

Through their network of friends, Alla's parents Naum and Bella heard rumors that admission for Jews was nearly impossible. Around the table, Alla's family made the decision that it was not worth taking the entrance exams for Leningrad State. Alla was ready to explode. Soviet reality kept attacking her dreams. It was she who needed to be in charge of her life, not the Soviet government. That conclusion fed her determination to escape this prison of a country. She would emigrate to Israel. Meanwhile, she had to decide where she could study. Her brother Gera had graduated from the Leningrad Institute of Finance and Economics. Alla had no desire to become an economist but reluctantly followed Gera's path to the Institute.

Meanwhile, across town, Papa Misha issued a similar warning to Vera that she was unlikely to gain admission to Leningrad State University. Even though Vera's mastery of science and math was topnotch, she would face an oral exam. It was during this oral exam that professors could arbitrarily choose questions designed to weed out "undesirables." Headstrong and highly prepared, Vera insisted on applying. Papa Misha was right. Vera had prided herself on her ability to spout propaganda, but she was thrown by the questions she was asked on arcane subjects. Of course, Vera knew she was going to be rejected, but she had to test the limits of the system. Still, it left her indignant.

Where to apply? The one institute that she knew accepted "Jews, disabled people, and little people," she later noted sarcastically. It seemed irrelevant that she had no interest in accounting or economics. She needed an education, and this school had an excellent reputation.

On registration day, Alla's trolley proceeded by some of Leningrad's most magnificent sights. She passed the golden-domed Kazanski Cathedral along Nevsky Prospekt, crossed the suspension bridge over the Griboyedov Canal, and paused to admire the beautiful wrought-iron railings crowned by two golden-winged griffons. Where once the griffons guarded the entrance to the treasury of the Russian tsars, they now welcomed students to the stately, yellow, neoclassical Institute of Finance and Economics. Alla checked her watch. Plenty of time before registration.

Thirty minutes after Alla's arrival, Vera rushed through

the Institute's wrought-iron gates. Vera had dressed as best she could, given the limited wardrobe choices of any Leningrad girl. Because of the extra time spent on makeup and hair and the unpredictability of the bus, she was running a little late. So what? As she approached the huge door of the Institute, she observed that it was in need of *remont* like every other building, but it still carried the grace and dignity of its European lineage.

This 2011 photo showing the majestic griffons that flank the Bankovsky Bridge leading to the Institute of Finance and Economics where Vera and Alisa first met.

She didn't notice the scenery she passed traveling to the Institute; however, once inside, no detail escaped her. Entering, her eyes were drawn to special areas where students were allowed to smoke. Pairs of students walked hand in hand undisturbed by faculty slapping them on their arms, saying *kak tebye ne stydna* ("you should be ashamed of yourself"). This was a grown-up place. As she headed down the hall to join the lines, she said to herself, *it smells like freedom.*

As Vera inhaled freedom, Alla tapped her foot in impatience while standing in line. Typical of all Soviet transactions, the registration process maximized time and personnel. There was a line to pick up forms and a line to hand in forms. Alla could feel her heart pounding as her eyes swept the room. As she waited, she wondered, *who would be a friend? Who was Jewish (svoi* chelovek*)? Who were the* stukachi *(informers)?* Finally, it was Alla's turn to confront the pile of "bloody registration forms."

Meanwhile, Vera edged herself forward, elbowing some timid people, to grab her forms. Papers in hand, she felt the usual irritation and impatience with Soviet bureaucracy. There were too many lines with too many questions, and the questions were just stupid. She scanned the crowd for familiar faces. Nobody she knew, but she noticed a sympathetic Jewish face near her.

Alla heard Vera before she saw her. Vera was loudly shuffling her papers as she approached, hovering a bit too close, peering over Alla's shoulder, and nudging her elbow. Irritated, Alla glanced up from her form to see a short, plump girl with a tell-tale Jewish face framed in shoulder-length, dark hair straining to read her name.

Vera glanced down at the pages in front of Alla. She shifted her gaze from the paper to the face and from the face to the paper, noting the classic Russian name "Ivanova, Elena Petrovna" on the paper that did not fit the face in front of her. Vera smiled at the serious, curly-haired girl in front of her, showing the same little gap between her front teeth that Alla had.

Vera sweetly asked with a little smirk, "Is this your form?"

Alla laughed, understanding the joke immediately. "No, I'm using this as an example. I'm Alla Naumovna Belenkaya."[2]

Ah, a Jewish name, just as Vera had assumed. Vera introduced herself. "The questions are stupid. I'll just take a look at your forms," Vera said.

They chatted a bit about their high schools and where they lived. They were surprised to find out they had both attended English-language schools. Conversation between strangers didn't usually proceed so easily or freely. They felt none of the wariness so typical of first meetings. Alla would remember Vera's candor and brio, and Vera would always recall Alla's laugh and openness. The girls exchanged phone numbers and recognized the possibility of friendship in each other.

When Vera returned home that day, it was not hard for

Mama Irina to read her daughter's mood. It was written in the velocity and angles of her body as she spun through the door. Vera flew in the apartment that afternoon, more ebullient than usual. A friend is a treasure. Vera knew that her mother had an unusually large collection of friends whom she had carefully cultivated throughout her life. Now it was Vera's turn. Her mother asked her the necessary questions. "Vera, what's her last name?"

"Belenkaya."

Irina blanched, caught her breath, and asked, "What is her father's first name?"

The sudden changes Vera saw on her mother's face did not bode well. *What did her mother know about this family? Had Vera misjudged Alla?* "Naum," Vera said meekly.

Irina's face regained color and deepened further to a bright red. She seemed to be emanating heat as she asked in a high-pitched voice, "Do you have the phone number?"

"Yes, yes. We exchanged phone numbers."

"Can I have it?" Irina said.

Strange, thought Vera.

By the time Vera handed her mother the number, their phone was ringing.

Just a few minutes earlier on Dekabristov Street, Bella and Naum returned home from their work at a dental clinic and sat down to dinner. Alla regaled them with her tale about meeting her new friend, pronouncing Vera's full name. Naum's face erupted in a smile while Bella suddenly stopped eating, noisily pushed back her chair, sat back, and crossed her arms. Alla's grandmother Rosa continued to silently serve the meal.

"Irina's daughter?" Naum said. He couldn't repress the growing smile. "I have to call. You understand, Bella?"

Bella retreated to wash the dishes, banging the pots mercilessly.

Irina answered the phone with the typical Russian phrase, "I hear you."

The male voice on the other line said warmly, "Irochka, is it really you? After all these years?"

Vera sat in wonder staring as Irina reverted to being a teenager in face and gesture. Vera listened to every word, mentally recording the data for further analysis. Once Irina put the phone down, she grasped her mother's hand; and, in a reversal of mother-daughter roles, asked the still-beaming Irina if there was anything she would like to share.

Irina took a deep breath, poured a cup of tea for herself and and one for Vera, then plopped down on the kitchen chair still flushed and smiling. She reminded her daughter that she and Misha had married in their late teens when she was already pregnant with Grisha. In fact, Misha had been so young, only seventeen, that they needed special permission. The Great Patriotic War had just ended. There was such confusion and devastation. Everyone was trying to resume a normal life, or in some cases, to begin a normal life since for many, their childhood had been usurped by war. Because of their wartime experiences, Misha and Irina felt they were mature enough for marriage even though they faced a challenging situation. Not only did they have a young son soon after marrying, but they had to live in two different cities while Misha attended the military academy and Irina was enrolled in dental school.

Irina knew that Vera idealized her father so she spoke with care. "Vera you are old enough to know now. Your father was young and handsome. Not only was he charming to me, but he was sharing his charms with other women."

Vera's attention was riveted. While her father was gallivanting around, her mother was studying and assisting her grandmother Baba Lyuba in caring for Vera's brother. Vera understood how her mother reached the point of saying to her father that she wanted a divorce. Vera felt as though her heart had stopped until she learned what came next.

In Irina's dental school classes, a distinguished young man always seated himself next to her. Each day this man approached Irina with a bit more conversation until he worked up the courage to ask her out. And the name of that man? Of course—Naum Belenky. According to Irina, Naum was intelligent like Vera's father but also very attentive and sincere. Vera felt chills rise when her mother then explained that over time, they fell deeply in love. She and Naum set their wedding date. Just about the time Irina was preparing to finalize the divorce from Misha, Naum made a startling confession. Although he loved Irina and was eager to have a child with her, he was troubled that he might not be able to treat Irina's son Grisha as his own. He suggested that Grisha remain with Baba Lyuba after they married.

Naum and Irina as they appeared in their
Dental School yearbook at graduation.

Irina cried, "How could I be with a man who wouldn't accept my son or who might treat him as second-class?"

Again, Vera was transfixed by her mother's devotion to Grisha but also confused. *Hadn't Baba Lyuba raised Grisha for his first six years? Could this story really be about her own parents, who always seemed in love?* Vera waited to hear the resolution.

Irina devised a simple algorithm. If she earned an "A" on her pharmacology exam without studying, then she would go to Misha's military college and convince him to give their marriage a second chance. If not, then Naum would be her future husband. Perhaps Irina knew what the outcome would be as she was already giving Naum the cold shoulder.

Fortune was good to Irina. Her oral examiner posed the one question that she could easily answer. Accepting this as a sign, Irina arrived in her better dress at Misha's military college without warning. Irina boldly approached her husband and said, "I almost married a man I thought I loved, but I want my son to have a real father."

"So we resolved that if your father could fool around less openly, then we could stay together. Your father readily agreed. From that time on, your father would announce to his mistresses 'You're wonderful, but I'll always love my Irochka.'"

This was the ending that Vera had awaited. She squeezed her mother's hand as Irina continued to smile warmly. But the story wasn't quite over. Irina recalled that Naum continued to beg her forgiveness, claiming he had reconsidered. He realized he could love Grisha as a son. Vera anticipated her mother's next words, "Too late." Irina continued to distance herself from the heartbroken man. That heartbroken man became the father of her new friend. Had it not been for today's encounter, she might never have known this dramatic chapter of her parents' life.

Vera and Alla did not meet again until classes began. Vera was privy to the uncensored, technicolor version of Irina and Naum's short-lived engagement. In contrast, Alla had only scraps of information garnered from the kitchen conversation and her own intuition to piece together the puzzle. Alla knew not to push. Some subjects were off limits in Alla's home. In September, Alla finally heard the entire story from Mama Irina, not her own parents. Later, Naum confirmed the essence of Irina's account. Bella maintained a stony silence, adding only a few details like the anguish of Naum's mother at the thought of her son marrying a divorcée with a child.

The young married couple Irina and Misha reconciled after Irina's rejection of Naum's proposal.

Vera and Alla reflected on this story throughout the years and never ceased to be amazed that this information came to light only because of their chance meeting. Vera reflects, "I sometimes tell Alla that if her dad had not been so honest, she would be me, and I would be her. We have a very special and deep relationship that is so rare. We almost lost it."

Alla says simply, "Vera felt like my long-lost sister."

After Irina spurned him, Naum found a life-long partner in Bella.

Notes

1. Thomas E. Sawyer, *The Jewish Minority in the Soviet Union* (Boulder, CO: Westview Press, 1979), pp. 165–166. In discussing the quota system implemented by the Soviets in 1970, Sawyer cites a rationale, which the Soviets termed "equivalent-balance." This meant that the number of an ethnic or national group in higher educational institutions should not exceed their percentage of the population of the Soviet Union. Jews were 1% of the population, therefore, no more than 1% of a university's student body should be Jewish.

2. In the Russian language, the middle name, "the patronymic," is the father's name. The endings of the patronymic and the family name are modified with a feminine ending for females. Naum Belenky's daughter Alla, would be formally named Alla Naumovna Belenkaya. A Russian would instantly discern that her dad's name was Naum and his last name was Belenky.

8

Alla: Growing Up Princess Alla

1960–1974

Skazki dlya detyei.
"Fairy tales are for children."

—Russian proverb

April 21, 1960

Winds whistled outside the naval barracks of Kaliningrad at the westernmost edge of the Soviet empire, isolated from the mainland of the Soviet Union. For little Alla, living here meant daily adventures outdoors and a constant stream of engaging pets like hedgehogs for her amusement. Her dentist father served as the base physician. Her mother, like the pioneer housewives of the American West, fished for their dinners, baked her own bread, and contended with the dust and cold of this ruggedly beautiful outpost.

In their drafty officer's hut on the night of April 21, 1960, Bella and Naum tucked three-year-old Alla into bed next to her older brother Gera. Neither child had noticed the parents' agitation when an official letter from the military arrived on the ferry that morning. The letter announced their abrupt departure from Kaliningrad.[1] It was an ironclad rule in Alla's family never to talk about unpleasantness in front of the children.

In September 2011 with our encouragement, Alla opened her mother's cache of official Soviet documents. Withdrawing the fifty-one-year-old letter from the box, Alla scanned the

Despite being a hero of Leningrad during the Great Patriotic War, Naum was still summarily dismissed from the army during an economic crisis.

official order, removed her glasses, and put her hand to her forehead shaking it back and forth. She could imagine the wound to Naum's pride. Had Naum been able to complete seven more months of army service, he would have received his military pension. That was precisely the point—the Soviet Union needed to cut costs, and military pensions were targeted. No doubt, her father's Jewish identity prioritized his termination. Alla gazes at her mother, now disabled by a stroke, and imagines her mother comforting her father fifty-one years ago but secretly relieved that they could return to the center of culture and to the arms of their family in Leningrad, 500 miles away.

August 1960–1965

Three-year-old Alla eagerly grasped her parents' hands as they returned to the mythical city, the city of "ahhs." "Ahh, when we return to Leningrad," her mother would sigh to her father. "Ahh, to be with family again!" And now they were arriving. After more than two days at sea, Alla would walk confidently again without pitching side to side with the heaving of the boat on the Baltic Sea.

Alla stared at the maze of colored buildings and winding

canals that was Leningrad. It was a magical world in Alla's eyes, far from the drab, dank naval base. The regal facades of the old imperial buildings were a Potemkin village of sorts.[2] Within the gray, coffin-shaped building on Marata Street that she would call home were communal apartments, chopped and diced spaces with one room for a family of four. Each family had a key to illuminate the dim bulb when going down the long hall to the smelly, shared toilet. Among the ten families, no one could agree how to share the cost of electricity. Community spirit was absent in the shared kitchen as well, where tempers could flare over a teabag. Alla missed the menagerie of animals that were allowed to roam freely around their Kaliningrad quarters. Alla couldn't verbalize the calculation, but the move had cost freedom and privacy.

Alla discovered the communal apartment was the "ech," not the lovely "ahhh" of Leningrad. She was introduced to another institutional "ech"—communal kindergarten. To Maria Montessori and Mr. Rogers, it would have seemed like toddler dystopia. According to the official kindergarten curriculum: Asking why—*forbidden*! Creativity—*bourgeois*! Individuality—*counter-revolutionary*! All this expressed in the army-like atmosphere of daily life in kindergarten. Cots were fastidiously lined up for the requisite nap hour. The *vospitatel* (teacher charged with enforcement of social conformity) patrolled the symmetrical rows. Everyone must sleep or there would be disciplinary measures. Of course, from the Soviet viewpoint, kindergarten indulged the little ones. From first grade onward, school was considered preparation for the serious business of life. No more coddling after kindergarten.

The *Manual for Instruction in Kindergarten* approved by the Ministry of Education, stipulated not just the overall goals but also the curriculum and proper methods of instruction. Art, for example, was considered part of political education. For one period each day of the month save one, all children drew exactly the same picture, for example, a child drinking milk. For one period per month (ten minutes), children were permitted "creative drawing."[3]

Little Alla was not a good toddler-soldier. To the teachers, she was raw material that needed to be molded into

Soviet citizenhood. But her imagination could not be squeezed into any pre-formed mold.

"My aunt is the Queen of England. Look what she sent!" Alla proudly announced to her fellow kindergarten internees as she showed off her beautiful new dresses. Even at age five, Alla prided herself on her appreciation of style and quality. Alla's fine, Western clothes set her apart from her classmates with their look-alike drab dresses. Alla's imagination had spun out of control with delight. Not Queen Elizabeth, but Uncle Aaron from South Africa was sending parcels. Alla was forbidden by her parents to talk about her relatives from South Africa. Connections to foreigners was considered anti-Soviet activity.

Her fellow students doubted her story and pelted her with their unkindness. "Alisa in Wonderland!"[4] they taunted. Alla feigned nonchalance and kept her head up and posture regal as befitted a relative of the British monarch.

The director summoned Bella and Naum to their daughter's kindergarten. "Your child is spreading decadent lies! It must stop!"

Even as Bella and Naum warned Alla about her boastfulness, Naum felt a secret pride that his daughter was different. Alla packed up her imaginary world and hauled it into the private sphere of home. The princess didn't disappear; she simply retreated temporarily. Vera would later refer to Alla's tactical retreats as "going underground."

Alla's boldness and imagination were a point of pride for Naum, but they were also dangerous. He needed a safer haven than the communal apartment. Furthermore, Naum was not going to allow his family to live in squalor and petty bickering with the thrum of the metro and the stink of diesel adding to the oppressive atmosphere. Within a year he brokered a deal by offering his communal flat along with Bella's parents' flat in exchange for a three-room apartment on Dekabristov Street. The communal experiment was over, and Leningrad once again became a city of wonder for Alla.

Unknown to Alla, Dekabristov Street had been the heart of the Jewish community before the Revolution. What a vibrant community those 20,000 Jews had built. The ghosts of Jewish life surrounded the apartment house at #54. In addition to the Grand Choral Synagogue, which bore witness to the past, were the buildings that could only whisper of their Jewish connections before the Revolution.

Alla's apartment building at 54 Dekabristov was designed by the Jewish architect M.K. Dubinsky in 1911.

Alla arrived on Dekabristov Street with Bella, Naum, Gera, her grandmother Rosa, grandfather Matus, and great-grandmother Tzipa. Naum opened the imposing wooden door to #51. Alla skipped into the building. They stood in a large entry hall with a fireplace to the left, a wide staircase to the right, and a lift straight ahead. Alla peered around the three generations of women and her gaze traveled upwards. "Ahhh!" escaped from Alla's soul as she stood transfixed. They climbed to the third floor, apartment #16, and Naum unlocked the massive door. Alla breathed another "ahhhh" as she made her way through the vestibule to the main living area. The plaster swans sailing across the ceiling captivated her. Each time she entered her new home, she felt their protective wings. Later, after water spots appeared on the ceiling of Alla's apartment due to seepage from the upstairs neighbor's toilet, her father painted the swans black with red beaks to enchant Alla and camouflage the encroaching decay in the once elegant building.

Forty-eight years later when we accompanied Alla back to her childhood home, we discovered an entry hall barely big enough to fit four adults, with only the outline of the original fireplace visible in the hallway. The swans were still frozen in flight above the living room although now they were bleached white.

To her kindergarten classmates, Alla boasted, "Our apartment is tip top!" It was hard to believe she could stroll through the whole apartment freely without the watchfulness of her communal apartment neighbors. All of Alla's classmates lived in one-room communal flats as she had. No one else could claim they had their very own apartment. Plus there were swans. She couldn't help but feel proud and overjoyed to share her good fortune with friends. Again, Bella and Naum had to remind Alla to keep her boastfulness at home, *doma*.

From the time Alla was four, her parents worked from morning until late evening. By day, both served their time in a government dental clinic, Naum as a dentist and Bella as a dental technician. Evenings, they converted their new apartment into a private dental clinic where they treated private patients. Employing his gifted hands, Naum fashioned a portable dental drill as he had in Kaliningrad using an armchair in the living room as the dental chair. Supper ended, then Bella and Naum quickly "redecorated" the living area, and Gera and Alla were banished from the space when patients arrived. The whir of the dental drill, paired with the ticking and tolling of the Prometheus clock were everyday sounds for Alla.

To operate the *levaya robota* clinic,[5] Naum and Bella needed more than Naum's inventive portable drill. They needed security. Their activities were illegal, and they could have been jailed for their capitalist initiative. Naum's enterprising and innovative spirit threatened the regime, and Jews, especially, had been imprisoned for lesser reasons. So, Naum and Bella made sure their patients were trustworthy and that word of their private enterprise would never leave the apartment. The patients were grateful for the excellent care. In addition to the payment, they demonstrated their thanks with favors when they could. The ability to trade favors and ask for help was the real key to success in the Soviet Union.

Until his retirement Naum worked as a dentist in a government clinic by day as seen in this 1977 photo and at home in the evenings.

With her parents working by day for the government and by night for the family, Alla's grandmother Rosa became the center of her universe. Although her grandmother Rosa was relatively young, beautiful, and well educated, she had retreated into the life of the devoted *babushka*. Alla came home from kindergarten and primary school to her warm hugs. Most of the day Rosa foraged for basic necessities in line after line. For Alla, this was normal life and better than the lives of many of her classmates.

Gera remembers his sister as "terrible and decisive." He vividly recalls the summer he was ten and Alla was five. Their parents arranged a modest vacation in Lithuania where they stayed in a primitive hut near a lodge. Guests could bring their own provisions to supplement their fare.

Naum had planned well and brought along a live chicken. It would lay eggs and then become soup. Unaware of the ultimate fate of the chicken, Alla befriended her, following her around the premises and chatting with her. She became a cherished pet. But the chicken had not laid an egg in a month. Everyone but Alla knew it was time for the soup pot to be filled with water and the root vegetables to be chopped. Once the water was boiling, the freshly slaughtered chicken would be added to make a rich soup.

Naum softly approached Alla and explained, "Allochka,[6] the hen is no longer laying. It's time for her to become dinner."

"Nyet! Nyet! Nyet!" shrieked Alla grabbing her beloved

chicken and racing to the straw. She put the hen on her bed of straw, stood back, pointed her finger and commanded, "Lay eggs!"

Gera, Bella, and Naum laughed at Alla's antics. Naum even snapped a photo. But, to the amazement of the entire family, the hen obeyed and laid an egg. The hen was saved. No one had any explanation for the entire incident except to ascribe it to Alla's determination.

Alla's "terribleness" was evident even in her play with Gera. Resting majestically on a shelf at home just within Alla's grasp was a gilded chafing dish. Bella didn't serve formal dinners with caviar blinis arrayed in the Imperial serving dish. So why was it in the apartment? An underground market flourished throughout the communist regime. A Russian might have salvaged an icon, a relic from a Romanov palace, or a family keepsake from the onslaught of expropriation of private property.

For Alla and Gera the chafing dish, rescued by their paternal grandfather was a superb plaything. Alla discovered that if she removed the stand with its precious metals and turned it upside down, it became a magnificent crown—fit for a princess like her. The only complication was Gera also saw it as a magnificent crown—for a prince like him. They tussled, they argued. Usually, Alla ended up victorious prancing around the apartment with the crown.

One afternoon when Naum was home, both Gera and Alla headed to snatch the crown and rule their realm. Alla was quicker and soon had the crown perfectly situated atop her curls.

Gera balled up his fists and threatened, "Alla, I'm going to punch you and . . ."

Thwack. Alla's tinier fist struck Gera in the chest while he was in mid-threat.

Alla raced away knowing she could always outrun her older brother. Before they collapsed from the chase, Naum intervened.

"Gera, you're the boy. You're five years older than Alla. Don't hit your sister. Don't even threaten to hit your sister."

Alla smiled to herself, knowing that in her father's eyes, she was a princess with or without a casserole crown.

The treasure trove of parcels from Uncle Aaron suddenly stopped while Alla was in grade school because the Soviet regime once again tightened restrictions. Alla's childhood lost its fairy-tale luster. But, like many children of Leningrad, she took great pride in the intellectual heritage of Leningrad, its culture, and the architectural beauty that distinguished her streets and offered relief from the utilitarian Soviet rectilinear gray box. Near her apartment on Dekabrisktov Street, criss-crossed by canals, were the towering Cathedral of St. Isaac, the Kirov Theatre of Opera and Ballet,[7] and the aristocratic Yusupov Palace. Alla's imagination could take wing walking anywhere in her neighborhood.

Gera gazes at his little sister Alla as she poses for her dad's camera.

Notes

1. Taubman, *Khrushchev: The Man and His Era*, p. 448. Two hundred and fifty thousand officers were dismissed following Khrushchev's trip to the United States and his anticipation of a limited test-ban treaty. The cuts were approved by the Supreme Soviet in mid-January, 1960.

2. According to a historical myth, the Russian minister Potemkin had false village fronts erected in the Crimea to impress Empress Catherine in 1787. A Potemkin village has come to mean a false front or something lacking real substance.

3. Susan Jacoby, *Inside Soviet Schools* (New York: Hill and Wang, 1974), pp.62–67. In her work Jacoby details the Soviet curriculum and ideology for *detsky sad* or kindergarten during Alla and Vera's childhood years.

4. Alisa is Russian for Alice. Russian children were familiar with the tale of "Alice in Wonderland."

5. *Levaya robota* is literally, work on the left, or, in the case of Alla's parents, moonlighting. This is, of course, an illegal activity in the Soviet Union.

6. Allochka is the diminutive form of Alla.

7. In 1988 the Kirov reverted to the name Mariinsky, the name it bore before 1937.

9

Alla: Living the Soviet Myth

1964–1971

Nyet huda bez dobra.
"There is no evil without good."

—Russian proverb

Even a small child came to understand the economic reality of the Soviet Union. Few goods or services were available. Grocery stores routinely lacked basic food commodities and rarely stocked meat or fruit. Even toilet paper was an uncommon sight on a store shelf. When it became available, a line formed immediately, and Russians pushed and shoved to buy it, carrying it home on a rope, strung like a precious pearl necklace. The Soviet Union publicly boasted about the number of doctors, but medical care was primitive due to lack of medicines and supplies. The artificial shortages were created by a centrally planned economy that focused on military production and limited consumer goods for families. Soviet teens, like adolescents everywhere, wanted to buy clothes, radios, music. The magic currency was party connections or *protektsi'a.*

In 1964, the world of seven-year-old Alla revolved around family and school much as it did for children her age in the United States. American children gradually learn not to repeat all they hear at home. Russian children had to learn that lesson, or the consequences could be their parents' imprisonment. Caution in the public domain (*na ulitze*) was imperative for Alla because her family was already suspect, having never joined the Communist Party. Only in the private sphere (*doma*) could Alla relax her guard.

By 1969 Alla could not speak outside the home about the family's central concern—Gera's impending induction into the army. Naum knew that his soulful, long-haired, Jewish, hippie son would be hammered by anti-Semitism in the army.[1] If he finished basic training, he could be deployed to any number of hot spots. Brezhnev had pushed Soviet troops like

chess pieces across the globe—to suppress the 1968 uprising in Prague, to bolster Ho Chi Minh's forces in southeast Asia, to protect the border from the Chinese, to support Marxist uprisings across the African continent. As in the United States in 1969, it took connections to avoid the draft. With no conscientious objector status in the Soviet Union, only a medical waiver could exempt Gera. Naum had to tap his best army and medical contacts. Fortunately, Naum and Bella had a lot of capital in

Young Pioneer scarf neatly tucked under her school uniform, eleven-year-old Alla is determined to find a way to escape assimilation into the Communist mindset and Young Pioneer camp.

the metaphorical Bank of *Blat* (connections). Many important people had very sound teeth and gums thanks to Naum and Bella. That was worth more than rubles. Before his eighteenth birthday Gera had his medical exemption, and his little sister had learned a powerful lesson about problem solving. There is always a way.

Although Gera avoided army service, Alla could not escape the Young Pioneers.[2] There was no chance of admission to a university or a technical institute without a good record in the Young Pioneers, so she dutifully attended meetings during the school year. But Alla chafed at spending any of her summer vacation at one of the 40,000 Young Pioneer camps. As a twelve-year old camper, she hatched a plan to run away before realizing that she had no money and no way home. Alla the individualist claimed Young Pioneer camp was a community of "brainwashed people singing communist songs." Pretending to be a good pioneer pushed her even farther away from the Communist Party line. The more the State pushed its propaganda, the more Alla seethed. From age thirteen on, her family's newly acquired dacha[3]—the small, blue–tinged, wooden country house with its neatly trimmed white windows and intricate wood carvings—was her escape from the "dreaded propaganda camp."

Alla's family's dacha in Skachki provided an escape from the city as well as an opportunity to grow and preserve fruits and vegetables for the long Russian winter.

Alla's dog also enjoyed the freedom of the dacha.
Alla fervently hoped to become a veterinarian.

For Bella and Naum, a summer dacha in rural Skachki meant fresh air, an apple orchard, and the possibility of growing vegetables, berries, and flowers. Most importantly, for Bella and Naum the countryside provided a place to relax from the pressures and dangers of Leningrad and a much needed respite from non-stop dentistry.

There was also work to be done at the dacha. Naum and Bella brought the urgency of survival to Skachki. Thirty-three apple trees required pruning and tending. Apples were picked and preserved for the winter. Naum's military discipline returned with a vengeance during the summer. Up early to work. No avoiding work detail. With a good harvest, the family would have fruit and vegetables to last them over the long winter.

Although Alla was well schooled in the *defitsit* of local grocery stores and the rigor of the queue, she did not really understand the frantic race to preserve food for the winter. For Leningraders like Naum and Bella, the memories of the *blokada*, the 900-day siege and stranglehold of the city by the Nazis, never faded. The flashbacks of hunger, of watching family and friends slowly starve to death were a constant companion. As a teen, Naum served during the war in the Pulkovo Unit, stationed just outside the city. Each night he went AWOL with his meager bread ration, stealing back into the city, searching out his parents and sharing his ration, so they would survive the siege. Making sure his family was well fed and adequately housed was his responsibility, and Naum embraced it.

Despite her reprieve from Young Pioneer Camp, Alla resented the hard work at the dacha and missed her friends and the entertainment that Leningrad had to offer. She did not experience summer at the dacha as a pastoral vision from Tolstoy with Russians living in concert with nature, singing to the accompaniment of the balalaika, and conversing in willow chairs in the warm summer light. "It was a boring prison. Naum forced me to go there. It was primitive with an outhouse and no comforts, not even running water in the house. And there was so much shared work inside and outside the dacha."

Yet, for Alla, the dacha at Skachki had one thrilling advantage over her family's Leningrad apartment—good radio reception. Living in the country meant hearing real news from the BBC or the Voice of America in Russian. They climbed to the highest point near the dacha with the small transistor. Following the radio broadcasts, Alla and her father set out on long walks. It began with an invitation from Alla to Naum,

"Dad, can you give me some 'political information'?"

"Political information" was the official Soviet term for brainwashing sessions. These briefings were conducted regularly in schools, institutes, and work places.

"Alla, here's the real truth. You must learn the difference between 'red media,' which is propaganda news and truth. Here's how to tell the difference between truth and lies. Remember to always read between the lines. Let's take an example . . ."

Naum talked to Alla as an adult despite her thirteen years. He respected her ability to understand and discern. She walked with her head high, trying to match Naum's long strides and ramrod straight posture. She was proud to be his disciple and was secure in his love. Although Alla frequently referred to the dacha as a "boring prison," over the years she began to treasure the precious time with her handsome father.

In 1971 while Naum was educating Alla at the dacha about Soviet double speak, she had no idea of his own cloak and dagger activities aiding Soviet dissidents. He hid this from the entire family until they were safely resettled outside Russia many years later.

Sheltered within the family, Alla could explore the wider world through literature. She read all the Russian classics and was attracted to Western authors who invited her mind to wander beyond the borders of the Soviet Union. She entered the imaginary world of Hans Christian Andersen's fairy tales. She traversed gas-lamp lit London with Sherlock Holmes. Most importantly, Alla was able to read the romantic, historical novels of Leon Feuchtwanger, such as *Spanish Ballad*, which introduced her to a Jewish universe non-existent in her academic classes. The Soviet regime permitted an odd assortment of Western books to be translated into Russian, and there were also the forbidden books. They were surreptitiously traded among friends and difficult to obtain. Alla enthusiastically read any Western book that she could borrow.

Nyet huda bez dobra. "There is no evil without good." That proverb seemed to turn on its head for Alla. All good seemed to have its bad side. Alla could lose herself in books and escape into worlds far beyond her apartment, but now she discovered it would cost her. At thirteen she would have to be fitted for glasses. Of course, there was no designer eyewear for non-party member children. The glasses would be the same as everyone else's no matter the shape of her face or her color preference. "Ech."

As if that were not enough humiliation, Alla was sent to a medical clinic. She literally looked like a curved bookworm with glasses, and she would have to be cured. Sitting in the clinic, Alla caught sight of another girl her age, also in an adolescent funk about her upcoming examination. They made tentative overtures to each other. After their examinations were completed, they exited with matching diagnoses: scoliosis. They also had matching prescriptions: gymnastics class.

Now the proverb reverted to its rightful order. *Nyet huda bez dobra.* "There is no evil without good." It was clear neither girl was headed for the Olympics as gymnasts. Instead, they learned to straighten their spine and enjoy their therapy.

Even more, they became true friends. In Russia a friend was everything. While the world outside one's home was suspect and dotted with potential land mines, especially for an outspoken adolescent, a true friend meant being at home in the world as long as you were together. Secrets, fears, and truth bound them together.

There was one secret the friends had not yet probed—sex. Sex was the biggest secret of all. More secret than the secret police. Despite the Russian educational system's emphasis on science, human biology—sex—was taboo. There was no class, no seminar in Young Pioneers, no Soviet approved booklet entitled, "You and Menstruation." Alla and her new friend Zina shared information and disinformation with equal abandon. In their later teens, they "learned by doing."

The day Alla's period began, she ran to her grandmother Rosa, shrieking, "I'm dying! I'm bleeding! I'm dying, Rosa!"

"Sha. No one is dying, Allochka; this is normal. It means you're a woman. It means you can have children some day. It happens to all women." Rosa extracted some rags from a drawer. "Allochka, take these and use them." Horrified, Alla's mouth dropped and she stared without comprehension at the wad of rags. Just when she thought she was beyond all humiliation, Rosa added a postscript: "This will happen once a month."

Alla had all the information Rosa would divulge, and she couldn't wait to exchange this secret intelligence with Zina. As Rosa's prediction about the monthly repetition of this dreadful state proved true, the Russian reality of *defitsit* slapped the girls in the face. No sanitary napkins, no tampons—only homemade "constructions"—meant monthly anxiety about blood spots on your clothes. You never felt clean, never felt comfortable. You couldn't do sports. The only remedy was commiserating with your best friend.

Notes

1.   Brutal hazing was common in the Soviet army. In 1985, 4,000 soldiers were tried for hazing, and this certainly represents a small fraction of the incidents. Jews were especially vulnerable. Katherine Bliss Eaton, *Daily Life in the Soviet Union* (Westport, CT: Greenwood Press, 2004), pp. 93–94.

2. Young Pioneers was the Communist youth organization that preached propaganda to children in grade four and upward. The children, clad in white shirts with red kerchiefs, were a feature of every patriotic parade and demonstration.

3. All land belonged to the State, but one could acquire a dacha by being registered as a union member enabling one to be part of a dacha cooperative (like Vera's family) in which case the dacha was a reward. The gardening cooperative allowed Russians, who had the means, to lease land from the government and construct a one-story, non-winterized cabin limited in size to less than 300 square feet. The property was usually about .15 acre and served the need of the population to grow fresh fruit and vegetables for family use throughout the year. For a comprehensive discussion of the dacha, see Stephen Lovell, *Summerfolk: A History of the Dacha 1710–2000* (Ithaca, NY: Cornell University Press, 2003).

10

Verochka: Early Childhood

1949–1969

T'zhelo ucheniy—legko vboyu.
"What is difficult in training will become easy in the battle."

—Alexander Suvorov

After Irina turned her back on her suitor Naum and forgave her husband Misha, the couple needed distance from Irina's mother who was not so quick to forgive. Only at such a moment could a military posting 5,000 miles away sound appealing. The destination was Sakhalin Island, just north of Hokkaido, Japan. Irina, dreading her mother's reaction, delayed sharing the news until the last possible moment. Still suffering under the implacable grief for her daughter Lusya, Lyuba stoically heard Irina out and sanctioned the move but only if four-year old Grisha would remain with his grandfather and her in Leningrad while they were posted in East Asia. Ironically, this was precisely the suggestion that Naum had proffered. Owing to the strong bond already formed between grandson and grandmother and the difficult living conditions in the Far East, Irina and Misha agreed it would be best for everyone. Childless, Misha and Irina set off for their remote posting, visiting Grisha just a few times a year until their return to Leningrad in 1954.

Misha, Grisha, and Irina and, seated in front,
a beautiful Baba Lyuba who reigned over the family.

Eleven years after her brother Grisha's birth, Vera was born in the heart of Leningrad and was quickly lodged in her parents' hearts. They now had a chance to raise a child together. Observing that Vera was an active, outgoing, and fearless little girl, Papa Misha and Mama Irina agreed that to avoid trouble, her energy must be well directed. Fortunately, Vera's parents could afford to hire a girl from an outlying village as a nanny.[1] This young woman lovingly encouraged Verochka's curiosity and engagement. She became part of the family, a natural process as she slept on the couch in their one-room communal apartment for three years.

When Vera turned three and was ready for preschool, Irina busied herself arranging for the nanny's next job in Leningrad so she would not lose her residency permit, could still earn a living, and remain close. This was Irina's natural way of taking care of the people in her circle. Irina and Misha felt fortunate to find a place for Verochka in pre-school, which, like most needs in the Soviet Union, was in *defitsit*. To obtain that slot, it helped that Misha was a party member. Soviet discipline had begun.

The best part of Verochka's day was skipping with her shoulders back and head held high to catch up with her big brother Grisha as he escorted her to school. The less desirable part was the nine-hour regimen. "Sarah," her teachers would call her and the other Jewish girls as if they didn't have to bother learning the names of the Jewish children. Jewish boys were *Isyas* (Isaac). Teachers tended to Verochka's physical needs, making sure she had her morning *kasha*, one hour of daylight outside, nap, snacks, and appropriate discipline. She was taught to color within the lines and to revere Father Lenin. Vera recalled a favorite game at preschool, played away from the teachers' oversight. Whoever spit into someone else's fruit compote could claim it. Vera didn't like it—"too unhygienic." Vera did her best to be a good member of the collective.

With remarkable calm and efficiency—without help from her mother— Irina performed the impossible: working overtime as a dentist, stocking food when she could find it in the refrigerator, cooking nightly, and still possessing emotional energy for her daughter. As she grew older, her health would bear the price of this lifestyle. Many of Irina's working hours were unpaid. Once she clocked her required time, she sometimes accommodated a friend from the office *gratis*. The time might come when Irina would need to approach her patients for a favor in return. This was how *svyazi* (networks) functioned. You had to be careful, though, if you lived with a military officer. Sausage, chocolate, or perfume was a form of acceptable payment, but Irina dared not accept money for fear of imprisonment. Even with a military salary and Irina's long hours, money was always tight. Each night, Irina penciled in a small notebook the account of every incoming and outgoing kopek. With each ruble spent, something else was sacrificed, a lesson Vera learned.

In summer, doting Russian parents sent their children to the countryside in droves to breathe in enough fresh air and soak up enough sunlight to fortify them for the rest of the year. Where to send Verochka? Without a family dacha at that time and only her grandparents' dark, Leningrad apartment humming with mosquitoes, camp seemed like the best alternative.

The government offered a ten-week summer camp for children, to which Verochka unhappily was dispatched from the age of four till she was seven. Vera marched to school like a trooper, but she drew the line at summer camp. Unfortunately, it took several years before her vehement protests were heeded. Vera winced when she recalled her painful camp nickname *chushka* (pigpen). A tomboy, Vera enjoyed her excavations in the sand and dirt so much that her dress was filthy by the end of the day. She begged her counselor for clean clothes. Instead, the counselor spanked her and relegated the little girl to the corner for failing to keep her clothes clean. Clearly, there were things boys could get away with, but not girls. Her little cheeks burned as tears rolled over them. Unaccustomed to humiliation, Vera would do anything to avoid it in the future.

Vera at her summer camp reciting a poem. This was the same summer she was humiliated as "chushka" by her counselor.

When Dedushka (Grandfather) Lev grew feeble from strokes, he and Baba Lyuba moved from their Blokhina apartment to a new "suburban" home on the outskirts of the city, an environment deemed healthy enough to serve as Vera's summer retreat. For Vera, this was a different kind of camp. She dubbed it concentration camp and her grandmother as her jailer. *Grisha would not have been bound by such a strict schedule*, she thought. Only in adulthood could Vera appreciate that in "serving her time," her grandmother had provided her a broad education in English, the classics, and art.

After Vera turned twelve, Misha was rewarded by his union with membership in a dacha cooperative, which gave him the right to garden on the property and build a dacha, moving closer to the trifecta of the "Soviet dream": a private apartment, a dacha, and a Soviet-made car. Lacking the funds to build, they procured a *kung* (an aluminum hut) for sleeping. Mama Irina soon befriended the villagers, who stopped by frequently to chat, and the family quickly became part of the community.

When "Uncle" Lyosha[2] inquired why they had such poor lodging for such a young daughter, Mama Irina explained the obvious—they were saving their money to build. The old man put his hand under his chin and stood for a few moments. "Wait. I will be back shortly." He returned to Irina passing her an envelope "Take this."

Mama Irina nearly fainted when she opened the envelope and found 3,000 rubles inside, the amount needed to erect a dacha. Being a butcher placed Uncle Lyosha in the perfect position to be a lender. His work allowed the chance to amass a great deal of cash by selling meat *na levo* (on the side). At that time Misha earned 300 rubles in a month, and Irina earned 90 rubles. It was unusual for them to be on the receiving end of such generosity. Week by week, Irina and Misha scrimped and saved. Russians lived rent free with the largest cash outlay for food. There was no buying on credit. Irina and Misha forswore luxuries and were able to save 100 rubles per month.

While her parents were in town during the work week, the dacha villagers cared for Vera. It was an idyllic life with a real sense of community and none of the usual mistrust. She ate well with Uncle Lyosha and his wife Aunt Klava, helped in the garden of another family, and slept at the family dacha of her older friend Klara. As their contribution, her parents scoured the city for the best meat each Friday to bring to the village. By the following summer, Misha and Irina had constructed their wooden dacha, gleaming with green paint; and after several years, they paid off their debt to Lyosha. Later, Uncle Lyosha would loan them the cash for a car.

In the country, the family could breathe. Misha and Irina had obtained a place of their own in the city only a few years earlier. Despite being well-educated professionals, Misha and Irina suffered from the housing shortage like everyone else. For the first eight years of Vera's life, her family occupied the largest room of a five-room communal apartment where up to twenty people shared a kitchen, toilet, and bathtub. Each family had one private room that served as a bedroom and living area. Vera adapted to lines early, starting with the communal toilet. A bath was a weekly, scheduled event in which each family had an assigned time not only to bathe, but to wash clothes in the tub next to the wood-fired water heater. *Shush, shika, tikha* are the words that Vera first remembers accompanied by the image of parents and grandparents touching their fingers to their mouths. There was no privacy, and everything could be heard. A nosy neighbor was apt to report to the neighborhood party official any disloyal comment, resulting in a reprimand before the local committee.

Vera may have lost the competition for her grandmother's affection to Grisha, but brother and sister had a deep devotion to each other. After the nanny left, Grisha was in charge of issuing orders and organizing play while their parents worked long hours. Fifteen-year-old Grisha was determined to cure his four-year-old sister of her pigeon-toed walk. To do so, he tied a jump rope around her ankles and, holding the ends in his hand, had her walk in tiny straight steps forward and backward down the long hall of the communal apartment.

"It was torture at the time. But I have to give him credit. He was very inventive, and I have a very nice walk now."

The theme music to Soviet life at that time could have been a strident, monotonous march called *Davlyenie* (pressure). Living in the communal apartment's tight quarters in a city with unforgiving weather, constant shortages, and daylight that was far too brief (for half a year), raised tensions to the breaking point.

Vera sensed her parents relax as they moved into their own apartment on Blokhina where Baba Lyuba and Dedushka Lev had lived. What a luxury to have the toilet and bathtub to themselves. No more shushing, though she was still reminded to keep information *doma*. The main drawback was that eight-year-old Vera now had a forty-five minute trek to school. She was proud to be independent, but, like her parents, she wearied of the tiring routine.

The bond between Grisha and his little sister, Vera, remains strong to this day.

The biggest *defitsit* in family life was free time. Everyone was always tired. Remembering this world of constant work and worry erases any nostalgia Vera might feel. Her family had no time to appreciate the culture of Leningrad, but they did appreciate each other.

It was not until the late 1960s that Russians were allowed a two-day "weekend." Sunday was the special family day when Vera snuck into bed next to her father, curling up to watch TV with him. When Mama Irina announced that breakfast was ready, they sat down to a "feast" of boiled potatoes with herring and onion—the only time of the week when they could eat and talk leisurely.

"Conversations with my dad were fantastic. He was like a walking encyclopedia." All topics were permitted around the table, but the rule was to repeat nothing outside of the home.

From the time Vera was eleven, she could sense her parents' anxiety about Grisha. Born in 1945, Grisha was a member of the patriotic post-war generation that revered the Russian military for the defeat of the Nazis. By Vera's account, Grisha was a soft boy who wanted to appear tougher than he was. Because he had a damaged kidney, he was eligible for a military exemption. Instead, after graduating university in 1968, he followed the family tradition and enlisted. After completing his training, he had thirty soldiers under his command. Eastern Europe was roiling with discontent against the Soviet monolith, and Grisha's cohort was fast-tracked to officer status without proper training. As Grisha awaited deployment, he and Papa Misha agreed on a code to identify his destination.

Late that summer, Mama Irina froze as she read the words on the cryptic telegram, "I am going to see Alexei."[3] This was the coded message signaling that Grisha was on his way to Prague. Based on his military briefing, Grisha thought Soviet troops would be welcomed. Instead, their tanks roared into the streets of Prague to face a popular and peaceful revolution of citizens, young and old, demanding greater freedom. The Czech army was ordered not to open fire, but the Russians had different orders and shot unarmed civilians, deepening the hatred of Eastern Europeans toward Russia.[4]

It seemed Grisha was posted wherever the danger was the greatest. China, during the border dispute over the Damanski peninsula in 1969, was frightening. However, the real danger in Mama Irina's eyes was the location of his permanent base in a small Ukrainian town with 1,000 young, female textile workers and 500 military men.

"Mama Irina was biting her nails not because of the danger of being in the military, but because she was afraid that her son would marry one of those *shiksas* (non-Jewish women) and would never return," explained Vera. "Mama Irina threatened to hang herself from the chandelier if Papa Misha did not use his connections to transfer Grisha back to safety. He humbled himself and tapped a precious military connection that could only be used once or twice in his life. Even with a posting back in Leningrad, Grisha's Jewish luck took him to Afghanistan."

At home, Misha was clearly the authority, but the love and respect he held for Irina made her a powerful partner. Unlike most children her age, Vera's voice was heard as well. Papa Misha would address her questions seriously and tenderly.

Baba Lyuba would visit bringing an onslaught of judgment and advice. Although they disagreed frequently, Papa Misha and Baba Lyuba agreed on the *milukha* (the government), always pronounced with the utmost disdain. Although they were talking about the Soviet leadership, the Yiddish word had been used for generations to refer to earlier political regimes in Russia, all of which made outcasts of the Jews. Vera would soon discover the workings of the *milukha* for herself.

Notes

1. "Children's clubs" accommodated fewer than 25% of children who needed them in the late fifties and early sixties, while 80 % of women worked. That left a lot of young children as latchkey children.

2. The terms, "Uncle" and "Aunt," are used for beloved adults by Russian children.

3. Alexei is the nickname for Alexander, in this case referring to Alexander Dubcek, the First Secretary of the Communist Party of Czechoslovakia, who supported reforms and a level of democracy that threatened Soviet domination.

4. The Brezhnev Doctrine was a foreign policy statement enunciated in 1968 justifying military intervention by the Soviet Union when socialism was threatened in any satellite country. The Soviet Union claimed to be a country of laws; therefore, they made a law to legitimize the invasion of Czechoslovakia.

11

Meryll: Mississippi *Dacha*

1960–1961

It's not good for you to be here.
—Mrs. Pell in *Mississippi Burning*

While Vera and Alla's parents ensured their daughters benefited from the fresh air, and the families stocked their Leningrad pantries with summer's bounty from the dachas, my parents had their own theory about a beneficial summer vacation. I was off to my paternal grandparents' house in Mississippi.

What made my parents think this was a good idea? I didn't even like being outdoors in an Ohio summer. Didn't they know the heat index for Tupelo? Couldn't I just stay home cocooned in air conditioning, sprawled in front of the TV to watch Rocky and Bullwinkle duke it out against the evil Boris and Natasha? Why did my younger brother and sister remain at home?

No explanations were forthcoming. I was headed for Tupelo. My grandparents' home was to be my summer dacha for two years. There my Barbie doll and I lived with my Grandpa

Irving, Grandma Rae, and her mother whom we called Baubie. My grandparents indulged me shamelessly, and I enjoyed their company, but I was still apprehensive about a month away in tropical Tupelo with my immigrant grandparents.

Grandma and Grandpa's house was a standard postwar brick rambler with matching homes lining the street. The grass looked spiky and dry, not like the lush lawns of our Columbus neighborhood. What was most surprising about the house was the missing basement. In Columbus, every house had a basement. There resided the mysteries of the house: octopus furnaces, old trunks, playrooms, coal chutes, a single toilet usually called "the commode." Some houses, like my maternal grandparents' home, boasted a bomb shelter that was completely equipped in case of nuclear war with the Soviet Union. Where would Tupelo's citizens go in case of an air raid? I supposed they would all hide under a kitchen table.

Tupelo in 1960 was a typical small town in the deep South with the requisite Confederate cannon located in the main square, a Jewish-owned dry goods store, and a separate "town" for African Americans. My grandparents joined two other families to form a trinity. Although I later learned that there were 110 other Jews, I believed then that Grandma had introduced me to all of Tupelo's Jews.

Peeking from the hallway into the open doorway of Baubie's room, I watched as she woke each morning, inserted her teeth, and patted my head as she padded down the hallway of the rambler on her way to the kitchen. She set tasks for herself. She baked in the searing summer heat; she weeded the garden and harvested the bounty of fresh vegetables. To relax, she dragged the white metal rocker to the back patio with her crocheting and rocked, hooking her needle in and out of the ecru thread. I wondered if she sweated. How could she stand the heat? I knew that Baubie came from Ekatrinoslav in southern Russia, but how warm could Ekatrinoslav have been?

My curiosity was piqued and in the languid Mississippi summer, I bombarded my grandmother with questions. Why did Baubie insist on driving to Memphis to buy meat each week? Why did she leave Russia? Why doesn't she speak English? Why doesn't Baubie crochet on Saturdays? Why is she shorter than me? Grandma Rae, although always bustling, patiently responded to my questions. She'd dig into the darkness of her suitcase of memories and draw out a thread, but she never relayed her memories as a whole cloth.

I kept Grandma busy whipping up knock-off Barbie outfits on her ancient Singer. She never reached the bottom of the remnant pile from the pants factory where Grandpa worked, but the ferocity with which she hammered the pedal on the machine cued me—sewing was not her preferred activity. Soon she decided I needed playmates, so she fixed me up with the two Jewish kids closest in age to mine, Steve and Susan.

I was awed by Susan who was older and so much more sophisticated than I was. She had a perfect beehive and posters of the hometown boy Elvis on her pink walls. That summer I discovered that terror could surface on Susan's front lawn and ripple through the Jewish community. On Friday nights I went to Temple with my grandparents and my Baubie, riding in Grandpa's large-finned Buick to Temple B'nai Israel on Marshall Street. Jews from small towns across northern Mississippi gathered for the brief service and lingered afterward for cake and conversation. One particular Friday night the atmosphere felt tense, no one smiled. Susan's father hurried through the prayers. After services, I learned what worried the grown-ups. The Ku Klux Klan (KKK) had burned a cross on Susan's front yard. Three years before Freedom Summer arrived in Mississippi, I began to learn lessons about race, religion, and the KKK.

Late one afternoon, the rain was pounding the roof of Grandma's house. In Mississippi that didn't mean it would feel cooler, just more humid. It was time for the maid to go home. White purse and shopping bag on her wrist, she was ready to leave. Baubie sprang up from her club chair in the corner and placed her crooked fingers on top of the maid's hand. Her sudden movements roused me from my reclining position under the demi-lune coffee table where I was helping Barbie prance in her gold brocade outfit. Baubie shook her head vigorously at the maid. Her tight gray bun seemed to swivel on top of her head. She called for her daughter. Instantly Grandma appeared, and I overheard a conversation in Yiddish between them. It sounded like one rhetorical question followed another. Then I heard my least favorite word in the Yiddish language, *shvartza*,[1] and realized they were talking about the maid.

By the end of the brief exchange, all four of us trundled out to the carport to Grandma's car. Then came the next Yiddish exchange with Baubie seeming to indicate that the maid should sit up front with Grandma, and she would sit in back with me. Grandma was opposing Baubie with *past nisht in Mississippi*. In my mind that translated to *not here in Mississippi*. Grandma won that round, and we took our assigned seats in the car as Grandma drove to the maid's home.

The ride took me through the now familiar areas, down the streets with brick ramblers, then through downtown. And then, it seemed, Tupelo ended. 1960 ended. We were in the nineteenth century and a different town, the "Negro town,"[2] unincorporated, whatever that meant. Grandma, already a brake and accelerate kind of driver, was taking us on a gut-wrenching drive into the wretched past. The unpaved street, the wooden shotgun shacks with outhouses in the back all seemed at odds with the gracious, syrupy manner of white Tupelo. But there it was. American apartheid.

Later that evening Grandma patiently heard about Grandpa's day at the factory in Okolona and in between ferrying dishes from the kitchen to the table, she told Grandpa that she took the maid home because "Mama asked me to."

Grandpa's admonitions were terse. Perhaps he was remembering the *milukha*.

"It's like Russia here. The Negroes are the Jews. You step over the line and I'll lose my job."

He pulled a Camel cigarette from the crumpled pack, opened the back door, and stepped out on the concrete patio for a smoke.

That was a lot for a nine-year-old to digest along with the surfeit of food at the dinner table. Pride in my Baubie kept bubbling up in my mind. She deferred to her son-in-law in almost all matters, but she had her principles. Whether it was driving all the way to Memphis for kosher meat or making sure that the maid got home safely and dry in the rain, she took her stand. That day Russian Jewish history and civil rights became fused in my mind. I was hungry for more information.

My sixty-year-old self wonders why I didn't jettison

the Barbie and create a Baubie doll, a 4'8" super-heroine with waist-length hair twisted in a gray bun, who could single-handedly convince her husband to uproot their family from Russia, stand tall to advocate for the rights of others, and hold fast against the pressing waves of assimilation.

Baubie at rest. It must be Saturday afternoon if Baubie's hands are still and she is relaxing outside Grandma and Grandpa's Tupelo home in July 1960.

Notes

1. *Shvartze* literally means the color "black" in Yiddish. The word was often used in a derogatory tone to mean African Americans.

2. I phoned former Tupelo acquaintances to see if they remember the name of the "Negro town." I remembered a separate name for this unincorporated area, but no one else remembered, and my acquaintances soon steered our conversation to happier topics.

12

Alla: A Special Education

1965–1972

Believe me, the drug of freedom is universally potent.
—Natan Sharansky[1]

Education is power. It was the only way to combat the *milukha*. This was a fundamental belief held by the families of both Vera and Alla. Navigating the Soviet educational bureaucracy could be a nightmare, but it was a family tradition to seek the best education despite all obstacles. Both grandmothers had graduated from gymnasium when few girls attended high school,[2] setting a high standard for their future granddaughters. What the girls didn't know was that their grandmothers had attended the same gymnasium in their small Belarusian village of Gorodok.

By 1961 reforms were afoot in the stodgy Soviet educational system. Instruction in English language was now viewed by the Soviets as a key weapon in their Cold War arsenal.[3] Math and science instruction were also upgraded. While Soviet schools typically inculcated rigid conformity,

English language schools were progressive enough to allow a bit of creative play.

Both families seized the opportunity to send their daughters to a progressive and competitive English school for grades 1–12. To do so, both families took advantage of their influence to bypass the quotas for Jewish children. The principal of English Language School #238 was Jewish and a private patient of Alla's father. He "put her on the list" and facilitated her admission. Alla remembers the high standards at the school. Junior high students read novels in English and spoke grammatically correct English. The curriculum in math and science was also modernized according to the newest principles of sequential learning.

View of Alla's school #238 surrounded by concrete and facing a military installation in the compound known as Dutch Harbor.

"I know I got lucky," Alla muses now, realizing that "Jews were really searching for better education, actively trying to get into better schools."

But there were limits to how many Jews would be admitted to the elite schools. Alla estimates one-fourth to one-third of the students in her school were Jewish.

Alla also was fortunate that her school was only five blocks away from her apartment. Most days she enjoyed the walk with her friend from the downstairs apartment past the candy factory and along the curving canal in front of Admiralty Island.

The focus on intensive English instruction and the

relatively large proportion of Jews did not shield Alla from anti-Semitism.[4] One twelve-year-old classmate taunted Alla when she dropped her pen by shouting, "you can't have your pen back—you Jewish pig!" Angered, Alla didn't flee or cry but stood her ground and surprised her tormentor by fighting back in what she characterized as "a boy fight." Alla punched the girl so hard, her hand stung from the force of the blow. Alla expected punishment and was not surprised to be called to the director's office. She was not dismissed from school. No doubt, the Jewish principal intervened for her.

Alla's second summons to the principal's office came in 1972 when she was a teenager. Frustrated with trying to understand the twisted world in which she lived, Alla stood in front of her class of thirty and announced, "There is no freedom to speak, write, or act in the USSR!"

Alla was sent directly to the principal's office. This time he summoned her parents to join her in his office. The principal admonished Alla. " That was a very dangerous statement." To Naum and Bella he said, "I advise you to make Alla stop talking like that. It could cost someone her freedom."

All three understood this was not a threat but a prediction. In his warning, the principal validated Alla's assertion. There was no freedom of speech. Alla did not repeat her protest aloud at school again. Like Vera, she now understood that the repercussions of her rebellion would be visited upon the entire family. Instead, she vowed to herself "to find a way to move to a better place in the world, where she could develop in a free, open society with opportunities, where she would give birth to a child who would grow up in a better world with multiple choices of her/his own, and be free to tell, write, and act." Alla never forgot that moment.

Alla had no illusions about her innate talents. She knew she had to work hard to succeed in school. Her tough and handsome father was her champion. He attended Alla's school conferences and heard morsels of praise from her teachers. Gentle Bella mediated with Naum for Gera. Resembling a thin, full-haired version of Alan Ginsburg, he was brilliant and talented but unmotivated in school. He wanted to be left alone to read literature. Bella absorbed the brunt of complaints from

Gera's teachers and then repackaged the comments in a more palatable form when she relayed them to Naum. Because the family concentrated on encouraging Gera's academic success, Alla was released from carrying the burden of the family's aspirations.

Leaving the outside world of taunts and restrictions due to her Jewish identity that was stamped on the fifth line of her passport, Alla enjoyed the Judaism that wafted through her household. Surrounded by her parents and her grandmother Rosa, she experienced her Jewishness. Her parents proudly told her of marrying in 1948 under a Jewish marriage canopy "with a rabbi, but in secrecy." She socialized with her family's Jewish friends in their unofficial Jewish neighborhood, close to the center of Leningrad and close to the synagogue. Alla claims that somehow Rosa always knew when the Jewish holidays fell.[5] Despite the danger, the family kept some Jewish traditions culled from her grandparents' memories.

For Rosa it was imperative that the family celebrate Passover complete with matzah. When boxed matzah wasn't available, she baked her own, enlisting Alla's help to stab holes in the dough with a fork. When matzah became available at the synagogue, Rosa walked the two blocks to Lermontovsky Prospekt to secure the family's supply.[6] She always managed to scrounge the necessary ingredients for gefilte fish and chopped liver. Remembering the feel of mixing the carp, matzah meal, and egg as she stood with her mother and grandmother, Alla later recreated the culinary memories for her own family.

The warm atmosphere of Alla's family's seder mirrored decades of past celebrations. The family cleaned the apartment till it sparkled. "We were around the table and we knew why," remembers Alla. "But we couldn't recite the prayers. We didn't know the words."

They may not have prayed, but the delectable scent of Passover hovering in the room evoked stories from the past. With curtains drawn against the outside world, they talked of Alla's great-grandparents' lives in the shtetls of Belarus and Lithuania. Her ancestors strived for education, to earn a living, to find love. The Revolution brought a flash of hope for redemption and then despair. Lenin had been a false messiah, and the family's life returned to a struggle for survival within a heartless system, a system that generated its own logic and devoured its own children. Without an awareness of the parallels, her family history and the family histories of their friends mirrored the story of Passover, the struggle for freedom and redemption.

Celebrating Passover sparked Alla's curiosity about religion. Without her parents' knowledge, her research included escapades with friends. By the time Alla was fifteen, she had become even more defiant of Soviet ideology than on the day she fought for her dignity in the schoolyard. Although most churches and synagogues had been closed by 1970, a few remained open. Alla and her friends boldly investigated two of the religious institutions left in their Leningrad neighborhood—The Grand Choral Synagogue and St. Isaac's Cathedral.

"The synagogue was just beautiful. I loved the atmosphere. I couldn't read Hebrew. I couldn't pray. But the atmosphere gave me a warm feeling. It was part of my history," Alla reflects. "I felt calm every time we snuck inside. The Church was not something that was mine, but, still, it is absolutely a beautiful building."

Alla's daring extended beyond touring religious sites. She wanted a boyfriend—Jewish, of course. She found a twenty-two-year-old university student. Mark was a dangerously attractive student of cinematography. At least she wasn't dating a non-Jew. Rebelling did not mean dismissing her Jewish identity.

Alla and her sophisticated boyfriend managed to secretly date a couple of times. Bella still had not discussed the facts of life with Alla, nor had Alla uncovered much information on the mysterious intimacies of men and women. She had no way of knowing that the Soviet Union had a *defitsit* in condoms and all forms of birth control. Venereal disease was rampant. And for most women, abortion was the only viable birth control.[7]

Blissfully unaware of the potentially dire consequences of romance with the cinematography student, Alla went out a third time with him. She knew they must return before the bridges that crisscrossed the city were raised at 1:00 a.m. The couple arrived in front of her apartment building at 11:30 p.m. As they approached the door, Alla saw a male figure pacing in front of the building. He was propelled as if steam were rising from his head. Was it Naum? Maybe the figure just had Naum's shape but was another angry man. No, it was Naum, and, ignominiously, Alla's secret boyfriend was discovered.

"Alla, upstairs. Now!" barked Naum.

"You," he yelled to Mark, "You stay right here."

Alla knew better than to debate Naum while he was in this state, and she dutifully headed inside the building but did not race upstairs. Instead, she left the massive, wooden exterior door to the building ajar and strained to hear the conversation outside.

"Alla is fifteen years old. What would a university student want with a fifteen-year-old?"

Mark knew that this was not an interrogation but a lecture, and he wisely maintained his silence. Naum did not want to hear anything that Mark might have to say: that his daughter was different than most Soviet girls, that she was an intelligent conversationalist, she was genuine, she was so lovely. Mark clearly understood that Naum was ramping up his rhetorical questions for a grand-finale threat.

"Don't you ever come near my daughter again." Naum did not need to spell out the "or else."

Cinematography students recognize when a father's anger is real. The romance was over, but Alla still did not completely understand her father's fears. She was grounded, confined to the apartment, and all she could do was cry. She couldn't even talk on the phone to her friend Zina. How could her father have humiliated her and reduced her to a little girl?

Although Naum did not tolerate Alla's amorous adventures, he turned a blind eye when she began to flirt with Zionism. She did not called herself a Zionist, but she wholeheartedly identified with Jews and Israel. Despite the extensive control the Brezhnev regime exerted over the press, knowledge of the struggles of dissidents like Ida Nudel,[8] Natan Sharansky,[1] and others to leave the Soviet Union for Israel reached the Jewish community and ignited the dreams of Jewish teens like Alla.

Alla enjoyed a special relationship with her dad. 1970.

By 1970, even the strict censorship of the Soviet press could not black out the stunning news of the "Leningrad hijacking." Such a thing had never happened before. Led by Eduard Kuznetsov and former military pilot Mark Dymshits, a group of twelve Jews purchased all the seats on an airplane. They intended to fly west to Finland. From there they would make their way to Israel. The KGB had tracked their elaborate plan and arrested them at Smolny Airport outside of Leningrad. For Soviet Jews, it was both thrilling to think of the hutzpah[9] and frightening to think of the retaliation.

The results of the trial were no surprise to Soviet Jews. The two leaders were condemned to death for high treason. The subsequent crackdown on Soviet dissidents was also no surprise. But what was unforeseen, was that the Soviet Union was vulnerable to world outcry. Pressure from foreign governments caused the court to commute the death sentences to fifteen years in prison. The refusenik movement grew stronger in Moscow under the bright lights of foreign journalists and diplomats.[10]

Until 2011 Alla was unaware of the part her father had played. One of the conspirators, Misha Kornblith, practiced oral surgery in the chair next to Naum. Despite the risk to himself and his family, Naum couldn't ignore his friend's imprisonment. Each week he prepared a care package, went to the prison, surrendered his passport so his information could be recorded by the desk clerk, and waited on the hard bench until he was summoned to leave his package. Whether or not Dr. Kornblith ever received the package, Naum didn't know. Naum kept this activity secret until he was safely settled in Sweden in 1994 and then told Gera the story. Pride spread across Alla's face when she heard Gera tell the story, and tears welled in her eyes as she sat in her Swedish apartment with her husband's arm drawing her close.

Although Alla did not risk demonstrating with the refuseniks in 1970, she and a friend secretly purchased a Star

of David necklace to announce their solidarity with refuseniks and their sense of identity. It became a talisman for the dream of emigration.

"This Magen David necklace was actually worn by an Israeli soldier. In battle," the seller assured them.

That was all the girls had to hear before they parted with their rubles to purchase the necklaces. Only the chain would be visible to the outside world.

Alla knew her father had demonstrated bravery and loyalty to his family during the Siege of Leningrad. She was surprised to discover how brave he had been to visit his imprisoned colleague.

Alla was proud of her Judaism, but she felt the constraints of being Jewish in Russia. Her professional goal of studying biology was snuffed out. At the same time, her identification with Israel sparked her dream of emigration. In 1974 at age seventeen, Alla's aim was clear—"get out of the place." She knew she had to attain any education she could to prepare for a future outside the Soviet Union. Unfortunately, following the Yom Kippur

War of 1973,[11] emigrating to Israel became more difficult. American newspapers wrote of Brezhnev's hard-line stance. By the time Alla sought an escape, Brezhnev himself seemed to have ossified into a statue, more rigid in bearing and policy. Brezhnev remained deaf to the soft voice of President Carter advocating human rights. The exit door closed for Jews just as it had in Stalin's time. No matter. Alla's dream landscape of Israel remained alive. She formulated Plan A and Plan B.

Notes

1. Natan Sharansky applied for an exit visa to Israel in 1972, was arrested in 1977, and sent to the gulag. Thanks to the efforts of his wife, Avital, who lived in Israel, his plight was constantly in the public eye. He was released and left for Israel in 1986.

2. In Eastern Europe in the early 20th century, a gymnasium was an exclusive high school for gifted students preparing for university. The final two years of study were the equivalent of earning a bachelor's degree in the United States and prepared students to enter university at the level equivalent to entering a program for a master's degree in the United States. It was rare for women to attend and even rarer for Jewish women to attend and graduate a gymnasium in tsarist Russia.

3. Stephen Lovell, *The Soviet Union: A Very Short Introduction* (Oxford: Oxford University Press, 2009), pp. 134–136. Lovell briefly discusses the 1960 educational reforms including the introduction of foreign language immersion schools.

4. Name calling was rampant. Benjamin Pinkus lists the common epithets used against Jews in *The Jews of the Soviet Union* (Cambridge, UK: Cambridge University Press, 1988), p. 95.

5. The Jewish calendar is based on the lunar cycle, and the years and months differ from the secular calendar. For example, 2011 corresponds to 5771 until the Jewish New Year, which occurs in September or October. From then until December 31, 2011 corresponds to 5772. Pinkus in *Jews of the Soviet Union* claims that no Jewish calendars were printed in Russia after the early 1930s (p. 105). The claim is made that "tiny calendars" were printed from 1955–1964 by the Moscow and Leningrad synagogues in a collection of essays edited by Lionel Kochan called *The Jews in Soviet Russia Since 1917* (London: Oxford University Press, 1972), p. 182.

6. Benjamin Pinkus, *Jews of the Soviet Union*, p. 317. Pinkus includes a detailed description of the Soviet Union's various campaigns to control matzah baking.

7. Abortion was legalized in the Soviet Union in 1955. By 1980 an estimated 16,000,000 abortions were performed. Even though it was common, many

women felt shamed by the procedure. (Eaton, *Daily Life in the Soviet Union,* p. 188).

8.   Ida Nudel applied for an exit visa to Israel in 1971 and while she waited for 16 years for permission to leave, she became the "guardian angel" to the prisoner of Zion movement, organizing aid for jailed dissidents and arranging contacts with the West.

9.   Hutzpah is a Yiddish term meaning a lot of nerve or gall. The term can have positive or negative connotations.

10. Gal Beckerman, *When They Come for Us We'll Be Gone: The Epic Struggle to Save Soviet Jewry* (Boston: Houghton Mifflin Harcourt, 2010), pp. 177–179 includes a thorough and concise account of the Leningrad hijacking and its impact.

11. Egypt and Syria, with the backing of other Arab nations and the support of the Soviet Union, launched an attack against Israel on the holiest day in the Jewish calendar. The Arab armies were repulsed. The Soviet Union was embarrassed and also fearful that its support of the Arab attack would engender pro-Zionist feelings in its Jewish population. It did not want its Arab allies to think it was encouraging Jewish immigration to Israel.

13

Vera: A Communist Education for a Future Capitalist

1965–1972

Proshla zima, nastalo l'eto, spasibo partii za eto.
"The winter's passed. The summer's here. For this we thank our Party dear."

—Russian joke

Baba Lyuba was at her most zealous when guiding Vera's education. Researching relentlessly, she discovered the proper school—School #316. She strode confidently into the principal's office at the competitive English language school, insisting that he interview six-year-old Verochka to recognize her gifts and demanding that Vera be assigned to the advanced A track even though Jews in this school were automatically assigned to the B track.

Vera explained the Soviet logic. "It was common to have one Jew in the A track to prove that Jews were not automatically excluded, and I turned out to be that Jew."

While other children were encouraged to fit in, Vera

groomed herself to excel. She enjoyed the idea of power. If there was to be judgment by a committee of peers, then she would be head of that committee. From a young age, she realized that she was not a good follower, but could be an excellent leader. Her body had always been active and solid, if a bit plump, and her mind was extremely agile. She displayed a confident style with the other children. Vera also could guard her speech. She knew what to say and what to leave unspoken.

Her first power position was star leader in the *Okterbryata* when she was in second grade. Every Soviet child was placed in a "star" of five children, and star leaders were responsible for keeping their fellow students in line. They served as teachers' helpers but had the additional task of reprimanding students whose performance was unsatisfactory.

Vera took to this role naturally. Hands on hips with her head tilted, she spoke to the offending child with the same serious intonation that her mama and papa would use with her when she was in need of correction; the words came easily, with the desired effect, "You have disappointed the group and need to work harder." This was remarkably close to the way she later would reprimand an irresponsible employee.

"Perhaps this explains the lack of friendships at that age," Vera says with a smile. "I wasn't very popular, but they obeyed. I enjoyed it. It was an achievement."

As Vera grew, so did her ambitions. The next rung on the ladder of Communist Party involvement for youths was the Pioneers. Fourth graders were divided into two *otr'adi* (military detachments). Vera ran for leader and was resoundingly defeated. She was already learning how grudges accrue and fester among the masses.

The election defeat was her first failure, and she received no sympathy at home. Papa Misha said, "What made you decide that everybody has to love you and that this determines whether you're the best? Even if you are the best, it doesn't mean that everybody will like you."

No wonder the Soviet leaders rigged elections. It was a vital lesson for her to understand that she might sacrifice popularity by doing the right thing.

Vera, as a proud pioneer, ready to lead.

By sixth grade, Vera was exploring a new career as President of the International Club. She and her classmates were corresponding with children from a sister school in Manchester, England. The English language teacher was fond of Vera and appreciated the skills that Vera had gained from the private tutor Irina and Misha had hired for her. The Manchester students arrived for a visit. Vera was put in charge of programming for the group, which gave her an opportunity to demonstrate her logistical prowess.

The following year Vera counted down the days until her class would choose delegates to travel to Manchester. There was no question in her mind that she would be selected. But she was wrong. As a Jewish student, she was denied the privilege of going to England. Vera fumed at the injustice.

Even as a little girl, Vera knew her family was "Jewish," but she didn't know what that really meant. There were Ukrainians, Belarusians, Georgians, and other nationalities, but somehow when people pronounced the word "Jew," it was with disgust. If a Ukrainian was nasty, he or she was just an unpleasant person, but if a Jewish person behaved poorly, then people would say, "They're all the same."

Vera's father gave a Darwinist explanation. Jews had learned to survive in whatever way they could, which usually involved working hard, finding niches of opportunity, and attaining the best education possible. So how should a Jew act? Papa Misha was committed to the notion that if all Jews were to be judged as a group, then he himself must behave as a mensch—a good, decent, and generous person.

And so it began. She started noticing the slights and the discrimination that would repeat unceasingly throughout her life under communism—the very ideology established with the aid of Jewish intellect, sweat, and blood. This was the ideology that was supposed to erase religious differences. No matter how hard she worked, she would always be in the category of "Jew" and would have to try twice as hard to succeed. This was true even in the most progressive of schools.

Vera couldn't blame her nationality for her lack of a boyfriend. At fourteen Vera remembers one Sunday weeping uncontrollably over a boy who didn't reciprocate her feelings. Her father put his hand on her shoulder and said firmly, "Vera, you're not blond, you're not tall, you're not slim. You're not a beauty. But you have an amazing personality. You need to let it out. You have an amazing mind. You will find the kind of person you want if you allow yourself to depend on this."

Vera swears to me that she was not offended. She knew she was fat in a world of slim adolescent beauties. Vera credits her father for helping her come to grips in a realistic way with her shortcomings and to enhance her strengths. She followed her father's advice and became more outgoing and reliant on her personality, but she did not overcome her wish to be desirable and attractive.

Vera thrived on responsibility, at least in school. By age fifteen, Vera was in charge of preparing the New Year's Eve performance, including scriptwriting, casting, and piano accompaniment. The remainder of her free time was spent studying for the critical tests to enter the college track in ninth grade. She didn't return home until late in the evening. Even after her father's first heart attack, she couldn't slow her pace.

"My dad was in the hospital, my mom was working, and Baba Lyuba wasn't well. My brother Grisha was in the military, but Mom dispatched him on this important mission to tell me how irresponsible I was. We were sitting in our kitchen at the tiny table next to the bathtub. With a serious tone, Grisha told me that I was not supporting our parents enough and

I was behaving irresponsibly by devoting too much time to my own activities. He managed to push a button inside me. I felt so guilty that I started to cry. It was winter and dry in Leningrad. We all had the flu and stuffed noses. A vein burst and blood came out through my eye. Grisha was appalled. He yelled,'Mama I can't talk to her. She's crying blood.'" He had made his point.

Papa Misha's job skills contributed a great deal to Vera's unique education. His first job in the late 1950s was jamming the Voice of America and Radio Liberty, two of the Western radio stations that broadcast news through the Iron Curtain during the Cold War. Therefore, he knew how to get the signal. Vera's lesson was identical to Alla's—read between the lines and understand that the official Soviet news was propaganda and keep conversations like this one *doma* (at home).

To correct Vera's lisp and enhance her language ability, her parents hired a tutor. She taught Vera in her private library filled with unusual volumes bearing interesting titles without the words "communist," "socialist," or "Leninist." Vera thirsted for knowledge.

At age twelve, Vera pondered the question: Why were Jews hated? Vera's tutor admired her intellectual curiosity and, from her shelves, removed a worn copy of the nearly seventy-five-year-old book, *Quo Vadis*. Fortunately, the theological questions posed by the book were threaded through a love story, which appealed to Vera's romantic nature. The tutor's next choice was *Jewish Wars* by Josephus chronicling the Roman conquest of Judea. For Vera, her new knowledge was groundbreaking as she reflected upon the resilience of the Jewish people despite the best efforts of the tsars and the Soviet regimes to marginalize or erase Judaism.

Vera read the tales of Sholom Aleichem[1] and wondered what in the world she had in common with these poor, but clever, provincial people from the shtetl. Amazed, she learned that this was the world of her grandmother's childhood and most Russian Jews of that generation.

Unlike her peers, Vera early on knew to question the truthfulness of the propaganda she heard in class, Young Pioneer meetings, and the slogans that pervaded the airwaves. A sense of familial conspiracy brought the family closer together. So began the two realities: the superficial self that would negotiate society and the inner self that developed through family narratives and covert operations such as Voice of America and forbidden or rare books, *samizdat* (self-published and exchanged hand to hand).

In high school, Vera's desire for leadership always kept her involved. She recognized the shallowness of the Soviet ideology, but she learned how to fit in. It was somewhat easier in her school because it was an island of relatively independent thought and excitement.

"We had our first détente in the sixties, and this was a time when writers and artists could flourish. I remember our Russian teacher taught us about Solzhenitsyn.[2] Our history teacher taught outside of the text, giving us a much broader picture of history than the official Soviet representation. The seeds of doubt were planted. Then, I could come home and talk about it with my dad and mom, and they would give me more insight."

Vera was ready for the wider world, and she hoped to find it at university. Her family expected her to achieve and have a good career despite the limits of the *milukha*, the system.

Notes

1. Sholom Aleichem (the pen name of Solomon Rabinovich) wrote the short story "Tevye the Milkman," on which *Fiddler on the Roof* is based.

2. Aleksandr Solzhenitsyn's wrenching novels of the Gulag earned him a Nobel Prize in 1970 and exile from the Soviet Union in 1974. He returned to Russia in 1994. When Vera was in school, it would have been unusual for his novels to be part of the curriculum since they were so critical of the Soviet regime.

14

Meryll: Russia—
Is it Good for the Jews?

1795–1917

*Yerehmiel Moses, the Hebrew teacher, blind in one eye
and short-sighted in the other, used to wear spectacles
without lenses. Asked "Why?" he would answer
triumphantly, "Well, it's better than nothing, isn't
it?"[1]*

—Adapted from a Sholom Aleichem
story

Homework: "Research your family history."

In our Columbus schools, that was a common social studies
assignment. We immersed ourselves in this homework,
badgering Grandma Rae with questions about her life in Russia
and why she left, paging through books that would illuminate
the past, and humming along with *Fiddler on the Roof.*

In Vera and Alla's youth, this was never an assignment.
It was decadent and bourgeois to think of your individual past
as opposed to the grand sweep of Soviet history. But in the

new Russia, a maverick history teacher on the recent TV series (2009) *Ranetki* threw down the gauntlet—"Interview your parents about your family history." It stumped the students and the parents.

To understand our common Jewish Russian past, we need to traipse backward in time to 1772. Catherine the Great, who could be dubbed "Catherine the Greedy," expanded the Russian border into the wheat fields of neighboring Poland. By 1794, after the third annexation of Polish territory, Catherine realized she had enlarged Russia's territory with the unintended consequence of increasing Russia's Jewish population. Life changed radically when Polish Jews became Russian Jews. They were confined to the Pale of Settlement.[2] The tsar doubled taxes for Jews, limited their occupations, and forbade them to own property. Jews turned inward but were not invisible to Russians. Government-sanctioned pogroms ravaged the Jewish villages, particularly at Easter.[3] Jews became the convenient and consummate outsiders, sometimes scapegoated, always exploited for taxes.

The pressing question of life in the Pale was "How do we survive?" With poverty, disease, army conscription, and pogroms as continual threats, death was a frequent visitor. Ironically, Russian policy reinforced and strengthened Jewish practice, community, and culture. Unlike the Russian peasants, the Jews were highly literate and, following the example of their Talmudic scholars, they valued debate.

The bomb that killed Tsar Alexander II, emancipator of the Russian serfs, in 1881 also ended liberalization. Jewish blood flowed throughout the Passover holiday of 1881 during an outbreak of vicious pogroms that were followed by additional restrictions aimed against the Jews. At this time 5.5 million Jews were living in villages that were bursting at the seams. There was no freedom to move from the congested shtetls. Jews were stuck unless they could gather the money to emigrate. From 1881 to 1920, more than two million Jews left the Russian Empire. Most left for the United States where the streets were said to be paved with gold, but others embraced Zionism and journeyed to Palestine to build a new Jewish homeland.

Our Stories

In 1914 before our paternal grandfather could be snatched for the military in the Great War, he fled his home, hitching wagon rides, and then trudging the remaining distance to the port of Gdansk, where he boarded a ship for America. His future wife Rae was sixteen at the time, living in New York. She had fled Russia in 1905 at age seven after a pogrom rumbled through Ekatrinoslav. During the violence she hid in a wardrobe with her mother and siblings, the children's faces pressed into pillows and down quilts to mute their crying. Grandma Rae recalled how terror galvanized her mother and made her plant herself in front of her tall and gentle husband and insist, "We're going to Newark, New Jersey, America, with or without you."

Back in the Pale of Settlement, in the small village of Gorodok, two young Jewish girls Lyuba and Rosa had no dreams of emigration, but they did achieve the rare dream for a girl of gaining a gymnasium education. The future would bring them together as the *babushki* of Vera and Alla. As the Revolutionary period progressed, the women, like the other Jews in the Pale, chose sides. Choices included from A to Z, anarchists, Bundists, conservatives . . . Zionists.[4] Many followed the Bolshevik siren song of a workers' paradise, promising a society where religion and ethnic heritage would not matter. The prospect of a more modern, egalitarian, and secular society seduced the teenage Lyuba. Rosa, bound more tightly to her roots, feared the changes and wondered: *Would it be good for the Jews?*

Notes

1. Howard Morley Sachar, *The Course of Modern Jewish History* (New York: Dell Publishing, 1958), pp.82–85. I first read this book in 1963 and discovered upon reexamination that I had internalized almost every word Sachar had written. It was Sachar's book that ignited my interest in reading history.

2. The Pale of Settlement comprised 4% of the Russian homeland. Jews were not allowed to settle where they wished within the Pale—they were limited to specific Jewish villages. Some Jews did acquire residency permits, which allowed them to live in cities, but these were exceptions, sometimes obtain by offering exceptionally large bribes. There were approximately 1.2 million Jews in 1815. The borders extended from the eastern demarcation line to the Russian

border with the Kingdom of Prussia and with Austria-Hungary. Included are present-day Lithuania, Belarus, Poland, Moldova, Ukraine, and some parts of western Russia. See the map on page 361.

3. Easter pogroms. Easter, frequently coinciding with Passover, was traditionally a time when European and Russian anti-Semitism peaked. Both the Catholic and Russian Orthodox Church reminded their followers of the Passion and the presumed guilt of the Jews in the death of Jesus. In addition, a false accusation circulated that Jews baked matzah with Christian blood, which fueled peasant anger and increased physical attacks on Jews.

4. According to Zvi Gitelman in *A Century of Ambivalence: The Jews of Russia and the Soviet Union* (New York: Yivo Institute, 1988), about 34,000 Jews joined the Jewish Bund (p. 90). By 1917, 2,133 Jews belonged to the Bolshevik Party (p. 95). Most Jews who affiliated with a political group were Zionists. The total membership for all of the Zionist groups combined was about 300,000 (p.90).

15

Vera: Dual Identity

1799–1974

Know how to take advantage of position.
—General Alexander Suvorov

Leslie, did I ever tell you that one of our ancestors fought alongside General Suvorov in 1799 against the French Revolutionaries?"[1] Vera looked away from the garment she was ironing in the Cayman Island master suite closet and glanced at the screen during our Skype conversation to savor the look of surprise on my face.

"What?" This was a completely different story than any I had ever heard about a Jewish family. Like most Ashkenazic Jews,[2] I was familiar with life in the Pale but had not heard much about Jews living outside its boundaries. Even more surprising was the fact that she possessed this knowledge. There was an effort in the Soviet Union to render personal history irrelevant. If it can't be forgotten, then suppress it or revise it, lest it lead to the Gulag.[3] This was a sacred moment. Vera understood the gravity of the storytelling and all the silenced voices that finally would be heard.

"This ancestor who fought with Suvorov converted to Russian Orthodoxy and was granted a title of nobility and the rank of officer." Vera then proudly narrated the tale of her father's side that linked every male back to military officers in St. Petersburg. An unbroken line until her son Lev.

"All these men married Jewish women, who, in Imperial times, converted to Russian Orthodoxy to gain permission to live in St. Petersburg."

Vera is telling me a story about men who were tied to the regime and achieved great success but, through their wives, were still linked to the fate of Jews in the Pale. Now I better understand her conflicted loyalties. Her ancestors were part of the *milukha* but were still weighed down by being Jewish.

Just when I thought I appreciated the assimilation of Vera's family into Russian life, Vera informed me that Baba Lyuba's father was a prominent and respected rabbi. In 1900 he was dispatched to America to help the Eastern European immigrants who had come to the "wonder land," as Vera called it, "like *Alice in Wonderland*." Tragically, he died soon after a return to Russia and before he could emigrate with his family to the United States as planned. *Again?* Vera never failed to amaze. *Could this all be true?* Later I verified her story with her elderly cousin.[4] Had her great-grandfather not died, he would have brought over his family, including her grandmother, and then our two stories would have merged. Vera is now setting up her favorite family story. Every family has World War II stories, but not every family shares their stories. To prepare for this moment, she stops ironing, moves to the dining room, sits down, and sips her wine. I watch her solemn gaze through our Skype connection.

"Both my parents were separated from their parents when the war first broke out." In June 1941, fourteen-year-old Misha, like many Soviet children, was in a Communist Party pioneer camp not far from Moscow. When it became apparent that the Germans were invading, Soviet officials evacuated the campers and staff eastward without informing the parents of their children's destination. Loaded onto railroad cargo cars, packed with about sixty people each, they traveled to the Russian interior with little food and water. The rumble of the train joined the sounds of children's cries.

After an excruciating four-month rail journey with prolonged stops, they finally reached Tavda, a small village in Siberia. Only forty out of the original three hundred people arrived alive.

During these months, Misha grew into manhood. By the time they reached Tavda, he had taken on the role of leader, one of the few males left who was strong enough physically and mentally to take charge. When the children finally were settled in the village, Misha assumed responsibility for gathering wood, finding food to eat, and obtaining clothes to wear. In Tavda, Misha also found the time and energy for scholarship. He felt lucky that the few adults around him devoted themselves to mentoring the youth in Russian language and literature, mathematics, chemistry, and physics. Misha attributed his passion for learning to this difficult time in his life and the few teachers who nourished him when he was hungry for knowledge. It wasn't until eighteen months after his arrival in Tavda that Misha managed to send word to his parents that he had survived. They had already mourned his death. It would be another two years before the family members reunited.

In May 1941, Baba Lyuba had sent Irina and her sister Lusya to their nanny's village, not far from Pskov, for the summer. When war broke out less than a month later, an uncle miraculously smuggled the girls back into Leningrad, already blockaded by the Nazis. Without formal training, the two teenagers served as nurses. Because Irina's parents were well connected, later the family did manage to evacuate together with their work units by crossing the frozen Lake Ladoga.

When the Great Patriotic War (World War II) ended, the Soviet Union was a country of dislocation and disorientation as survivors made their way home to recover what remained of their former lives. Twenty-three million were dead, and millions suffered physical wounds or mental trauma. In the spring of 1944, Irina and her family reached Volkhov, 100 miles from Leningrad. They were delayed there, stuck like many others, awaiting a permit to return to the liberated city of Leningrad. With millions of Soviet citizens and former POWs migrating back to their homes, they had nowhere to sleep but the railway station. One day, close to desperation, Irina, who tended to be gregarious and a bit flirtatious, exchanged words with a handsome young man, standing just ahead of her in line for a permit to return to Leningrad. His vigor and enthusiasm stood out from the other men—young and old—who looked haggard and defeated, despite their country's certain victory. He introduced himself as Mikhail Grigorevich, also a Leningrader.

Nobody would have known from Misha's confident stance that he was only sixteen, one year younger than Irina. His experience had matured him. Irina mentioned that her sister was diabetic and needed a place to sterilize her needles. Misha immediately took charge, saying he was staying in a house where a room would soon be available. Until that time, Irina's family was welcome to his room; he would find a bed elsewhere. Irina was touched but embarrassed; however, for her sister's sake, she gratefully accepted.

Misha and Irina began a conversation that day that continued for many days to follow. The attraction was so strong that even when Misha finally received his permit to return, he waited a month so that he could accompany Irina and her family back to Leningrad. Misha and Irina decided to marry in the spring of 1945, but they could not do so legally because Misha was only seventeen. Instead, they had a traditional Jewish ceremony under a ḥuppah (canopy) followed by a civil wedding a few months later, just before Vera's older brother Grisha was born.

Vera's chimerical identity suddenly made sense to me. Her ancestors had been military officers in St. Petersburg. Misha's father had been head of the Communist Party in Pskov and then trusted enough for Stalin to send him to Spain with the Propaganda Department during Franco's

Grisha, according to Vera, was the last of a long line of military officers going back two centuries.

time. Her parents married under a ḥuppah. And her brother, whom she viewed as anti-Semitic until recently, was raised by her mother's parents—the daughter of a rabbi and her husband, who secretly worshipped in synagogue every Saturday. When we met, Grisha explained that he knew this well, but his grandparents were trying to protect him by hiding their Jewish observance during the height of post-war anti-Semitism. With Vera's encouragement, he is now pursuing Israeli citizenship.

For Vera, Jewish ethnicity was not always a source of pride. She considered her family modern and unfettered by religious superstitions but weighed down by the label of their nationality. This fit with official policy. Marxist-Leninism had replaced religion, and Lenin had deposed God. A relic on display under Plexiglas,[5] Father Lenin was put to rest in his own mausoleum in Moscow's Red Square, a humidifier inserted in his chest. The idea of the embalmed Lenin both fascinated and appalled Vera. When she was born, Stalin inhabited the mausoleum as well.

Vera could never deny that she was Jewish because Soviet society continued to remind her of that fact. This meant that her father, Misha, was passed over for promotions despite the quality of his credentials. Misha understood that the system was broken, that authorities would rather promote a fool because he wasn't Jewish than a qualified man who was Jewish.

Discrimination based on nationality was illegal according to the Soviet Constitution, but contradictions abounded. Jews were highly respected for their skills and knowledge yet mocked as avaricious and untrustworthy, following the centuries-old stereotype. The underlying presumption was that Jews were different. Better or worse than others? Papa Misha wanted Vera to believe they are better.

Like many American Jews, my sister and I viewed Israel as a core part of our Jewish identity. For Vera, it was the Soviet government that reminded her family of their connection to Israel. In 1964 the KGB requested that Misha move his family to Israel to promote Soviet political influence. Misha refused to work as a spy for Russia and did not want to live in Israel. He told his superiors he was honored by the invitation but could not leave his "beloved motherland."

Vera did not understand the motivation for Zionism

until the 1970s, well after the Six-Day War when little Israel prevailed over Russia's Arab allies. Russian Jews took pride in their Judaism following this war, and a strong Jewish dissident movement was born. Some wanted to leave Russia because of their Zionist idealism. Those who were important to the Soviet government and deemed to know state secrets were refused exit permits. Others applied to emigrate to Israel for economic opportunities or personal reasons and then chose an alternate destination after reaching the transfer center in Rome. Papa Misha's younger sister Lena requested a visa for Israel in 1973. The cumbersome process required Lena to have her brother, Vera's father, sign the *OVIR* (Office of Visa and Registration) documents.

"Papa Misha could not refuse his sister," according to Vera.

Her scheming husband Meyer, he could have refused. Misha's sister tearfully claimed that her seven-year-old son, who suffered from severe asthma, was unlikely to survive into adulthood without better medical care. Misha knew the personal cost of signing these papers. His loyalty to the Party and to the Soviet Union would be suspect. He would eventually lose his rank but considered himself fortunate to be able to keep his military pension, which provided his family with some economic security. There was no other employer but the State. Lena's exodus in 1974 remained a black mark on the family, which later would have repercussions for Grisha.

*Photo (2011) of Vera with Grisha considering his future in Israel
and the pleasure of finding old friends there. Regarding his past
anti-Semitic remarks, "It was the times."*

Notes

1. Alexander Suvorov was a brilliant Russian general who never lost a battle, even one fought in winter in the Alps. He also authored a book on military tactics. Upon Suvorov's victorious return to St. Petersburg, Tsar Paul, threatened by his popularity and power, dismissed him from his post.

2. Ashkenazic, a Yiddish and Hebrew word that literally means "Germanic," designates Jews from Eastern Europe who follow religious traditions that diverge from Sephardic (lit., Spanish) Jews. For example, Ashkenazic Jews do not eat rice on Passover, whereas Sephardic Jews do. Their liturgical melodies differ as well. Ashkenazic and Sephardic Jews also pronounce Hebrew differently.

3. Gulag is an acronym for the Soviet agency responsible for the system of forced labor camps that imprisoned both criminals and political prisoners.

4. Coincidentally, Vera's cousin Roma is a congregant at the Stockholm synagogue Alisa now attends. While eating cookies after services, Leslie interviewed Roma in Russian.

5. Both men were embalmed and placed under plexiglass as a modern day relic for the thousands who would file by their bodies in Red Square. Stalin was removed from the mausoleum in 1961, five years after the cruelty of his regime was exposed during the time of Khrushchev.

16

Vera and Alla: *Druzhba*[1]

1974–1976

Zapretni plot—sladok.
"Forbidden fruit is sweet."

—Russian proverb

Rolling their eyes, smirking, and developing other tics to cope with their torpor, Vera and Alla shared their suffering through Red history and the many courses laced with Marxist-Leninism that infested their curriculum at the prestigious Institute of Finance and Economics. About 500 hours were lost on a course whose text book was called *A Short Course of the History of the CPSU* (Communist Party of the Soviet Union). Facts were sifted through a political sieve with new "information" added as deemed necessary by the Kremlin. It wasn't easy to separate the wheat from the chaff, but Vera and Alla succeeded.

Fortunately, there were also first-rate classes in statistics and accounting that would come in handy. However, the glaring omission of texts about the free market system would render what they learned in their economic courses obsolete.

At this time, capitalism was viewed as a way station on the road to socialism.

Academic demands did not interfere with Vera's newfound freedom and social life. Her initial goal was not to excel but simply to attain a degree and enjoy herself. By examination time, she realized she was overdoing the partying and had to settle down to intensive study if she wanted to remain at the Institute and assure herself a decent future.

Meanwhile, Alla soldiered through her courses, satisfied with nothing less than the highest score. She worked diligently with a private math tutor throughout her time at the Institute. Someday she would escape the nightmare of this system. But, until that day, she would play the game to win but still have what fun she could with Vera as her comrade-in-arms.

Like true sisters, they gossiped, argued, and laughed. Trust was the bedrock of their relationship; they would never betray one another. They opened doors for each other to new adventures and new perspectives in life, beginning with the doors to their homes.

When Vera first entered Alla's apartment, her eyes widened. She gasped with admiration. "It was a museum," she recalled. She entered a brighter, airier world with large rooms and a unique aesthetic. Vera could picture Baba Lyuba shaking her head in disapproval of this gallery of bourgeois pretensions. But Vera loved it. Her own home seemed like "poor *intelligentsia*"in comparison. Vera quickly calculated the reason. Both Mama Irina and Naum were dentists, but Naum could accept cash from patients whereas Irina could not. In this odd, upside-down society, status was disadvantageous. Although Vera's father was a military officer and Party member, his privileged access to special stores and spas, discounts on utilities, and his military pension paled in comparison to the opportunity to earn hard cash.

When Alla stepped into Vera's building on Blokhina for the first time, she did not notice the dark stairway nor the decor. Her curiosity gravitated to Mama Irina, her father's first love. How easy it was to understand her dad's attraction to the vibrant, engaging, open-hearted Mama Irina, so different from her own guarded mom. No need for secrets here.

Vera had chosen the international track at the Institute, an interest that dated back to her sixth-grade stint as president of the International Club. Now, Vera was studying alongside students from exotic countries like Zaire, Benin, and Vietnam. Alla felt fortunate to gain entree to the larger, albeit Soviet-aligned, world through Vera. Although foreigners were treated with the same disdain most Russians displayed toward ethnic minorities, anti-Semitism remained primal and trumped xenophobia. One day, while quietly working next to her Russian lab partners Olga and Katya, Vera heard Katya snickering and saying:

"Can you imagine Omar has to share a room with a Jew. Poor boy."

Olga nodded her head in agreement. Vera was seething, thinking, *One guy is black and another guy is Jewish. Why should anyone be sorry for either?* Vera leaned over to Katya and Olga and said, "Don't you feel sorry for yourselves that you are sharing a table with a Jew?"

"Who's Jewish?" Katya asked, startled, quickly scanning the room. Olga was already slinking down in her chair. Maintaining unnerving eye contact with Katya, Vera edged in closer and with teeth clenched, said, "I am."

Katya hastened to repair her *faux pas.* "You don't look Jewish, and you don't behave like a Jew."

Vera snorted and replied, "I'm not continuing this conversation with you because I can't guarantee that I won't beat you up." Vera had never been violent, but Katya seemed like a deserving first victim. Alla understood perfectly. In her younger days, she had punched classmates for less offensive remarks.

Vera found herself drawn toward the lively, cosmopolitan attitudes of the foreign students. Linked arm in arm, she brought Alla to the spirited parties of the African students. Gaining admittance to the dorm and scooting past the *dezhurnaya* was a challenge. Russians were generous but only within their tight-knit circles. Foreign students freely shared possessions with acquaintances expecting nothing in return but the pleasure of their smiles. Long after Alla received the Abba cassette *Dancing Queen, young and sweet—only seventeen* from an African student, it reverberated through her head. Vera's way of learning about the world was heart first, and she dove into relationships beginning with Marcel from Benin as her first case study.

For both girls, dissidence neatly coincided with their own adolescent rebellion, not against parents but against the constraints of the "stupid Soviet system." Vera was thrilled to take risks for the first time. Alla was already a veteran rebel. Her decision in 1972 to leave the Soviet Union as soon as she could was the ultimate defiance of the Soviet regime. Vera's experiments were a gamble, especially for a girl with a lot to lose. Vera harnessed all the energy that she had once generated for Young Pioneer leadership to organize her own fun.

When Vera approached Lars and me (Leslie) in the summer of 1976, she was primed to break the taboo against speaking to Americans. There was no doubt in Vera's mind that our friendship was destined. Even Mama Irina and Papa Misha approved. Vera's life expanded with her connection to us, the Americans. During the following year, Vera faithfully and emotionally wrote to me of falling in love and the associated heartbreaks. I was running through my own United Nations of men, and my friend Vera had a competitive streak. Vera told me that the upsurge in her social life coincided with meeting me. If it was possible for Vera to get bolder, she did. Having watched my sister marry at twenty and about to give birth to her first child, I realized I wanted a more adventurous life. I had no desire to establish myself and no reason to settle down. Feminism was flourishing, and my interpretation of it was that no one was going to be the boss of me.

Alla, too, exercised her boldness. At age seventeen Alla headed out on a Saturday night with another friend to a café. Glancing around, Alla spotted a well-dressed man at the bar who she suspected at first glance was Jewish; she coyly made eye contact. He approached and as they talked, Alla investigated further and probed deeper. After Boris identified himself as Jewish, an "absolutely very important" quality for Alla, she allowed herself to warm to him. After just a few dates, she confided to Vera she had found true love.

Studies in economics had not been wasted on Vera and Alla. Passion aside, they analyzed the balance sheet. Boris's well-crafted Hungarian shoes and suit broadcast his status. He was charming and Jewish, and he didn't seem to be an alcoholic. Due to the high rate of intermarriage, there were few eligible Jewish bachelors. Due to discrimination, some Jewish men tried to pass as Russians. To cope with the struggle of living in the Soviet Union, many young men embraced alcohol at a young age and loved their vodka more than their women. Boris was a decade older, but that bestowed on him more maturity. As a manager of a major food market, he had access to produce, meat, and connections. He seemed to be generous and came from a good family.

Alla's parents later filled in the negative side of the balance sheet. In Bella and Naum's eyes, a son-in-law who worked in a store was not *intelligentsia* and, therefore, stood lower in the social pyramid. After Alla's parents evinced their disapproval, Alla took the relationship underground and did not talk further with her parents about it until she announced her engagement at age eighteen.

Shocked, her father said, "Why so early?"

Her mother and her grandmother Rosa echoed the same question.

"Love," retorted Alla, tolerating no challenge.

Naum and Bella made their peace with Alla's choice and encouraged Boris and Alla's decision to marry under the huppah, still risky in the Soviet Union. Alla's parents acknowledged that Boris was a good provider, and Alla seemed happy. Things could be worse. Many newly married couples camped out in their parents' apartments while rental applications wended their way through the elaborate Soviet bureaucracy, but Boris and Alla were fortunate enough to have a place of their own— one room in a collective apartment with two other families.

For Alla, married life was not quite the romantic adventure she had dreamed. Initially, the worst part was living in a communal apartment with the obvious disadvantages of a shared bathroom and kitchen for three families. This collective had additional drawbacks including undesirable neighbors: a sloppy drunk and a self-righteous informer.

The alcoholic neighbor drank, smoked, and passed out while smoking, making Alla fear he would set the apartment ablaze. The informer neighbor was covert in her machinations.

One evening Alla and Boris invited friends to share a special Western treat—*Monopoly*. It was rare enough to indulge in a game from the forbidden West, but even more so since *Monopoly* glorified capitalism. What fun!

Alla landed on Boardwalk and announced. "I'll pay the $400 for the property."

In the adjacent room, with an ear pressed against the wall, her neighbor was aghast. Dollars were criminal. Buying property was criminal. It was her duty to phone the *militsia* (police), the only institution in Russia known for its promptness. Within half an hour of the call, the police tromped up the stairs, banged on the door, and stormed into the room to find sober young adults hunched over the Monopoly game board with the play money in front of them. The "Go to Jail" card was not played that evening, and the *militsia* trooped back down the stairs muttering about the stupid informant.

Alla laughed as she recounted the story to her parents. Naum and Bella were concerned for Alla's safety, so Naum played his own game of monopoly, trading the Dekabristov Street apartment for a new apartment for the young couple and a smaller apartment for Naum, Bella, and Rosa.

Alla and Boris were now the proud residents of a private apartment, but disillusion resided in the apartment as a third occupant. Perhaps if she acted more like a wife, she could revitalize her marriage. After a month eating their main meals at noon at the *stolovaya* (cafeteria),[2] Alla decided to cook at home for the first time. She'd begin with basic chicken soup. How hard could that be? She brought home fresh chicken from the market, complete with innards and pin feathers. She dumped the chicken straight from the shopping bag into a pot of boiling water. *Abrakadabra*, this should make chicken soup. Several hours later, a smell like Rosa's delectable soup wafted through the apartment, but the feathers, gizzards, and chicken skin floating in the broth warned Alla that chicken soup would not cure her disillusion.

After only a month of marriage, Boris did not return

home one evening. The next day he shrugged his shoulders and said, "You know how it is. The tram was delayed. The bridges were up. I couldn't get across the river. I slept at a friend's."

The "raised bridge" excuse could hold water only so long. In the ensuing years, Boris no longer bothered with excuses. Alla had always been cherished. She never anticipated that Boris would take her for granted and that her marriage would not seem "real." Her father's question echoed in her mind, why had she married so young? Because she craved independence, but she never guessed it would come with such loneliness. Her only confidante Vera would listen and understand.

Alla still had friends, and she refused to stay home alone awaiting an unreliable husband. She was still attractive and vibrant and felt like her old self when she went out with Vera and her friends from the Institute. Alla relied more and more on Vera's friendship for emotional survival. According to Alla, "The entire world around can harm you. Friendship is absolute trust."

Divorce was not an option in Alla's mind although it was relatively simple in the Soviet Union. The complication was living space. Alla lived with Boris in their comfortable apartment in a sham, but relatively polite, marriage for ten more years.

Vera sadly observed Alla's journey from romantic love to resignation. Their bubbles of hope were bursting one by one. Vera felt her friend's anguish and tried to resist her own growing cynicism about men. *How few Jewish men there were.* When she least expected it, Vera's two interests, dissidence and men intersected.

Before Alla married, she and Vera engaged in illicit activities that didn't necessarily involve romance. One October day the smell of fallen leaves was in the air. Alla had that old look of conspiratorial glee as she met Vera in their designated spot after classes. She implored Vera:

"Come with me to the synagogue for Simḥat Torah."[3]

"Alla, you're crazy. We could be arrested. What is this holiday anyway? You know I'm only Jewish on my passport. I don't observe."

"Vera, this is the one holiday when over two thousand

Jews our age come out and celebrate together without having to be afraid. Even though the police are watching us, we form such a big group that they don't dare break us up. It's amazing, Vera. You'll feel something you've never felt before."

Vera was intrigued. She had heard about this but to see it for herself and to feel that sense of pride and belonging was irresistible forbidden fruit.

On the night of Simhat Torah, Vera heard the sounds of Hebrew singing from the Grand Choral Synagogue just around the corner from the apartment building where Alla's parents lived as she hurried into the building.

Alla grabbed Vera's hand, drew her into the bedroom, and said, "Vera, try this wig on."

"Alla, why are we wearing wigs?"

"It's our protection. The KGB will be watching, but the wigs will be enough of a disguise. You know they might sprinkle good-looking young *stukachi* (informers) in the crowd. I'll take chances, but I don't want us to be dismissed from the Institute."

Across the street from the synagogue in the uppermost floor of the City Service Center, the KGB set up a temporary observation post to photograph the celebrants.

"Last year the KGB photographed my cousin. The dean called him to his office, confronted him with the picture, reminded him of his obligation not to practice religion, and expelled him. End of story. That won't happen to us."

The girls arranged their new hair, lovingly mocking each other's appearance. They pranced in front of Alla's family and laughter rippled through the room. As they made their way down Dekabristov Street toward the synagogue, they could feel the ground pulsing with the exotic rhythms of Hebrew songs. Walking through the courtyard gates, Vera's eyes filled with tears. Truly, she had never seen a mass of so many young people ecstatically celebrating their Judaism. Alla grabbed Vera's hand as they melted into the crowd, becoming part of the waves of people surging in and out of the circles. Vera and Alla had to strain to see the velvet covers of the Torah as the scrolls bobbed overhead like buoys guiding ships in a harbor. Alla and Vera were caught up in the frenzied movement. Classically trained violinists bowed frantically, quickening the pace for the dancers. The celebration snaked from the courtyard into the synagogue and back outside again. Even the capacious Grand Choral Synagogue could not contain the absolute joy of the moment.

Vera leaned closer to Alla and whispered, "This is the first time in my life I don't feel alone."

Alla whispered back, "That's why I wanted you to come."

As the celebration wound down, Alla and Vera headed to the elegant Astoria Hotel with Boris and their group of Jewish friends. Vasya, a handsome, twenty-six-year-old man, joked about his brief stint in jail for hitting a policeman. Vera was unfazed, intrigued, and hooked. The fact that he was sitting with a girlfriend did not deter Vera from flirting with him or slipping him her phone number. Vera suspected that Alla thought it foolhardy. But Alla understood Vera's attraction and admired his commitment to Judaism, even mentioning his circumcision the previous year.

Vera's boldness was rewarded. Vasya did call and the relationship took off at high velocity. Vera threw herself into love affairs focused on the moment. Besotted by this Zionist, she ignored the implications. Although she had no personal dream of moving to Israel, Vasya was her hero—a passionate idealistic man worthy of her attention. Most importantly, he was in love with her.

While Vera was floating on a cloud, Irina shuddered as she watched storm clouds gather. Vasya, like many who had applied to go to Israel, could no longer obtain work. Worse, he might fill Vera's impressionable head with crazy ideas. As usual, in times of trouble, Irina came up with a plan. She shrewdly told Vera it was time to bring her new beau home. The warm hospitality captivated Vasya, and he felt complimented when Irina pulled him aside to talk with him privately.

At the time, Vera did not realize that her mother proposed a deal that Vasya accepted. Vasya was to extend his deepest apologies to Vera and tell her that he didn't truly love her though she was a wonderful and attractive girl. Next, Vasya would say that he had reunited with his girlfriend who also planned to emigrate to Israel. In return, Irina would arrange an apprenticeship for him as an optician so that when he arrived in Israel, he would have a skill.

The plan unfolded without a hitch. Vera's heartbreak saddened Irina, but it served the greater good of the family. Hadn't they had enough trouble with Lena's departure to Israel years before? Irina and Misha packed Vera off to a resort to recuperate. Thinking Vasya had already left the country, Vera spent her first days in the country in mourning. One evening, Vera responded to a knock on her door. Seeing Vasya's face, she stood dumbfounded as tears welled up in her eyes. She felt his arms encircle her and he, too, was crying as he told her, "I couldn't leave the country without seeing you. If not for your mom, we would still be together." Vasya was the hero of her personal fantasy. She wouldn't accompany him to Israel, but he had still come to say farewell.

He explained the "agreement" between himself and Irina and how it seemed to be to everyone's benefit. Vera was no longer obsessed with "what might have been" or aggrieved by her mother's interference but, rather, deeply touched by the effort he made to find her and the knowledge that he had reciprocated her love.

In a recent conversation, I challenged Vera. "How could you not be angry at your mom?" *It's not only the Soviets who rewrite history*, I thought. Vera said, "She did it for my own good." Even then Vera knew that ultimately she would never emigrate to Israel because she didn't want to destroy the family. At that time, her life was in Leningrad. It was painful. Vera claimed she wasn't angry at her mother, but grateful. "Even if I had left the country with him, I would have realized that he wasn't the right man. Simply put, I would have outgrown him." I wondered how many years it took for her to reach this point.

Vera had spent her life thus far perfecting survival in the Soviet system. Despite the glory of adventure calling her, she was not interested in living in Israel or having to learn another system from the ground up. Most important, she was not interested in leaving Misha and Irina. After Vasya left, Vera sank into depression and cynicism. In Vera's mind, life dealt out only one true love per person. There would be no love anymore, only sex. Attention and affection from temporary liaisons kept Vera afloat.

Vera was vulnerable. "Red," her next-door-neighbor, noticed. The fact that he was Jewish was irrelevant given that he had grown into a "total hooligan" who was probably already a member of a gang. For a young, unemployed man, he had a suspicious amount of cash on hand. When Red started his flirtations, Vera was unable to resist. Alla warned Vera about this liaison. To go outside a group of friends for companionship was dangerous. It could be deadly.

Vera recalls the trip on Trolleybus #7 when she confessed to Alla the humiliating details about her relationship with Red. From Alla's stern expression, Vera could already anticipate her *I told you so*. The words followed a moment later.

"He's a thug. He treats you like garbage and now you're telling me that he hit you? Vera, your morals are going downhill. You're losing your dignity. You need to get married."

"To whom?" Vera asked with desperation in her voice.

Alla replied, "I'll look into it."

Alla followed through with her promise and introduced Vera to Sergei, a friend of Boris. Vera seems repelled when asked to reflect on that period. She'd prefer to erase Sergei from her mind. Sadly, he is now erased from life. With my prodding, Vera unearthed the buried memories. "On the surface Sergei was from a nice Jewish family. He had no obvious vices. He was handsome enough, though not my type," Vera said, referring to the compact, athletic build she preferred. Certainly, Sergei did not sweep her off her feet. On the positive side, Sergei was not completely brainwashed by the Soviet system. He was an artist and respected her. Perhaps simply to push herself forward into adulthood, Vera resolved to marry right away. "I was oblivious to feelings. I talked myself into this marriage because I didn't expect to love again. Maybe that is all I expected at that time—a Jewish husband who would be good to me and not be a drunk."

Before marrying, there was one more matter—ridding herself of Red. "I started to avoid Red, but he began to stalk me. One day, I found him lurking by our staircase. I asked him to leave me alone. Like a true hooligan he said, 'I will if you give me your sweater.' It wasn't over until another evening when he cornered me and, with cold eyes, promised 'If you give me your Jewish star, I swear from my Jewish roots and blood that you will never see me again.'"

Vera had little choice but to give him the necklace that had first drawn her to me as a safe person, *svoi chelovek*. At that time neither she nor Alla would allow a Jewish star to be visible to others. This was her punishment for bad choices.

The pressure to find a suitable mate had been yet another challenge in a system with a *defitsit* of acceptable Jewish men. Even for Vera, there was something familiar and secure about choosing a Jewish man. Alla arranged for Vera's wedding under a ḥuppah. Alla already knew her own marriage did not measure up to her dreams or even an acceptable version of reality. Though Vera expected less, she, too, would grow disenchanted.

Alla and Vera's next step was to prepare for the treadmill of work awaiting them after graduation. They were united by reluctance to feel trapped in their lives.

Grown-up life had begun.

Vera and Alla are both unhappily married by the end of their Institute years. Left to right: Boris, Vera, Sergei, and Alla.

Notes

1. The Russian language has many words for friendship. *Druzhba* connotes the closest type of friendship.

2. Russian universities, institutes, and workplaces generally provided a subsidized lunch for students and employees. This substantial lunch at the *stolovaya* (cafeteria) served as the main meal of the day. In the evening some women cooked a light meal for their families; other families ate a cold meal. When Bella and her mother Rosa cooked on the weekends, they always sent food home with Alla and Boris. This is typical for Jewish families and some Russian families.

3. For a thorough discussion of how Simhat Torah became the central holiday for Russian Jews in this time period, see Kochan, *Jews in Soviet Russia since 1917*, p. 184.

17

Vera: Living the Soviet Dream

1976–1985

S volkami zyt', povolchi vyt'.
"If you live with wolves, you have to learn to howl."
—Russian Proverb

Interrupting the tedium of everyday worries of life, and the rumbling of the trolleys that carried Vera back and forth to the Institute, were the letters and visits with the Americans. After Vera met Lars and me, she had a lifeline to the outside world.

I sensed a change in Vera from her letters of 1976 and 1977. Crafted in eloquent Russian, her distress calls and descriptions of heartbreak arrived on thin, crackling paper. It would take days for me to decode her innuendos and then construct my answer. Due to the Soviet censors, a month might be required to complete the circle of communication.

Our lives were a study in contrasts. I wrote to Vera that I had chosen to move to Minneapolis to be closer to Meryll and her family. She was appalled by my post-college "career" of temping as a Kelly girl, serving as a copy boy with Lars at the *Minneapolis Star* newspaper, and as a baker. To my good, Soviet-raised friend it was declassé. To me, it was fascinating. I was never trapped by a job but, rather, was given a new perspective that would be helpful to me later as a psychologist. Of course, I had no plan of what would happen next. Paying only $85 per month for an apartment made getting by easy. Status was not at the top of my list nor at the top of Meryll's. Meryll had curtailed her graduate studies in Arabic to support her husband, a medical student, by teaching and lived a modest life.

Vera learned how I succumbed to an ill-fated engagement and then was surprised when a year later, I extricated myself from it with my family's support. I had choices. There were plenty of Jewish men and if I decided not to marry, so be it. Vera was pleased for me when I went to graduate school to learn to teach English as a second language. The letters were important, but the best thing Lars and I ever did for Vera was to send RD to her.

RD had been teaching English to Russian immigrants in Texas before he accepted a job as a guide for the USIA (US Information Agency) Agricultural Exhibit touring the Soviet Union. This was a plum job, a training ground for future diplomats including ambassadors to Russia. Unfortunately, he knew this career path was closed to him unless he could be satisfied with a closeted gay life. So far he had maintained the secret, but he hoped the need to hide part of his identity was temporary.

In 1978 toward the end of his nine-month tour of the Soviet Union, RD dodged his KGB minders, found a phone booth, and took out the encoded phone number. Vera's "Oys!" were effervescent as she heard his gravelly voice announce he was a friend of Lars and Leslie. She had been waiting for this call for weeks, gathering hard-to-find delicacies to serve him. One look at this well-built and blond young man with bangs falling into his sincere blue eyes, and she was smitten. His fluency in the Russian language and culture was striking. What touched her most was his genuine interest in her. She felt significant. Despite the fact that he was a guide for such an important exhibit, he was unpretentious. RD understood his importance to Vera and the drama of meeting an American. "It was like having a touchstone to the outside world."

From RD's viewpoint, Vera was "warm, articulate, and extremely smart." She had insight and a perspective that few Russians possessed, likely gained at the family table where her father, privy to Western radio broadcasts, would analyze the latest moves of the Soviet system. Vera could view her country and the Russian people with objectivity and compassion despite their life of *vranya*.[1] Vera inspired a character in RD's 1984 thriller *The Cross and the Sickle*. Using Vera's words, the character expressed conflicting feelings of shame and pride in her country.

"All our friends think as we do and see clearly as we do, but we don't talk—certainly not openly—and we don't act. . . . Don't get me wrong. I love my country, and I will support and defend it forever. I don't want to live anywhere else . . . not even in America."[2]

By the end of RD's three-day visit, the bond of friendship was sealed. RD remembered Vera's tears as she said goodbye. Having no idea whether they might meet again, she clutched his arm, embraced him tightly, and repeated the words she had said to Lars and me: "Don't forget us."

RD would never forget Vera; in fact, he would try to convince her to move to the United States many times. RD became Vera's closest confidante and most trusted investor. She would return the friendship and every penny she borrowed with interest. A decade passed before RD returned to the Soviet Union and eleven years before Vera and I were reunited.

RD brought more detailed news of Vera's situation to me. I knew that marriage had sobered her. The family situation grew more serious with Papa Misha's second heart attack and then another rupture with her brother, Grisha. In 1978, Grisha reported to the military office to reenlist, only to be threatened with dismissal because of "disloyalty" for failure to report his aunt's immigration to Israel in 1974. That evening Grisha stomped angrily into the family apartment, interrupting dinner, and shouted at his parents, "Why did you make me a stinking Jew?"

Misha and Irina were stunned by his words but understood his rage. For the second time Misha reached out to an old military connection for a favor—to reinstate Grisha. Grisha's words could not be retracted or forgotten, causing bitterness to linger among family members for years. The words fell onto the pile of upsetting memories that included Grisha telling his father that he looked like an "old Jew."

"Yet," Vera noted one afternoon years later, "had Papa Misha not been forced into early retirement by Lena's emigration, we would have been unlikely to open our home to Americans and I would not have known you, Lars, and RD."

"It's ironic," I tell Vera that afternoon on Skype.

She shrugs her shoulders and responds, "Jewish luck."Vera shifted into high gear at the Institute, studying intensively during her last two years. Her future depended on it, and her best bet would be graduate study. She proposed a dissertation topic to her enthusiastic adviser. Like every Russian college student, Vera received a stipend that could be rescinded at the whim of the administration for even a trivial offense. Her future seemed set until she received a notice that her stipend was terminated, effectively slamming the door on graduate studies.

The next day, Vera knocked on her adviser's door with one question—"Why?"

The professor shrugged her shoulders, removed her glasses, and explained the facts of Institute life. "Vera Mikhailovna, when the director looked over the list of proposed graduate students, he saw your last name 'Abramovich,' and asked, 'Don't we have someone with a better name to take this spot?' I am so sorry."

Vera thanked her professor for her honesty and left knowing that a "better name" meant a non-Jewish name. It was devastating. No matter how sympathetic her professor was, Vera knew both of them were powerless to change the system.

Because she could not continue with graduate studies, Vera was compelled to join the vast Soviet distribution machine. Institute graduates were placed in appointed positions, and Vera was assigned to the Soviet version of a pawn shop as the accountant.[3] Nothing could be less interesting to Vera.

As Vera's graduation approached in 1979, her life was at a new low. Her marriage to Sergei was steeped in tension. The research position at the Institute that had seemed so certain had slipped through her fingers. Her assignment to the pawn shop was humiliating and, much to her surprise, she discovered she was pregnant.

Adding insult to injury, when the personnel manager at the pawn shop learned she was pregnant, he refused to consider her for the job that she had never wanted. In Vera's mind, there were no options. "Most of the jobs were mindless bureaucratic jobs in which you had to pretend that you were fulfilling the plan. We were all pretending then."

Just when she thought she could not survive any more disappointments, the ultimate blow occurred—a miscarriage. Sergei's words, "It's for the best," hit her like a slap in the face and planted the seed that a future with him was "utterly hopeless."

When the spring thaw of 1978 began, Vera woke up one day with a horrible pain like scissor blades cutting into her leg. The next phase, numbness, was even more frightening. Psychically, she felt paralyzed and now she was physically paralyzed as well. Her legs were no longer obeying her orders. Vera needed a wheelchair, but none was available. So she stayed in bed day after day. Her weight shot up to 200 pounds. She sank into a deep depression. This was to be the first of several medical crises for her. As Vera discussed this period, she was fighting back tears. "I had no job. I had no hope of immigrating because I didn't want to ruin my brother's career. I was done with my husband though not yet separated."

By summer the paralysis abated. But each spring, when most Leningraders looked forward to enjoying sunlight again, the paralysis would return as an unwelcome visitor dressed in different guises. No doctor could explain the unusual and disabling symptoms until 1995 when a herpes virus was diagnosed, which was treated with vitamins and medicine. Not only did Vera feel betrayed by her body, but she also felt let down by her husband. For Vera and her family, it was imperative that Sergei be a good provider and the fact that her parents had to remind him of the need to contribute was a bad omen. Although Sergei was grateful for the military exemption, he groused daily about the lithography work that Vera's family had secured for him. The chemicals were hazardous, but Vera sensed other dangers. She couldn't figure out where their money was going.

It is not one, but a cascade of events that leads to the end of a marriage. Sergei's moods had become unpredictable. One evening his eyes would be glassy, and his energy seemed manic. Another evening he would be withdrawn and vegetative. Vera could not forgive Sergei for encouraging her to have an abortion and his indifference to her miscarriage. She believed that after two failed pregnancies, she would never be able to have a child. But the final straw was Sergei's snide insinuation that when money was tight, Vera could steal from work.

"He might have sold all his principles, but I had not. I told him to pack his bags and leave."

Sergei did not leave right away, but eventually he left Vera's life for good. For Vera, no feelings remained—"complete emptiness, weight off my shoulders. Nothing more." Over time, she learned that their money had slipped away to support Sergei's drug addiction. Finally, his emotional volatility made sense. When Vera received a call from Sergei's sister six years later, telling her that Sergei had been found hanging from a tree in his hometown of Pushkin, Vera felt nothing. "I don't know if it was suicide or a murder related to his drug use. What a waste of life."

As her health improved, Vera still had to face the question, *What next?* It seemed delusional to think she could preserve herself and her values in this system. The logical conclusion for Vera was "to give up, which meant trying harder to fit into Soviet life, even to become a Party member. I felt very distant from myself as a Jew." Vera lost the connection to her Jewish friends. She and Alla were no longer close. From the few times they spoke (nobody trusted the phone), she suspected dramatic changes were occurring in Alla's life. Though they lived less than two miles from each other, Vera did not have the energy to keep the friendship alive and assumed that Alla was struggling with her own problems and did not have much time for her.

On the heels of this desperation and resignation, Vera had a sudden inspiration. Vera knew RD coordinated the English Program for Russian immigrants in Minneapolis and that I taught English as a Second Language (ESL) at the University of Minnesota. The English language had been her first love after all; so, why shouldn't she teach English to people who were waiting to leave the country? In 1979, Vera requested textbooks from us so that she could prepare a modern curriculum for teaching English privately, *na levo*. Through word of mouth Jewish students arrived, interested and eager to learn English and prepare for their new lives abroad. To pay for their tutoring, they were willing to sell their possessions. For Vera, this was a different frame of reference. Russians didn't plan ahead, but these students clearly did, and their optimism fueled hers as well. Through this experience, she might have empathized with Alla's longing to go to Israel, had she known that Alla had actually applied to emigrate. Not only was the work enjoyable and interesting but, financially, it was much more rewarding than laboring under the planned economy. "By the end of six months, I was earning 400 rubles—unheard of and about four times as much as I would have earned at my first assignment at the pawn office."

Vera proved to herself that she could be successful by pursuing interests she loved and by relying on no one but herself. Vera's tutoring business continued for about a year until the spigot was turned off in 1980. Immigration came to a halt. I succeeded RD as the director of the ESL program for Russian immigrants, and that year I felt the results on the other end of the pipeline. All three of Vera's American friends were on the cusp of new careers. RD devoted himself to writing full-time. Lars left the torpor of technical writing to begin a degree in architecture. I entered a PhD program at the University of Minnesota in clinical psychology to study cross-cultural adaptation.

Vera's choices were more limited. She had to enter the Soviet workforce. Although Alla and Vera seldom saw each other, Alla's husband helped Vera land a job as assistant manager of one of the better grocery stores in the city.

"The truth is that the experience was horrible—my worst nightmare."

Vera was responsible for opening the store and ensuring shelves were stocked with the little that was available. The first morning, she approached three employees sitting on crates, sharing a bottle of vodka. She greeted them and politely requested them to move five cases of apples to the fruit counter and ten cases of milk and four boxes of butter to the dairy counter, and so forth. "They looked at me as if I were speaking a foreign language and kept talking among themselves. At 8:00 a.m. the store opened, but no progress was made because the men continued to ignore me."

At 9:30 a.m., the short, pudgy, forty-year-old manager from a neighboring store strutted in, wearing a faded dress and a fur hat. She had heard the customers' complaints about the empty shelves. After Vera explained the situation, this seasoned manager instructed, "Watch me!" She marched over to the makeshift bar where the men had emptied their first bottle of vodka. Shoulders back and hands on hips, she bellowed:

"You motherfucking bastards, get off your lazy asses, stand up on your fucking feet, and fucking go to the fucking storage area and move those fucking cases or I'll kick your sorry asses out of here." Startled out of their drunken trance, they snapped to attention and followed orders.

Vera was impressed. "I asked my new friend to write down an exact transcription of the words she had used to facilitate the process. I had never before heard so many different useful words of Russian *mat'*.[4] That may have been my first lesson in effective management. In two months, my mom told me that she could not stand my language because I now articulated very few meaningful words, and the majority of my words were cuss words." Working at the grocery meant that the family always had access to food, but there were serious challenges.

"My job was to survive, and to do so I would have to be like everyone else. We sold meat, vegetables, milk and fruit—food that was constantly in demand but in poor supply. This made it a ripe opportunity for people to steal and take advantage, as is typical in Russian workplaces." Russians rationalized that if they took anything from a government entity in this socialist state, they were, in fact, simply taking property that belonged to them. Thus, the best meat would go out the back door at a higher price, and the money into the pocket of one of the butchers there or, for the more daring employees, in cases or satchels that went home with the workers.

Vera explained that she was accustomed to having adults who were close to her treat her kindly. Perhaps that was due to her family connections but, more likely, she concluded it was because of her charm, intellect, and hard work. That changed in the spring of 1982 when, following a routine inventory, her boss informed her that money was missing and she was responsible. The blood rushed to Vera's head knowing she could go to prison for this. Shaking and in tears, she called her parents at midnight. Awakened by the call, Misha listened calmly though he was inwardly raging, knowing that his daughter was being set up. Misha asked one question: How much? Vera said, " 2500 rubles," almost the price of the new car for which Misha had been saving. Misha told her he would pay them the missing money, but she must quit immediately. Vera had been scapegoated by her boss once and it could happen again.

One connection could make all the difference in Soviet life. Vera was rescued by the personnel director of the grocery store headquarters who, in 1983, offered her the position of Director of Production Education. She warned Vera that it was not a high status job, but "offered a degree of freedom and opportunity to use her brain." Vera would write speeches for the bosses and reports about the latest Marxist-Leninist economic achievements for the continued education of middle managers. The two women got along well, sharing their sense of irony for touting the mythical achievements of their inefficient system.

Vera was ready to go along with the "Soviet Communist bullshit," giving up her resistance to join the Communist Party. Without party membership, her opportunities for advancement would be limited. Vera's boss championed her application. Vera quips, "You'll be surprised what a joke my Jewish luck played on me."

Usually blue collar workers were favored for Party positions. Ironically, that year this job, the most intellectually stimulating to date, was graded as blue collar, but the quota of one Jew was reserved for a white collar position. Vera shrugged, "Once again, I didn't fit the system."

Even this could not break Vera's optimistic mood as she had succeeded in achieving other, more meaningful goals. She lost sixty pounds and regained a sense of attractiveness. She noticed, as did her parents, that her flirtatious overtures were reciprocated. Through a barter with friends, Irina and Misha found a small apartment for Vera so they did not have to witness too much of her social renaissance.

After Vera's application for party membership was rejected, Vera's boss continued to support her, recommending her for a new job opportunity at the Moscow Research Institute, where she would be involved in a radical new project applying market research tools to understand consumer demand in Russia. Never before had consumers' needs been studied in any methodical way. Certainly, marketing had never been taught at the Leningrad Institute of Finance and Economics.

For Vera, using capitalist theories and measures was nothing short of revolutionary. She felt at home on the leading edge of economic research (at least in the Soviet Union). It was intriguing, stimulating, and also her idea of fun. Vera achieved the equivalent of a PhD in marketing.

"I had lost weight. I looked great. I felt confident. I was in no hurry to get married. Finally, life seemed good."

Notes

1. *Vranya* is derived from the word for a lie, but it is so much more than that. It is deception, double-think, often with the knowledge that listener and speaker are sharing in this deceit. The speaker pretends that something is true and the listener pretends to believe it.

2. Robert D. Zimmerman, *The Cross and the Sickle* (New York: Kensington, 1984), pp. 52–53.

3. Pawn shops in the Soviet Union served a banking function by providing a credit line. One would bring some form of collateral to the store and receive 60% of its appraised value; then after receiving one's salary, one would repay the original amount interest-free.

4. *Mat'* refers to obscenities. It is part of everyday language for the *nekulturni* (uneducated) but also appreciated by the educated for its richness and elaboration of a few basic Russian words. It is difficult to translate *mat'* word-for-word so the translated sentence is written to convey the general tone.

18

Vera: Love and Politics

1984–1986

"I will never share your stupid beliefs, but I will respect them."

—Vera

It seemed like Vera's real life, the one she had planned, had finally begun. These days she felt not only successful in her research position, but beautiful. She had no expectations of marriage or any wish to marry. She had a tacit agreement with her friend Andrei to meet once a week for a romantic encounter with no commitment.

On April 14, Vera knew Andrei was assembling a group of friends, and she was sure they would be interesting and well-educated people. She put on a borrowed dress and admired her reflection in the mirror. Then she wrapped herself in an expensive white, fur-trimmed coat and donned a matching fur hat, overly generous gifts from her parents. Vera strode confidently into Andrei's small apartment, crowded with people. She was immediately captivated by a handsome, animated man surrounded by a small groups of rapt listeners.

Vera edged herself closer to hear the story. The speaker's blue eyes noted the new audience member. Nodding to her as he continued, Vera felt that his attention was directed to her alone.

"Alexei was hilarious," Vera remembered. His intelligence and wit would meet even Baba Lyuba's high standards. It seemed that the attraction was mutual.

Andrei took one look at Vera's starstruck face and said, "No way will this happen. Don't even think about it. He's married. He has two children. He's a loyal husband and a great father. Won't happen." Andrei's warning only emboldened Vera who had just set a new goal for herself.

When the party ended after 1:00 a.m. and Alexei was leaving to escort his drunk boss home, Vera offered to keep them company. By the time the boss was deposited at his apartment, Alexei had already missed the last train to his parents' home where he lived during the workweek. His wife and children lived seventy-five miles away. Vera thought it only polite and rather strategic to offer him the couch in her apartment. After walking Alexei to work the next morning and exchanging phone numbers, Vera counted down forty-eight hours before she called him.

Alexei told Vera he would be stopping by Andrei's house later that day. Vera appeared at Andrei's house at the time designated by Alexei. When Andrei left the room, Vera whispered to Alexei like a conspiratorial teenager, "Do you want to go to the movies with me?"

Alexei's eyebrows shot up, and he said with amusement, "What are you going to tell your boyfriend?"

Vera jauntily said, "It's none of his business. But if you want to go, you need to leave immediately. I'll meet up with you in ten minutes."

Exactly ten minutes later, Vera feigned a headache, expressed her apologies, left Andrei's apartment, and ran down the steps to meet Alexei at the corner. As they walked to the movie, Alexei said, "Will you also buy me a drink?"

"The movie ticket, a drink, and chewing gum!" Vera responded. She was willing to take a risk for a good return on her investment. Since that night in 1986, they have rarely spent a night apart.

Dreamily, Vera confided to Alla, "Alexei is the most wonderful man I have ever met in my life."

Alla sighed. She had heard this before. Alla could not be sympathetic to her friend falling in love with a man who was not Jewish, still married, and had two children. She would be driven away further as she learned about Alexei's politics. In this case, her opinion did not seem to matter.

After the first torrid month, Vera and Alexei planned a two-week get-away, which her co-workers and Alla predicted would inevitably dampen the infatuation. The couple found an idyllic forested retreat in Lithuania. Arm in arm, they strolled along the Nieman River breathing in the fresh pine-filled air. Everything was serene and romantic until Alexei opened the heretofore unspoken topic of politics. Alexei chose a romantic moment with Vera to criticize Alla's husband, Boris, for "cheating old *babushki*" by giving the best cuts of meat to friends from the store he managed.

Vera was shocked. She suddenly felt like she was talking to someone from another planet, a communist planet, one she didn't care to inhabit on vacation. The fact that this topic arose testifies to the complexity and unique randomness of Alexei's mind. Following Alexei's train of thought was like meandering on unmarked trails in a deep forest, never knowing if he was leading you to a destination or simply enjoying his companion's disorientation.

Indignant with his hypocrisy, Vera reminded her lover, "You're benefiting from this same system. Either use your connections to your advantage and shut your mouth or queue up for meat behind the old *babushki*, and then you can protest in solidarity with them."

In case that wasn't completely clear, she added, "If you can afford to buy from the back door, that means you have revenues that you got in not such an honest way." His jaw dropped. He had never been talked to this way before. He suggested a change of subject. Vera's greatest dilemma was now clear. She just happened to fall madly in love with someone who actually bought the Communist Party line—hook, line, and sinker. He didn't inhabit two realities like her close friends but only this one—the one scripted by Soviet propagandists. She made peace by telling him she would never share his stupid beliefs but would respect them. "In the meantime," she reminded him, "if you feel that strongly about it, don't buy from the back door."

Alexei's position was not unusual. The goal of a Soviet education, after all, was indoctrination. History was rewritten era after era to eliminate inconsistencies, to clarify and legitimize the current regime's stance. Information was controlled, and anything foreign was suspect. Alexei, like the majority of Russians, had never considered the concept of hypocrisy. To survive, he had learned to parrot the party line. Or, as Vera would rationalize, "When he was discussing political issues, he automatically brought up all this garbage from his mouth." He continued to buy from the back door, but stopped criticizing Vera's friends. In time, he realized that he, like everyone else, participated in the corruption in a society in which an underground economy was necessary to meet the most basic demands of daily life.

However, something deeper was occuring here. Alexei had learned different survival techniques growing up. In Alexei's family, with good reason, no one discussed politics or challenged Soviet ideology. His mother had grown up with terror. Her father, a loyal, well-positioned Communist, was forced to abandon his family when an informant alleged that his father had owned boats twenty years earlier. For the crime of his father's bourgeois past, Alexei's grandfather was arrested and sentenced to hard labor in Siberia where he died. Members of the family were labeled political enemies, *CSVR* (Members of the Family of an Enemy of the State), and were treated like outcasts. This label remained in the KGB files until amnesty was granted under Khrushchev in the late 1950s. Alexei's mother carried this trauma with her constantly, and she desperately sought safety for her children without telling them why. Alexei did not learn of this family history until he was an adult.

In the end, it wasn't Vera who changed Alexei's mind over the next year but Vera's father, Mikhail Grigorevich, a former party member. As Alexei said, "No doubt if Mikhail Grigorevich had been a rabbi in a synagogue, I would have become an observant Jew. He was that persuasive and influential a man. Mikhail Grigorevich was one of the few people who was *nezashoren* (without blinders). All of the people in the

Soviet Union were like horses with blinders on, living with half-open eyes and seeing only the things they were allowed to see. I was like the majority. I, too, had blinders on, as did my parents. Mikhail Grigorevich could analyze information clearly because he was looking with open eyes, and he taught me to do the same."

Although Alexei felt freer after the blinders were removed, he also felt angry at the system and the deceptions it forced upon him. Misha advised self-restraint. Expressing anger openly would lead to danger.

"If you want to survive," Misha told Alexei as he paced the room, "the most important thing is to know your way through this horrible system, and the strategy is to do your job as well as you can. Be valuable to the system and use the system to your own benefit." Misha also counseled him regarding personal responsibility. Alexei must choose between Vera and his family and stop living a double life. Alexei felt torn. Divorce was common; life in Russia was very hard on a marriage. Alexei was concerned about the welfare of his wife and children, so it took courage to finally tell his wife he wanted a divorce. His wife declared she was in love with his best friend. The desire for a divorce was mutual. As usual with these situations, living space was the issue. When Alexei offered an apartment in the city to his first wife, the divorce could proceed.

To Vera's surprise she became pregnant in January 1986. Vera described their May wedding as "perfect" although the bride and groom may have been the only ones who enjoyed it. For Vera, it meant an opportunity to use her connections at her new job at the State Fashion House to design the ideal dress of imported pink fabric for her five-month-pregnant figure. She and Alexei personally hosted a lavish reception at the Grand Hotel Europe.

By this time, Vera and Alla were so distant that Alla was not invited. Vera would say that Alla had gone "underground" as she did when trouble brewed. Alla would say she was questioning whether she could trust Alexei at that time regarding her illegal plan to leave Russia, so she kept her distance from the couple.

"Alexei's mother was spitting mad," according to Vera. "We were breaking too many rules. Alexei was a criminal for leaving his family for me. I was more of a criminal. I was clearly not a virgin, and I was divorced and pregnant. Because Alexei's mother was unhappy, his father was not allowed to enjoy himself." Alexei and Vera didn't even discuss a huppah because "I thought it would give Alexei's mother apoplexy."

Vera's parents loved Alexei and hoped Vera would be happy and that her mother-in-law would come to adore their daughter. Vera remembers crying at the words "husband and wife." She never imagined having a second chance to feel such love again. Vera recalled a favorite picture of Papa Misha kissing Mama Irina on their thirty-seventh anniversary and thinking, *I want my husband to kiss me that passionately when we have been married thirty-seven years.* It's very likely that he will.

Alexei and a pregnant Vera surrounded by their parents at their wedding. From left to right: Standing–Alexei's father, Alexei, Vera, Misha. Seated–Alexei's mother, Irina.

19

Alla: The Game of Risk

1979–1986

Never give up. Everything is possible, the impossible only takes longer.

—Alla

By 1979 anger enveloped Alla. Boris's routine infidelities humiliated her. Her work was meaningless. Had she worked this hard to complete her degree with honors at the Institute only to find herself in a mind-numbing internship as an economist, where she was now just a cog in the planned state economy? Granted, most graduates were resigned to their fates, but she and Vera learned from their fathers to question the system. For seven years, she had vowed to leave this country for Israel. Now was the time to act.

Alla's dilemma was to identify a trade that could provide a comfortable living in Israel's capitalist economy and wouldn't require fluency in Hebrew. Her work had to allow her creative freedom and not bore her. Alla researched through her network of friends. Her decision was one that would surprise every university friend—hairdressing school.

Although unfaithful, Boris was loyal to Alla in his way and promised his financial support if she wanted to return to school following her internship. Alla was grateful, and the marriage evolved into a tolerable contract for Alla—settling for a relationship without love to get out of Russia. Boris's offer also enabled her to save face by not revealing to her parents that she had made a mistake when she thought she had found true love at eighteen.

Hairdressing school was a steep step down in status, and Alla's parents were aghast. Purposely lowering one's status was simply not done in Russia. An institute graduate did not enter trade school. Alla deflected her parents' criticism although she, too, was secretly mortified. No matter. This was part of her campaign to leave, and nothing would dissuade her. To succeed she needed to keep her own counsel, play the Soviet system, and win without harming anyone else. She needed an impermeable shell to hide her motives and her feelings.

"Never give up, everything is possible, the impossible only takes longer," Alla whispered to herself and continued to whisper year after year until her slogan became her truth.

Alla accepted the humiliation of "downgrading" her status. Once she entered the hairdressing school in 1981, her competitive juices flowed. Her goal was to be "the best of the best and work in the most renowned salon in Leningrad." Academic classes were "like a game" for her. In those classes she sat in the front row and raised her hand to answer all the questions. Finally, the instructors simply said, "Alla, okay, we know you know all the answers. Can you put your hand down and let someone else answer?"

To further her rise to the top in hairstyling, she sought out a mentor, a renowned hairdresser who worked on Nevsky Prospekt. He, too, had applied to emigrate to Israel, but still had a year or two before his visa would be approved.

For their final exam, the aspiring hairdressers competed to create a hairstyle before a jury. Alla was nervous. She set her sights on the gold medal but finished with silver. Not bad for a Jewish economist. It was clear to Alla she had been the best, but coming in second was nothing new. Having a Jew finish in first place was not considered "appropriate" to a panel of Russian judges. Alla earned a prize more valuable than a first-place certificate, a job at the prestigious Salon #120, known among the cognoscenti as The Salon on Nevsky.

The Salon on Nevsky where Alla worked was located on the corner. (2011 photo).

Even before establishing herself in her new profession, Alla was working on step two—to make her dream of emigration a shared dream among all her family members. How could she leave them behind? She began an all-out campaign to convince her family to apply for visas to Israel. After eight years, and perhaps worn down by Alla's relentless campaign, the struggle ended with Alla victorious. Alla's graduation from hairdressing school in 1982 was a minor accomplishment compared to her family's acquiescence to begin the process of filing to leave for Israel.

It would take Alla four years to leave the Soviet Union from the time she first submitted papers in 1982, and it would be a different route than she ever had imagined. Getting out of Russia was not as simple as buying a plane ticket, packing, and saying one's good-byes. First Alla needed to procure an invitation from an "Israeli relative." For those like Alla without *bona fide* relatives, there was a network of names and addresses provided by sympathetic Israelis who would become "family" and sponsor a Russian emigrant.

Next Alla assembled her family's *spravka*—the massive

pile of documentation, certification, and notarized papers. It was no mean feat to compile this mountain of paperwork, chasing after minor officials at school, work, and in the apartment building, as well as obtaining signed permission slips from all relatives permitting the family to leave. Just as the Soviet system intended, it also meant having to tolerate the harsh judgment of minor bureaucrats, job loss, and the possible risks to the relatives who had signed. After all the forms were sent to OVIR (Office of Visas and Registration), there was nothing to do but wait with the family's life hanging in the balance. Alla steeled herself for the wait and the repercussions. In 1983 the official envelope from OVIR arrived. In it lay the fates of Alla, Naum, Bella, Gera, and Rosa. Alla raced to her parents' apartment to discover their future. No one breathed and even the air in the apartment seemed absolutely still. "Denied. Your request is invalid." The thin paper fluttered to the floor from Alla's hand.

The stark, official denial pierced Alla to her soul. *Why go on? Nothing would ever change.*

"It was the end of life," remembers Alla when she recalls her feelings after the refusal.

Alla was not aware of how few Russian Jews were granted permission to leave in 1983—a paltry 1,315 out of tens of thousands who had applied. In 1979 over 50,000 Jews had been granted permission to leave. What had changed? Without a free press, Alla had no way of knowing that her refusal could be traced back to the Soviet invasion of Afghanistan. The Soviet Union had opened the doors for Jewish emigration to improve relations with the United States. When the United States protested the invasion of Afghanistan, the Soviet Union reverted to a hard-line approach to emigration. Alla's application dropped into the pile at OVIR in the midst of the Kremlin's 1982 directive to erect barriers to emigration and to jail more dissidents.[1]

Now what? She had to escape this life of constraints. She would not remain in this prison of a country. It was a place where you could be seduced into thinking one day that you were living well. The next day, the hammer and sickle could fall on your head. Bribes and connections were the currency.

Every day she had to censor her thoughts and censor authentic Alla.

Day after day she tried to concoct an escape route. While cutting and coloring at The Salon, Alla had plenty of time to ruminate over her exit strategy. After months of brainstorming one impractical plan after another, an opportunity to leave presented itself, and Alla exploited the chance despite the risks involved.

Meanwhile, she had to admit that although hairdressing had been a pragmatic choice, she enjoyed it. She had never expected to laugh at her job or have fun in a Soviet workplace. Sure, it was a low-status job, but this also meant there was no pressure to be a Communist Party member. Alla reveled in the creativity, simplicity, and openness of her coworkers. Most importantly, she could remain under the radar of the Soviet authorities while preparing her visa request. Ironically, Alla was earning far more than she could have as an economist, due to tips under the table.

However, even in Alla's fashionable salon, danger lurked. Something so trivial as accepting a tip from a grateful client was against Soviet law and punishable by a five-year prison sentence. Yet, everyone from government functionaries to doctors expected a tip for a personal favor or special treatment to supplement their meager income. When the police or KGB wanted to exert control over a Russian citizen, they could arbitrarily invoke Article 153 forbidding tips.

Salons not only provided a creative outlet in a pleasant atmosphere with cash tips but were also a hub of black market activity. This was the place to find quality clothing as opposed to the shoddy apparel in government stores. You could also exchange rubles for foreign currency, a wise investment, but another forbidden activity.

By nature, Alla was observant, especially of style. In 1983, still depressed the year after OVIR denied her visa request, she noticed Larissa, a dark-haired Russian woman outfitted in expensive designer gear at the salon. Bit by bit, Alla was trying to piece together her story. Where did she get these clothes? How did she travel freely? What gave her the freedom she seemed to flaunt? Larissa was a regular at the salon, conducting her business in leather goods *na levo* (on the side). Although

Larissa punctuated her speech with vulgarity and had the look of a woman who enjoyed her drink and probably was familiar with a variety of illicit drugs, Alla admired her entrepreneurial courage. Through the grapevine, she learned that Larissa had married a Finn and then moved to Sweden. This was key to her business success as she could come and go freely, collecting her merchandise cheaply in Scandinavia and then traveling to Leningrad frequently to sell it for twice the price. It was more than the clothing that intrigued Alla.

Alla wondered whether this woman could be trusted as she watched Larissa operate in the salon. Deciding it was worth the risk, she plotted her strategy carefully. She invited Larissa for a drink in the safety of her apartment where they could talk freely. Alla had already prepared Boris. That night, Alla gathered her courage and, after a few drinks and small talk, leaned over to Larissa, gently interrogating her on the details of her escape from Russia. Larissa's responses were simple and direct. She married a Finnish man in Leningrad, secured the visa, and moved to Finland. She divorced him and then settled in Sweden. At this revelation, everyone in the room fell silent. Boris glanced at Alla, wondering how far she would take the conversation. Alla breathed deeply and then continued her questioning, "Could you help me to leave, too?"

Without missing a beat, Larissa responded as if this were simply another routine service she provided to her best customers. The price was 25,000 Swedish *kronor* (approximately $3600 at the time), and Larissa would furnish her current Swedish boyfriend as Alla's husband. Alla could even live with Larissa and her boyfriend Sven for the first month after she moved to Sweden.

Based on her observations of Larissa, Alla felt she was completely untrustworthy; however, in the matter that concerned her, she hoped it would be in Larissa's self-interest to keep quiet and honor her part of the deal. No doubt, this was a lucrative deal for Larissa; for Alla, it was a risky step. It felt like this was her last chance to leave the stifling Communist regime. Without wavering, Alla agreed to all the terms. It was a fortune for her at that time. In the next months, Alla sold as much jewelry, crystal, and vases as she could. With the proceeds plus her tip money, she could pay half the stipulated fee to

Larissa. The rest would be due later. She had just sold herself into marriage. And she wasn't even divorced from Boris.

Her family thought this was the craziest idea yet. It was not enough that her parents had to hide Alla's career change from economist to hairdresser, but now this? They were mortified and terrified in equal measure. Evenings were filled with tears and pleas and "oys." Alla shut the door and was afraid to question her own judgment. She had come too far.

"They couldn't stop me, and there was no point to discuss it. They cried and they cried."

Boris readily agreed to a civil divorce in 1984. They filed the requisite forms with the Department of Civil Status. Done. He kept Alla's secret along with the apartment. In return, Alla received the divorce document, her books, and some cash. Until she would leave, Alla moved into her parents' apartment and closed her ears to her parents' entreaties to remain with them.

Most of Alla's acquaintances were shocked to hear about the divorce. They could only assess the relationship from a pragmatic viewpoint. Boris was a good provider. He wasn't alcoholic or abusive. Alla's divorce made no sense in the Soviet world where it was the norm for men and women to cheat if they wanted "love." She didn't dare tell them about her planned escape.

Vera was the one with whom she wanted to discuss this whole scheme, weighing the risks and benefits. But there was no way, not with this new Soviet boyfriend of Vera's. Who knew whether he could keep quiet? She missed their friendship. Vera's life was moving in such a different direction. After much hardship, Vera seemed to be finding a place for herself within the Soviet system and now that she was also divorced, she was reinventing herself. The two women kept in touch, but the contact was superficial. Alla was no longer sharing her deepest secrets with Vera, remembering their longstanding arguments about Jewish identity and believing that Vera would have disapproved of her visa application to Israel.

Alla now focused all her energies on her exit strategy. Fortunately, Larissa was a one-stop black market expert. Aside from offering leather goods and a husband, she had another business—foreign currency exchange. One of her foreign customers was Kalle, a successful Stockholm businessman who had arrived in Leningrad to sell construction machinery. He needed to exchange Swedish *kronor* for rubles and contacted Larissa, who then arranged for Alla to meet Kalle, so she would have a contact in Sweden.

Alla knew the rules she was breaking. Russians were not permitted to meet with foreigners. With manufactured confidence, she strode into the Park Inn and saw a man about the age of her father nod at her. Alla had a sense about people, and Kalle inspired trust and openness like Naum. Her shoulders relaxed, and she began to talk to him as though they were already friends. It felt so good to be freed from her self-imposed secrecy even for a few minutes. She revealed all the details of her plans to him from the phony marriage to the proposed *ménage à trois*.

Alla concluded, "I am looking for freedom."

He listened intently, hearing her desperation to leave. Kalle implored her, "Just let me know when you are coming. Send me a postcard with just your arrival date."

"I fully understand, just the date." Alla nodded and embraced him.

Tears of gratitude for her luck welled in her eyes as she placed the address carefully in her purse and set out on the return journey to central Leningrad.

The late autumn wind was blowing off the Neva River. In the dark chill, Alla walked with determination up Nevsky Prospekt to The Salon on Nevsky. She was deep in thought on this, her wedding day, November 1984. It would not be romantic or spiritual. No fairy-tale bride today. Alla would close the deal with a civil ceremony in the ZAGS office,[2] and then she could submit her request to join her husband in Sweden. Alla had to remain cautious. There were so many people to consider and to protect.

Walking to work, she considered the salon manager, a Communist Party member. The manager had been kind to her, and Alla wanted to reciprocate with honesty. At least partial honesty. Like most Soviet dissidents or refuseniks, Alla operated in two systems of morality. Breaking the Soviet law and lying to authorities was often necessary, but it was absolutely immoral to be dishonest with friends or endanger them.

Alla walked in the door and, in a quiet moment, motioned to the manager. They moved to a quiet corner. Alla explained she was marrying a foreigner and then would emigrate after she received permission to leave. She offered to resign as a hairdresser so she wouldn't cause problems. Everyone knew a story of the police or KGB bursting into a business and arresting people who were awaiting visas. Knowing that it could take a year or longer to obtain her visa after the marriage, the manager offered Alla work in the back room, which she gratefully accepted.

In 1986 while Alla still awaited papers to travel to Sweden as Sven's wife, Vera introduced her to Alexei, her Communist boyfriend. When they were alone, Alla listed the problems. Alexei was married when they met. He was not Jewish.[3] How did Vera know he wouldn't cheat on her if he cheated on his wife? Vera bristled at the comments and waved her hand in front of Alla indicating she was not the least bit interested in a cost/benefit analysis of the relationship. She just wanted Alla to be happy for her.

To further that goal, Vera invited Alla to get together with Alexei and her one evening. Alla felt she owed Vera that. Vera had never looked so happy. The evening began with cordiality but spiraled into a disaster once the talk became political. Alexei spouted all the party nonsense that was anathema to Alla. Alla was insulted by his arrogance. He mocked her job as a hairdresser, and he lashed out at Boris for "selling out the back door." Alexei's talk underscored for Alla why she couldn't live in this crazy country where people could no longer think for themselves. What was happening to her friend Vera? Who was she becoming? Alla slowly began to close herself off from Vera. She was hurt that Vera refused to listen to her concerns about Alexei. Vera could feel the distance, and it stung. It would be years before Alla would understand the political transformation of Alexei that Vera had undertaken and for Vera to forgive Alla her secrecy.

Following her marriage to Sven, it took eighteen months for Alla's emigration papers to move from desk to desk through the serpentine Soviet bureaucracy. In the summer of 1986, her visa was in hand and she could board a ship for Sweden, not

as a refugee but, as the wife of a Swedish citizen. At least that
was what Larissa promised.

Notes

1. In 1981, a year before Alla submitted her request for a visa to Israel, Soviet
Premier Andropov wrote a memo to the Communist Party leadership urging the
Soviet Union to "thwart the plans of the adversary [Israel] in sending out more
invitations to Russian Jews to Israel." By 1983 an anti-Zionist committee was
formed by the Soviet government with thirteen employees to track refuseniks.
Boris Morozov, *Documents on Soviet Jewish Emigration* (London: Frank Cass,
1999), pp. 236–237. For an extensive account of the Soviet Jews' struggle to
leave for Israel, see Beckerman, *When They Come for Us We'll be Gone*. Although
mainly an account of the movement outside of the Soviet Union, it provides
a clear picture of the situation of Soviet Jews as well. Both Morozov and
Beckerman had access to the Soviet archives that were opened under Yeltsin.

2. ZAGS is the acronym for the civil registry for marriage and divorce.

3. Alexei's father was Jewish but according to Jewish law, a child is Jewish only
if his mother is Jewish. Alexei had not been raised with Jewish traditions, and
he listed his nationality as "Russian" on his passport.

20

Alla: Leavetaking

Summer 1986

I was going into the nowhere.

—Alla

lla felt like she was about to disappear. Absolute fear seized her as she surreptitiously visited each friend and memorized her cityscape.

"I was so undercover," she remembers. "I didn't know anything. I was going into nowhere. I was absolutely terrified, but I was so determined to go."

Leaving her family and friends was bittersweet. There would be no bon voyage parties for Alla or even a quick cup of tea and a hug good-bye with a promise to write. To protect herself and her friends, Alla had to leave without formal farewells. A stray word could prove dangerous. Even though Alla and Vera's friendship was flagging by the summer of 1986, it pained her to leave Vera with a whiff of dishonesty, withholding the entire story of her fake marriage. Alla still distrusted Alexei, but she felt the pull of her sister-friend Vera. She called Vera when she knew Alexei would not be present.

Vera, surprised by the call and hopeful that the distance between them could be bridged, invited Alla to her apartment. Vera was aching to share with Alla the hardships and excitement of her pregnancy. For Alla, the prospect of this visit was unbearably painful because only she knew its significance as a final farewell. She would have to guard her words instead of pouring out her heart to Vera.

Alla arrived with a small package concealed in her purse. They chatted, but Alla couldn't offer Vera her full attention and empathy. Had Vera not been so preoccupied with her pregnancy, she would have surely picked up the signals that Alla was hiding something. Before parting, Alla handed Vera the gift.

"It's not my birthday, Alla. Why the present?"

Alla shrugged and encouraged Vera to open it—a wooden box, so Vera would not forget her. Ignoring Vera's puzzled expression, Alla hugged her friend and tried to hide her tears as she said good-bye.

What do you take with you when you close the door on your old life, leaving your past behind? Bella would help with practical comforts and advice. Which memories would Alla select? Which memories would return unbidden in dreams? Alla had one more glance over her shoulder at her Leningrad before leaving. Her head was bursting with details and fears, but she could not ignore the casual invitation from her friend Natalya to visit an artist's studio. Art could always feed Alla's soul. The vibrant underground art scene in Leningrad would be a distraction. Artists dared speak freely with their brushstrokes and composition.

A beautiful woman opened the door to Sergei Potapenko's studio.[1] Alla and Natalya peered in and saw a room stripped bare except for the paintings leaning against the wall. Instantly, one of the paintings drew Alla. As she moved toward the portrait, her fears retreated. All the empty space was filled with wonder as she opened herself to the soft, gray and brown tones of the paintings. Staring back at her from the most captivating painting was a woman with a mysterious smile and deep, dark eyes—her own Mona Lisa—whispering to her "Everything will be all right." Alla moved closer to the painting and declared, "I love it! Can I buy it?"

"Of course. You know, that's a portrait of me that Sergei painted."

Disheartened, Alla dutifully asked, "Are you sure you want to sell it?"

"Sergei has already left for Italy. I need to raise the money to leave, so you will be doing me a favor if you can buy it."

Maybe it was self-indulgent to buy this painting at a time when she would need every bit of cash, but she also needed to bring her Mona Lisa with her to remember Leningrad with its creativity locked underground but impossible to restrain. She and Potapenko's Mona Lisa would be leaving soon.

Twenty-two boxes surrounded Alla and her family the night before she left. Her parents' apartment became the launching pad for her new life. Implacable Alla would not be dissuaded from leaving. Her parents couldn't stop her, so they helped her. She

This painting was Alla's talisman keeping her hopeful even in the dark days to come.

packed carefully not knowing what she would need in Sweden and what was available there. Into the boxes went bed quilts, dishes, winter coats. Bella kept adding items to the inventory. Alla was headed into the great unknown, and it was best to be prepared. Each item was duly listed on an inventory, values noted, and, when required, Alla secured the proper papers from various authorities. She scrupulously followed every rule, so the Soviet customs officials would not be able to accuse her of even the smallest infraction of the law.

There was one document Alla wanted to pack but could not obtain—a *get*,[2] a Jewish divorce. She knew that according to Jewish law, she could not remarry a Jewish man without it. Boris was indifferent, but Alla and her mother tirelessly explored every avenue. There were not three rabbis in Russia who could constitute a rabbinical court, nor was there a scribe to write the *get* according to the proper procedure. Witnessing the *get* could be dangerous for friends. Alla had to leave with only her Russian civil divorce.

It had been a comfort for Bella and Naum to have Alla close to them for the year between her divorce and departure. Alla wanted her mother to embrace her and murmur, "Allochka, everything will be all right." But Alla knew her mother couldn't lie to her. There was no assurance that everything would be all right. At a loss for comforting words, Bella bustled and helped with the packing adding more and more "you might need this" items to the boxes.

Then, two nights before departure, Rosa and Bella broke down in tears. A funeral was in progress with Alla the living corpse.

"We'll never see you again, Alla," they wailed again and again.

Naum's stoicism was cracking. Would he see his Alla again? Naum forced himself to focus. He was a military man, after all, and had to maintain his military bearing. He hadn't cracked during the siege of Leningrad. He would not show his feelings now.

"It's not a funeral, Bella. Stop the tears. Alla, you have to be strong. Write as often as you can," Naum said from his rapidly eroding position as supreme commander of the family. How could a general allow his daughter to venture into "the nowhere," an unknown world with unknown people, with only one hundred dollars in her pocket, the maximum allowed by the Soviet authorities? Naum was not in control of this situation, he realized. Alla was leaving the ranks. His face twisted in pain, his eyes closed for a moment. But no tears.

The final night Alla arranged a farewell dinner. The funereal atmosphere still pervaded the apartment. Around the table sat Rosa, Naum, Bella, Alla, and her brother Gera and his wife. The table had always been the heart of Alla's home. On holidays, friends and family gathered and talked. The table was a touchstone where opinions and feelings could be freely expressed. Dinner was served along with earnest conversation. Alla knew when she thought of home after she left, she would imagine this very sight—the family around the table.

That August evening everyone knew the rules—no talking to anyone outside their immediate family about Alla's plan. The pain could only be shared among themselves. It was different when friends left for Israel or the United States. Reports circulated about what life was like in those countries, about jobs and community. Moving to Sweden was traveling into "nowhere." There was no information about what life was like for Russian emigrants in Sweden. The family would experience separation for a time, but Alla believed she could remove all obstacles and bring her family to her. She believed with perfect faith in her words that became her prayer, "We will fix it."

On a gray day in August, Alla left her home with her boxes and her memories. Remaining behind were her brother and his family, her parents, her ailing grandmother, and her friends. Sweden is a day and a half boat cruise or an hour's plane ride from Leningrad, yet the psychological distance was beyond time and space. Could Sweden become home without her family? How would she ever bring her family members out of the Soviet Union? This was not the time to dwell in doubt, and Alla slammed the door on her questions.

Before Alla could reach the "nowhere" of Sweden, she had to pass through No Man's Land, the purgatory of Russian customs. Ahead of her, the Stockholm-bound ferry rocked in the Neva Bay. Beyond, lay the Gulf of Finland, then the Baltic Sea. The customs zone was crawling with *militsia* and customs agents. It did not mean the lines moved more quickly, only that more eyes were trained on the erstwhile travelers and their belongings. The agents aggressively hunted for contraband and suspicious faces. Maybe Alla looked too smug, maybe the agent had indigestion that day. In the end, the whim of a custom agent could determine everything.

Arriving at the port with twenty-two boxes plus a feeling

of absolute terror turned her departure into a nightmare. Alla reminded herself as she neared the stern customs official, "I did everything 100% correctly according to the book. Everything is perfectly documented. Even my art has an official certificate of value with a stamp. Everything is correct from my visa to my marriage documents. All the paperwork is done."

Alla peered ahead and thought she saw a passenger pass some rubles to the agent.

"I would never bribe anyone because that could be the end of the beginning. And I will not need to bribe anyone because I have done everything correctly."

Alla's turn. She waited, expressionless and quiet, while the official examined each document. "You're leaving," he said to Alla.

She could feel his anger pulsating. She calmed herself and in her most neutral tone, she responded, "Yes."

Minutes ticked by—twenty-two boxes to examine, each perfectly organized and packed. The contents of each box were listed—all within the framework of what was allowed. He looked offended that he could not find fault with Alla's paperwork. The exit stamp crashed onto the documents.

"*Proshchayete*," the official barked as if to tell her to get the hell out of here.

Alla and her boxes moved forward to the waiting ship. Now she could breathe the sea air. *Would it smell the same in Sweden?*

The ferry was enormous, and delights abounded on every deck. There were restaurants, bars, discos. The duty-free shop was a revelation with an abundance of cigarettes, liquor, perfumes, and designer goods. Was this real? It was dizzying. Alla couldn't shake the fear that had accompanied her these past few months and had boarded the boat with her. Aboard the ship, she talked to no one. She sat like a frightened chicken on the ferry for thirty-six hours as she sailed from nightmare to dream.

Notes

1. Born in 1962, Sergei Potapenko attended art school in Leningrad and

immigrated to Italy in 1986, settling in Turin. He continued to work as an artist until his death in Italy in 2003.

2.   Among traditional Jews, obtaining a *get,* signed by a rabbinic court (*bet din*), is essential before a Jewish woman with a civil divorce can marry a Jewish man. Alla was determined that if she remarried, she would remarry another Jewish man within the Jewish legal framework. She was aware of the Jewish law even though it was impossible to obtain a *get* in the Soviet Union. In Israel and in all major major cities of the Diaspora, it is a common request to convene a *bet din* of three rabbis, who require the man and woman to come together, so the man can physically hand the woman the divorce decree that has been written in Hebrew by a scribe and witnessed by the *bet din*. It is very difficult when the man will not or cannot appear in person.

21

Meryll: The Iron Curtain Rusts Away

1985–1991

In a restaurant a patron asks his waiter:
"Why are the meatballs cube-shaped?"
Waiter: "Perestroika! (restructuring)!"
"Why are they undercooked?"
Waiter: "Uskoreniye! (acceleration)!"
"Why are they half-eaten?"
Waiter: Gospriyomka! (state approval)!"
"Why are you telling me all this so brazenly?"
Waiter: Glasnost! (openness)!

—Russian joke

To teach Russian history in a US high school during Gorbachev's tenure was a heady experience. Newspaper reporters and television commentators lauded the youngish new leader, and it was common to hear Americans discussing *perestroika*[1] and *glasnost*[2] as if they were old Russia hands. Students' eyes lit up in class as they asked, "How quickly would Russia be "just like us?" They wondered if they would see a real revolution on TV. I shrugged my shoulders and encouraged their speculation. I had no idea, and history does not present a blueprint for the future.

I was not alone in wondering what lay ahead. In Russia, reactions were mixed. Although Brezhnev's era of stagnation drew no rave reviews, it was clear to Soviet citizens that the Russia to which they awoke each morning under Brezhnev was the same Russia they had experienced yesterday. The prevailing uncertainty animated many of the young but frightened some of the older population.

Gorbachev took the reins of the country in 1985 but until 1990 the impact of *perestroika* (restructuring of the economy) was hazy. New laws were passed that sanctioned joint ventures with foreigners, private business, and less control from the State. At first those who benefited had been part of the old power structure, the *nomenklatura*; however, soon intellectuals, industrial managers, and those who had operated in the shadow economy exploited the opportunities of restructuring. Although Gorbachev intended to move to a more humane socialist economy, the unintended consequence by 1987 was the rise of the Russian mafia who extorted, "protected," and enforced with violence.

Another type of restructuring paralleled economic changes—the communist iron fist started to unclench. By 1988 in the Soviet Union, elections to Party posts were democratized, the Communist Party lost control of state organs, and a real Parliament was created. The dictatorship of the Party was gone. Outside the Soviet Union, the satellite countries were flexing democratic muscles that would lead to the dissolution of the Soviet bloc and then the Soviet Union itself by 1991.

While scholars and foreign policymakers debated whether *glasnost* was real, Russians tentatively tasted free speech. It was a heady banquet for some Russians; however, others were fearful that the freedoms were chimerical. In all likelihood no reformer could have switched off the command economy, booted out the *nomenklatura* in 1985, and seamlessly flipped the switch to capitalism and democracy. Inflation plagued Russia. By 1991 the ruble was falling 2–3 % each week.[3] For anyone on a fixed income, the situation was a disaster. The food shortages were so dire in Leningrad that ration books were issued. Many bemoaned the loss of the old social contract that offered citizens "job security, welfare, and equality."[4]

The stage was set by December of 1991 for the next act, and soon Russians would learn a new term: "shock therapy."

Notes

1. *Perestroika* literally means restructuring and was the term used under Gorbachev (1990s) for the restructuring of the Russian political and economic systems. One of the leading theoreticians was Tatyana Zaslavskaya, whose work had been banned for years. She developed the idea of restructuring the economy and coined the term *perestroika*, which Gorbachev embraced as his platform.

2. *Glasnost* literally means transparency. Under Gorbachev, this meant both more freedom of expression in the Soviet Union and more contact with the West.

3. John Keep, "Gorbachev Era in Historical Context," *Studies in East European Thought*, 49 no. 4 (December 1997): p. 285. See also Archie Brown, *The Gorbachev Factor* (Oxford: Oxford University Press, 1996), p. 128 for a discussion of Gorbachev's intentions.

4. Linda J. Cook, "Brezhnev's Social Contract and Gorbachev's Reforms," *Soviet Studies* 44, no.1 (1992): p. 37.

22

Vera: Labor Rules

1986

Luck arrives when it is least expected.
—Russian Proverb

As fall came, Vera felt like a brooding chicken. She patted her swollen stomach contemplating her good and bad luck. She was happy with Alexei and never dreamed that she could still have a baby after an abortion and miscarriage. The bad luck was that she and the baby must endure the ordeal of childbirth in a Russian hospital. Not even Mama Irina's connections could guarantee a comfortable stay in the maternity hospital. Without Mama Irina, she would need to bring her own sheets and blankets and provide her own food. Worst of all was that Baba Lyuba was dying, and Mama Irina would not leave her side, partly out of devotion and partly due to a fear of bringing germs into Vera's home. Vera gritted her teeth in a momentary wave of anger that Baba Lyuba was commandeering her mother's attention. Alla was God-knows-where. Vera suspected she had left the country, but no one was telling her anything.

Vera felt most comfortable when she was in control or when she delegated control to the people she truly trusted—Alexei or her parents. She was decidedly out of control when it came to childbirth. Two weeks before her mid-October due date, Alexei was accompanying Vera to a check-up when Vera froze in her tracks with a horrified expression. She felt the gush of liquid between her legs and looked at Alexei with her eyes widened, whispering, "My water broke." They ran quickly to the adjacent building to enter the hospital waiting room. Vera remembers the time—10:00 a.m. Like any Russian official, the surly nurse wielded the small amount of power she possessed to its full degree. She banished Alexei from the waiting room. This was no place for husbands. She snapped a list of questions at Vera ignoring Vera's distress. She then pointed to the hard chairs in the crowded, spartan room and barked, "Sit until your name is called."

Vera still cannot recall what went through her mind while she waited hours to hear her name. Her best guess is that in the complete absence of loving support, she numbed herself and retreated within to a place of great sadness and wordless fear. The sun was already setting when Vera startled as the nurse called her name. Then, in a casual aside to a co-worker, the nurse remarked, "We forgot about this one. The baby might be in crisis." Vera was seized with panic as an orderly pushed her through the double doors into the ward. "Women were screaming like they were being interrogated by the Gestapo. There was no medication available for anesthesia." Another *defitsit*. A nurse gave her an injection to initiate labor without explaining much. Fifty-five minutes later, her son was born. "Too fast," Vera explained. She wasn't ready to give him a name yet. A Jewish name or a Russian name? She wasn't sure.

The baby was scooped up and taken away immediately. Vera, weak and mute, noticed that she was the only one of the nine women in the room who was not given her baby to nurse and hold. She was "unnerved" and feared he was dead. She pleaded for him but was told he was weak and tired and had to be placed in an incubator.

"Nobody could find out what happened. When I finally saw my boy, he looked very small and very quiet."

Bringing this tiny baby to a home without Mama Irina nearby felt overwhelming. Alexei was helpful, but he had increased responsibilities at the State Furniture Plant. Alla, the one friend on whom Vera could have relied, had vanished into thin air. Ensuring that Lev was adequately nourished became Vera's daily work. She knew nothing about infants and had no experience with small children. Alone, she had to push aside feelings of inadequacy with logic. Lev wasn't able to nurse and seemed unable to suck properly from a bottle. She cut a larger hole in the nipple and felt victorious when he finally swallowed enough milk to sate his little appetite. Diapers had to be boiled and bottles sanitized. She watched her tiny boy grow over the next two months but was still worried about his poor muscle tone. One leg was spastic and the other leg limp. Twenty-six years later she demonstrated the position to me.

Vera recalls one episode at two months that started ominously but turned out to be quite fortunate. Vera was swaddling Lev before a walk, but his cry this day was more plaintive, and none of her usual tricks comforted him. She gently unwrapped him and discovered a bubble around his navel. Paging through her treasured copy of Dr. Spock's book, she concluded that he must have a hernia. Vera feared exposing him to the germs at a children's clinic and called Emergency Care. Apparently, the dispatcher had written her last name incorrectly, so it matched the physician's name. Curious, the doctor rushed to her door, setting a record for emergency response time. He introduced himself as a pediatric neurologist who moonlighted for Emergency Services to supplement his meager income.

Vera grabbed his arm pleading, "You are the first doctor we've seen since I came home from the maternity hospital. Please examine my son, and I will pay you. Tell me what's wrong with him."

He carefully checked over the little boy, first verifying Dr. Spock and Vera's diagnosis of a hernia, and then tested his reflexes and muscle tone. After hearing the history of his delivery, he explained that in all likelihood Lev had suffered neurological trauma from his quick birth.

"I have seen this before, and I know how to treat it," the physician said.

Finally, someone validated her fears that something was not quite right and could offer her a diagnosis and a plan. The doctor's wife became part of the team of specialists that assisted Lev through physical therapy, massage techniques, and diet. Vera was told not to inoculate Lev, which meant that she had to be careful that he not come into contact with too many children. Vera was encouraged but also afraid for Lev. The next two years passed like a "horrible movie."

"I was so unprepared. And now I was thinking that he might have a lifelong disability. I read a lot about what I could expect and do."

The Soviet Union was a harsh place to raise a child with a disability. Although medical care was free, there would be few therapies offered. Education would be a problem. She shuddered to think how his peers would treat him. Vera couldn't change the past, but she applied all her managerial talent to ensure that Lev's future was as hopeful as possible. Mama Irina and Papa Misha were now a part of Lev's daily life though they were home only in the evening and on weekends. Vera missed her former life in the business world, and she ached for Alla. How many times she had wanted to call Alla after the birth! She couldn't believe that Alla's family, who knew and, she thought, trusted her, would tell her nothing. When Vera learned that her parents would celebrate New Year's Eve with Alla's parents, she begged Mama Irina to investigate Alla's mysterious disappearance. Successful in her mission, Irina reported that Alla had arranged a marriage to a Swede in order to emigrate and was now living in Stockholm. Vera cried tears of relief that her friend had escaped and was safe and tears of sadness and hurt for the abandonment she felt.

Left to right: Vera, Misha, Lev, Irina, and Alexei—
a happy moment with little Lev.

23

Vera: Private Enterprise

1986–1989

Byla ne byla
"Whatever the consequences—I'll try it"
—Russian proverb

Nothing in the drone of the newscasters' carefully censored scripts caught Vera's attention long enough to interest her much until Gorbachev was elected General Secretary in 1985. Before Lev's birth, she had witnessed the revolving door of jaded party officials taking a seat briefly on the Communist throne before dying. As much as Vera detested Brezhnev, his successor in 1982, former KGB director Yuri Andropov,[1] promised to be worse. Vera was relieved by Andropov's demise fifteen months later and barely blinked when Konstantin Chernenko bit the dust after thirteen months in March 1985: three rulers in fewer than three years in a country that could not feed its people. She was disgusted by her country's failed leadership. But Gorbachev seemed different, not only because he represented a younger generation reaching the top at the youthful age of fifty-four, but because he seemed willing to challenge the system. Her ear was attuned to the news for the first time.

The Soviet information machine slowly transformed from broadcasting canned announcements of Soviet production and superiority to reporting about a piece of truly counterrevolutionary legislation—the resurgence of legalized private enterprise in May 1987, the first time private enterprise had been allowed in sixty years.[2] It made complete sense to Vera. Since the Soviet system could not meet consumer demand and enterprises operated illegally, why not legalize them? In truth, it was Russia's only hope to shake the economy out of stagnation. To purge any whiff of the capitalist stench, the Soviet government dubbed these private enterprises "cooperatives."

Vera studied this new Law of Cooperatives, discussing it in depth with Alexei over morning coffee and, again, in the evening after hearing Alexei's litany of complaints about production at the government furniture plant. While her job was relatively interesting at the State Fashion House, like everyone else she was at the mercy of the inefficient State bureaucracy. She had a few more months left of her year-long maternity leave but wasn't eager to return to her job. As she toyed with business ideas, she could feel the revival of the old Vera, the energetic girl who wanted to play the leading role in a play she wrote for herself.

Valya, the daughter of one of Mama's Irina's close friends, dangled a tempting offer in front of Vera. Would she like to serve as Business Director of the first private fashion design house in Leningrad? Before accepting, she began a ritual integral to her relationship with Alexei—a careful analysis of the pros and cons, including weighing their trust in the potential partner and identifying any hidden motives.

Valya was a talented designer and obviously serious since she was willing to invest her own money. *But where did she get her money? How could she travel in and out of the Soviet Union so freely?* Alexei and Vera knew that Valya's situation seemed shady, but no more so than usual. Mama Irina was a friend of Valya's mother, which weighed positively in the equation.

In her Marxist-Leninist life, Vera never envisioned directing her own company, but now that it was becoming a reality, she extended that dream to others. She tapped the best seamstresses from the government fashion house offering them a salary three times greater than the pittance they received inconsistently from the State. Thrilled by the opportunity, the seamstresses rewarded Vera with their loyalty.

Vera, the same woman who grew impatient and bored with registration forms, transformed herself into the likes of a business lawyer, carefully perusing every word of documents and methodically planning her strategy to launch the private fashion house.

"We set it up very quickly. At the end of three months, we had registered the business, hired people, found equipment, and renovated the premises."

In the summer of 1987, the business opened and quickly turned a profit. Success bred its own problems—ones common in the Soviet Union—envy and greed. Alexei and Vera had built good careers that had enabled them to purchase a high-end car, still a luxury to most citizens. Valya felt entitled to the same, financed by the cooperative account. Status symbols in Russia were essential to gain respect but reinvesting profits back in the business was the first priority for Vera. This was a foreign concept in a land where as soon as a ruble hit your palm it was spent.

Valya fumed at Vera's attempt to rein in her spending, and her spite spilled out in front of the staff as she blamed Vera for minor problems, "What can you expect from a Jew like Vera Mikhailovna?"

Here it was again, the ugliness—the word "Jew" spoken as a nasty epithet. It was particularly galling to Vera, given that Valya was raised by a loving Jewish step-father. After months of tensions, the final straw snapped. Vera was fed up and, seven months after opening the business, she walked out. She had succeeded once, and surely she could do it again. Unfortunately, there were some threads unravelling. In spring 1988, she heard that Valya had fled to Turkey with all the cash. A seamstress had tipped off Vera that criminal investigations had begun.

Angry that she was still registered as a partner, Vera vowed to protect herself better in the future. In hindsight, her instinct to mistrust Valya had been correct. She managed to emerge from the criminal trial with her reputation intact thanks to the supportive testimony of the seamstresses. In the future, she had to be mindful that her freedom and reputation were at stake. She needed to have more control in a partnership and to surround herself with trustworthy people. Furthermore, she realized she couldn't simply walk out of a business in which she was a partner.

Alexei did not realize that he was itching to resign as Assistant Director of the government furniture factory until a mutual acquaintance introduced him to Genrik Slutsky in 1988. Slutsky offered him a position in a private cooperative. Alexei had never envisioned such an opportunity outside of the monolithic State system. The norm was job dissatisfaction for professionals, but at least Alexei had a lot of perks that went with his high level position. He recalled his first day as Assistant Director at the government factory. Pacing nervously outside his boss's office, he heard shouts reverberating through the dusty, echoing space. A booming voice blasted, "You're a horse's ass," followed by an equally loud voice, "You're an even bigger horse's ass." Next, he saw the previous Assistant Director slam the door. Alexei's only thought was, *What have I gotten myself into?*

One year after leaving State employment to work with Genrik, Alexei heard of his successor's suicide. Sadly, he understood exactly the pressure that could drive a person to this extreme. No power, but all the blame. All over this country, managers and directors waited months for their paperwork to circulate around the Moscow bureaucracy before receiving an essential machine part or raw material. If the factory didn't meet the government-assigned quota, someone had to be blamed, and it wasn't going to be the boss.

Alexei was finally free from dealing with government hemorrhages. Genrik was seeking someone to direct the wood-processing division of his business. The lumber business was proving to be a headache. Although one third of the world's forests are located in the former Soviet Union, it was difficult to obtain a logging permit because Soviet forests were under protection. Permits also required "proper" connections and "fees" to accompany those connections. Genrik was confident that Alexei could take that on.

Alexei agreed to the deal if he could work with the

smartest, most trusted person he knew—his wife. Genrik agreed to pay generous salaries that far exceeded government pay plus 10% of the profits. From the beginning, Vera insisted on an international connection in order to base their business on hard currency. Soviet banks were undependable because the ruble performed a daily dance in value. Credit was not routinely extended. She had been following with interest the Soviet Joint Venture Law established in June 1987, allowing foreigners to invest and share joint ventures with Russians without having to go through the National Ministry of Trade.

The obvious international connection was her father's younger sister, Aunt Lena, now residing with Uncle Meyer in Belgium after their initial move to Israel. Whenever Meyer was involved, caution was required. With a long résumé of scams and a history of spending time in prison in Russia, Germany and Israel, Meyer had earned so much respect among criminals that he needed no protection himself.

Meyer was a charmer to boot, "a better relative you couldn't have," Vera wryly said. "We all love him."

With gigantic ears protruding from the side of his "handsome, sweet face" and possessing a huge bear-like frame, he towered above his once-slender, blond wife. This couple lived life to the fullest, but Vera did not want too much information about how they supported that lifestyle. Meyer and Lena were now surrounded by good people and financed by solid banks; and, to sleep better at night, she and Alexei chose to believe that her aunt and uncle had gone legit. Meyer was incredibly successful, but he got bored easily, which led to his attaction to less savory business enterprises. "His Achilles heel was that he never overlooked a 'good opportunity,'" Vera explained. They were not the ideal foreign partners, but they would have to do for now.

So Aunt Lena and Uncle Meyer became 50-50 owners in this new joint venture and were cast in a supporting role as European brokers. Alexei directed operations, and Vera had expected to be cast as Chief Accountant. Apparently, Genrik was not comfortable with Vera having access to the books and instead decided to assign her a different role as Director of International Business Development. Vera didn't have time to dwell on this insult because just then news of an international opportunity for which she had waited her whole life dropped at her feet.

Notes

1. Andropov was known for his strong efforts to suppress political dissidence.

2. Limited free enterprise had been permitted briefly under Lenin's "New Economic Policy" in agriculture, light industry, and services. This was a response to a desperate economic situation and poor agricultural output. It began in 1921 and was abandoned in 1927 by Stalin.

24

Alla: Alisa from Wonderland

1986–1988

Ne govori gop, poka ne pereskochish.
"Never say 'hop' before crossing the river."
—Great-Grandma Tzipa
and Russian proverb

Alla now realizes Sweden is not Wonderland; however, in
August 1986 it brought her closer to the utopian vision
she had imagined on the boat from Leningrad to Stockholm.

In the early August morning light as the end of
her odyssey neared, Alla looked toward Stockholm. Her
Wonderland glimmered in the distance as if to beckon her. She
blinked and pinched herself. Spread before her like a necklace
were the fantastical islands of the Skägård archipelago. The
shining sun seemed to spotlight the myriad of islands. All told,
there are 24,000 islands in the archipelago but for Alla it was
not the number of islands, but rather their storybook look—
emerald green forests studded with summer houses with ruby-
red roofs—that impressed her. Each one seemed to have a
garden, one more colorful than the next.

This is a fairy tale right out of Hans Christian Andersen! Alla simply could not believe her eyes—*Wonderland.*

So-called news in the Soviet Union had not prepared Alla for the crisis atmosphere in Sweden that lay beneath the charming architecture and lovely landscape. According to the Swedish press, the country lost its innocence on February 28, 1986 when Prime Minister Olof Palme was murdered, walking home from the movies on a quiet street. Two months later, Sweden found herself coping with the after effects of the worst environmental disaster of the twentieth century— the Chernobyl nuclear reactor accident that irradiated the air, water, and soil far beyond the Ukraine. There was a growing wariness among Swedish people toward new immigrants. By the time Alla arrived in this once homogeneous country, 9% of Swedish citizens had been born elsewhere. Five years before her arrival, Sweden had suffered through its own version of impending Armageddon similar to the Cuban missile crisis. A Soviet U-137 Whiskey class submarine loaded with nuclear warheads ran aground in Swedish waters. The stand-off, referred to in the press as "Whiskey on the rocks," lasted ten days, but the fear of Soviet attack and the suspicion of Russian spies remained for years. Alla would soon confront those prejudices.

Swaying unsteadily down the gangplank, stunned by Sweden's natural beauty, exhausted, and nerves on edge after thirty-six hours at sea, Alla's mind was far from politics. She was trembling all over. She began to cry, thinking of her meager supply of cash and her twenty-two boxes. From the ferry Sweden may have looked like a fairy-tale kingdom, but Alla could not foresee a "happily ever after" and the question, *What now? What now?* thrummed through her mind.

Her eyes swept the quay. Her new husband would not be there with flowers and a hug to welcome her. Through her tears, Alla saw a car in the handicapped spot. She wiped the tears away and, yes, it was Kalle with his cane in one hand and his wife, Inga, next to him. They were waving at Alla! That small rectangle—a postcard—had miraculously reached them, and her confidence in their goodness was justified. Alla assumed everyone outside of Russia would be trustworthy.

Only honest people like the Voice of America announcer or American exchange students populated Wonderland.

Alla felt her shoulders relax as they embraced her. Her trembling stopped and her tears of apprehension turned to tears of joy. Immediately Kalle said, "Alla, stay with us. You'll enjoy the country. Inga could use the help. We have twenty horses, two houses."

Instinctively Alla responded, "I'm a city girl, and I'll go to Sven and Larissa like we planned."

She was grateful to Kalle but wary that she might end up a housekeeper, and her future plans would be compromised. She had heard stories of Russian women with big plans that swirled in their heads while they mopped floors in their new countries. That would not happen to her. Still, she carefully tucked away Kalle and Inga's phone number as they drove to her new home in the suburbs of Enskede,[1] knowing she had one month to stay with Sven and Larissa and adapt to life in Sweden before she must fend for herself. She tried to push away her worries about the money she still owed Larissa and concentrate on enjoying the grace of this sparkling city and celebrating her success at arriving in this new wonderland.

On the drive, Alla stared through the car window marveling like a small child at the tidiness, the openness, the green. Kalle announced that they would stop for gas. Spotting a convenience store at the gas station, Alla decided to buy something to eat. She entered the mini mart, surveyed the store, and burst into tears. The clerk turned to watch the young woman's shoulders heaving. He would never have guessed the shock that Alla experienced as the thought raced through her mind, *I have never seen this much food before in one place.* And this was a gas station mini mart! She had yet to visit a supermarket or department store.

Alla and her twenty-two boxes made it to Sven and Larissa's villa in Enskede, constructed as a workers' suburb in the early twentieth century. Cautiously optimistic that things would work out, she moved into her new villa where Sven and Larissa greeted her. Alla had landed in the middle of a typical bourgeois lifestyle except that Larissa was still her vulgar self. Alla liked Sven although she had no romantic interest in him. Their relationship was purely business, she reminded herself.

Still, she felt companionable with him. Alla wondered how this good-looking, cultured Swede could be happy with Larissa and her crassness. *Sex and alcohol, that was the answer.*

As Sven and Alla bonded over music, wine, and convivial conversation, Alla saw Larissa scowl and cross her arms over her low cut blouse. She would march across the wood floors with her heels clicking, slamming cabinet doors, downing more alcohol than usual. *Jealousy? Perhaps*, thought Alla.

One evening, to Alla's surprise, Larissa brightly announced, "You're very tense, you know. You need to have some fun. I'll take you out to the clubs. Go on and get ready."

Alla had no idea why Larissa's attitude toward her had changed although Larissa was a colorful personality with mercurial moods. Nor did Alla know anything about the club scene in Stockholm, but Larissa was offering, and it would be an adventure. They headed to a local club. When they arrived, Larissa pushed Alla into a room with flashing strobes and pulsing music and directed her to start talking to men. Fortunately, before Alla could feel too awkward, a Swedish man approached Alla, asked her to dance, and they began talking in English. Dancing was a release, and it was lovely to be admired again by a man.

"Your English is really good. Where are you from?"

Without missing a beat, Alla responded, "I'm from the USSR."

More cautiously, her dance partner asked, "How did you get here?"

Employing her newly gained knowledge to joke with her partner, she said, "By submarine, of course."

Apparently Alla's partner lacked a sense of humor and was spooked by the idea of dancing with a Russian. His arms dropped and he ran, leaving her stranded on the dance floor. The U-137 incident had occurred five years earlier, but Swedes were still wary of Russians and many assumed they were all spies. Alla laughed with Larissa about the incident but had learned that Swedes would not welcome her with open arms.

Within days of her arrival, Alla received her permanent green card and personal identification number. She began paying Swedish taxes and was eligible for Swedish social insurance because she had arrived as the wife of a Swedish citizen. She was also eligible for language classes and a subsidy while she studied.[2] To verify that the marriage was legitimate, every six months Swedish police interviewed Alla and Sven. Alla and her husband were placed in separate rooms and asked similar "ordinary but intimate questions" like what color are your mate's pajamas? What did your spouse give you for the Christmas holiday? Answers were checked and rechecked. Alla had learned of these interviews from others who had traveled the same path. She and Sven meticulously prepared for each interview.

Only three weeks had passed since Alla's arrival when Larissa delivered a metaphorical punch to Alla's stomach.

"Out! Get out now, today."

With no explanation, Larissa kicked her out. Alla's body felt like it had been set ablaze. Heat traveled from her scalp to her toes. She couldn't think. There was no possibility of return to the villa. Alla was homeless. She had thought she had one more week to arrange new housing. Later, Alla realized that her enjoyable conversations with Sven had rekindled Larissa's jealous fire.

Alla's first panicky thoughts focused on her legal status. She had to maintain Sven's address as her own permanent address to remain in Sweden. *What if the Swedish police checked up on her?* Two years must pass before Alla and Sven could legally divorce and Alla could change her permanent address. She had to keep her green card secure for three more years until she could apply for citizenship. Alla's legal worries were compounded by survival needs. At this point Alla had no job, no money, could not speak Swedish, and now she had no place to live. She didn't understand how the vaunted Swedish social system worked. Alla was shocked and terrified—she had sold everything she wouldn't need in Sweden except her wedding band from Boris to pay Larissa. Alla had no bargaining chips. Her contract with Larissa and her husband was over, and she had to swallow her anger and fear and focus on figuring out how to survive in Sweden. Wonderland faded away. In its place loomed a foreign and lonely land where she had to quickly solve practical daily problems. Through it all, Alla never regretted her decision to leave Russia.

With no other resources, Alla retrieved the slip of paper

with Kalle's phone number. She smoothed out the wrinkled souvenir from her first day in Sweden and made the phone call. Her chest felt tight, *Should she ask for help?* It wasn't her nature. It wasn't a "Swedish" thing to do. *Would he simply offer the housekeeping position again as he had at the quay?* She had no choice. She remembered that Kalle owned a small construction company and some apartment buildings in Stockholm. She dialed and waited for Kalle to pick up the receiver, hoping he could provide counsel or a job.

"No question," said Kalle, "Come to us. We can help."

Inga and Kalle again invited Alla to remain with them in their pastoral setting, but Alla carefully explained to them she needed to study. To study, she needed to be in the city. Doubts about Kalle's motives gnawed at Alla. *Did he want her as a servant?* Kalle seemed to accept Alla's reasoning without taking offense and proposed that she rent an apartment in his building in the northern suburb of Sundyberg, a twenty-five minute subway ride from Stockholm's city center. Overwhelmed by his generosity, Alla felt compelled to offer something in return. She wanted to pay, but only 100 *kronor* (about $14) remained from her original stash of $100. Kalle understood and suggested a business proposition.

"Alla, I own the apartment building. You will get a one-room apartment on the sixth floor and you can clean my office on the first floor in exchange for rent. We'll meet once a month or so, and I'll check how you're doing."

That was an honorable arrangement in Alla's eyes, and she gratefully accepted. Still, she had not left Russia to become a cleaning lady, she reminded herself.

From the time she was booted out of Enskede until she was settled in Sundyberg, Alla was a nervous wreck. Her stomach hurt. Her hair began to fall out. Her nails broke. She even had problems with her teeth. As each physical symptom emerged, Alla knew she wasn't ill. It was stress—stress in the extreme.

No matter how demeaned Alla felt by her cleaning work, Alla's spirits lifted with a walk through the aisles of Hemköp, the grocery store. The abundance and variety, the polite demeanor of the clerks, and the pristine cleanliness of the store returned her to Wonderland. Alisa's head spun with the dizzying abundance and excess of Hemköp. In Leningrad, sound echoed from one empty shelf to another. Choice! Sweden was a carousel of choices no matter which store she entered.

The reality of having no extra money rudely intruded upon her elation when browsing the aisles at Hemköp. In fact, her finances were so limited that before she began her Swedish language classes, Alla had only enough *kronor* for cheese or a new pair of stockings. She wavered between the two. *Should she eat or look presentable?* It would be another year before she could indulge in salmon or meat. Alla sustained herself on dreams and hopes. She bought the stockings.

Slowly, Alla began to thread her way through the Swedish bureaucracy and take advantage of her rights as a new immigrant. She began studying Swedish daily. In 1975 Sweden had set up a comprehensive system to deal with immigrants, and language instruction was part of the entitlement package for all new immigrants. The language instruction came with a small stipend.

Most days Alla rode the *T-bana* (subway) to the Old City (Gamla Stan), exiting one stop early. Even in her dire straits, Alla enjoyed walking through the twisty, narrow cobblestone streets of the Old City. How different these streets were from Nevsky Prospekt or Dekabristov. Alla could dream and imagine while ambling in Gamla Stan. Leningrad wears her history like a set of manacles, chained by the pockmarks of the Leningrad siege that scarred the buildings. Leningrad is a city hunched over with shoulders pressed close together. Stockholm is a city with its arms flung wide, with all its treasures dangling before Alla. To find beauty in Leningrad, Alla's imagination demanded crayons to color away the gray days and restore its glory. Stockholm didn't demand anything of the imagination; it nourished Alla's soul. Gamla Stan's ancient streets sang with fresh color. Store windows were chic; orchids and candles peeked out from the lacy curtains.

The charming old world streets of Gamla Stan captivated Alla. As she walked the streets on her way to Swedish class, she had no way of knowing one of the windows in Gamla Stan belonged to her future husband.

Although Alla could enjoy the pleasures of the city without language, she knew she must learn Swedish and learn how to operate in a free market economy. In Swedish class Alla encountered a difficulty she had not anticipated—her name. The teacher followed the introduction of each new word with the command, "*Alla, upprepa!*" Alla was on the spot, *What should she do?* It didn't take her long to realize that the phrase so often repeated in her class meant "Everyone, repeat!" Alla's name meant "everyone" in Swedish. How could she succeed with a name that meant "everyone"? It was laughable. At first she tried explaining.

"Alla is a Russian name."

"Oh, sorry," a stranger would intone, then think a moment and ask, "like Alla Pugacheva?" *Ugh*, thought Alla, *they all associate my name with that cheap, drunken Russian singer. I can't stand even thinking about her!*

Alla renamed herself Alisa. She could have selected her Hebrew name, Hana (Anna or Hanna), but the memory of her grade school nickname, "Alisa in Wonderland" resurfaced. For Alisa it had a dual meaning. She felt like Alisa from Wonderland. *I wonder what the hell I was doing in that land of Russia?* And she had arrived in a real wonderland of plenty and freedom. So Alisa it was.

Alisa recognized immediately that most Swedes were not open to strangers. "It was difficult to make new friends. People are introverted." Alisa was learning quickly that the Swedish proverb *Tala är silver, tiga är guld* "to speak is silver, to remain silent is gold," was the guideline for social interactions.

Studying Swedish turned out to be more than a linguistic education. In class Alisa discovered three new friends. Endlessly, they discussed feeling like outsiders in the company of Swedes. Hands encircling their coffee mugs, speaking their newly acquired Swedish, the women admitted their difficulty in feeling accepted. The most reassuring phrase for Alisa at the time was her British friend's remark, "It's exactly the same for me" in describing how shut off she felt from Swedes. They shared tips about studies, jobs, and how to get back on their feet. Beneath the conversation Alisa felt they were "damaged souls" because they had amputated themselves from their motherlands. While all of them had immigrated to Sweden in hopes of a better future, there was a cost. Sometimes their homeland felt like a phantom limb beckoning them back. Sweden's social policy was a help to immigrants, but they all felt the ache of longing for families left behind and the hardships of alienation and starting over. No social program covers that longing.

Language class was not enough to gain Alisa entrance into the Swedish job market. She continued her education in a program designed to retrain and upgrade the skills of foreign academics. Alisa held the equivalent of an MA from the Leningrad Institute and was considered an academic by the immigration authorities. In the government-sponsored retraining program, Alisa had her first formal introduction to the capitalist economy, human resources management, and business administration. The Swedish economic and business outlook suited her personality. She was far more comfortable in a world where merit and competence reigned supreme rather than in the Soviet system of *svyazi* (party connections) and *vranya* (double think). Still, it was shocking to learn that in Sweden, managers were expected to know how to wordprocess on a computer. In the Soviet Union, typing indicated low status. Personal assistants did the typing. There were no personal computers in Russia, so Alisa had to familiarize herself with the latest Western technology and take her own great leap forward.

Alisa realized that her immigrant stipend would not suffice for her expenses. In her budget Alisa allocated a small amount to be saved each month to buy her family an apartment when they moved to Stockholm. Through her network of Russian Jewish acquaintances, Alisa met salon owner Gita who hired her part-time. Alisa also arranged private appointments for styling and cutting hair in her apartment. There was always a way.

She would have to do more than cover expenses; she would also have to learn the Swedish culture. Although it seemed overwhelming, she would not remain on the margins of Swedish society but penetrate the barriers.

Notes

1. Enskede was built in 1904 as part of Stockholm's progressive city planning efforts. The villas are attached wooden houses with pointed roofs, surrounded by gardens along winding streets, reminiscent of an English village.

2. The Swedish government had created an elaborate immigration administration by 1975. In addition to the immigration office, there were language institutes, immigrants' associations, social service offices, and labor market institutes and organizations. Masoud Kamali, *Distorted Integration: Clientization of Immigrants in Sweden* (Uppsala: Uppsala Multiethnic Papers, 1997), p. 11.

25

Vera: Coming to America

1988–1989

America is the best country in the world.
—Grandma Rae Levine

Vera's life was stretching beyond its seams. She needed more fabric and time to redesign a plan. Her country was also busting out of its rigid frame. The changes drove Vera to become a news junkie; she scoured the newsprint and, for the first time, listened attentively to Russian news for any opportunities opening in this unfamiliar, morphing Soviet world.

Something wondrous was happening as Gorbachev ascended to power. Vera felt nascent hope for her country. For the first time since Vladimir Lenin, Russia was led by a university graduate. Gorbachev appeared to be intellectually curious, pragmatic, cosmopolitan, and unafraid of change. Could she dare to believe that this country could be reformed? She was already benefitting from the opportunity to have a private enterprise. She thought he was on the right track with *perestroika.*

Vera and Alexei had surfed the highest wave of possibilities within the State system. But she hated this system—the system that had botched Lev's birth, the system that transformed its citizens into petty criminals because it couldn't deliver basic needs and because it outlawed free markets, the system that constantly demanded *vranya*—deception and hypocrisy. Everyone was living this lie. It was hard to believe that even a man like Gorbachev could change such an entrenched system.

Yet, change was happening day by day. In August 1988, Vera called out to Alexei that soon ordinary Soviet citizens would be able to travel to the West legally. To do so required an external passport, which could be requested after obtaining an "invitation." Vera was on it immediately. Too important for a letter, this news demanded a long-distance phone call to explain the particulars.

"Leslie, how are you?" Vera asked in her British accented English.

"Great, Vera, what's happened? Is everything okay? How is Lev?" International long-distance calls were still very expensive at that time and usually saved for life and death matters. I waited for the sound to travel under the ocean.

"Lev is improving day by day. I have a big favor to ask of you. Would you be willing to procure for me an invitation to visit the United States?"

I leapt off my chair. "You're kidding. Is it really possible to visit?" Eleven years had passed since we had seen each other. I assumed I would be the one traveling if we were to reunite.

Vera dictated the particulars and, although out of character for me, I followed the instructions to the letter. I expected it to be a year before the efforts would deliver the intended result but within four months, the invitation was complete. Dated November 29, 1988, the document was covered with stamps and a big red ribbon and appeared to be signed by Secretary of State George Shultz himself. It was actually signed by an underling. It took another nine weeks, the blink of an eye in Soviet time, for the Washington DC-based Soviet embassy to authenticate the document. When Vera proudly displayed the invitation to the officer at the Ministry of Internal Affairs, he gently weighed it in his hand, examined the stamps, the ribbon, and the signature with great interest and then nodded his respect to Vera as if to say *molodetz* ("good job"). He expedited the final step of obtaining the external passport. Vera was giddy. This was the treasure of a lifetime—an external passport.

People of her parents' generation considered themselves fortunate to visit an Eastern Bloc country and even that was usually reserved for high-level party members. Going to the United States was like going to the moon. Although hypothetically possible, for most people, it remained science fiction. When Vera made her initial request, she was in the vanguard. She called me five months before Gorbachev's December 1988 visit to New York City. Not even Vera could anticipate the sea change that would ensue from Gorbachev's speech at the United Nations when he announced the end of the Cold War in the most eloquent of terms. He emphasized that the interdependence of the East and West should take priority over the Marxist struggle for world revolution.

Vera and Alisa never dreamed that they would hear such words from a Soviet leader. This speech presaged the democratic changes that would shake the Soviet hold of Eastern Europe the following year, symbolized vividly by the fall of the Berlin Wall. Vera's country had already changed its relationship with the West between the time her invitation to the United States was signed and the day she arrived.

Vera and Alexei sold valuable possessions to obtain cash for the trip, and the date was set for summer 1989. When Papa Misha died on April 23, 1989, Vera made a second long-distance call to the States, this time weeping as she announced the death of her father and the sad news that she must cancel the trip.

"I'm too depressed. Mama Irina is struggling and I need to be home."

I wept with her, "Vera, I understand how sad this is for you. Just take your time and think this over before canceling your trip. You've looked forward to it for so long, and I think this could be a tribute to your father."

Over the next month, she thought it over, discussed it with Mama Irina and Alexei, and received their blessings to go forward with the trip. Vera had done all she could to make her parents comfortable; and, this time, unlike during high school, she had been present and attentive to her Papa Misha. She would journey to the United States in honor of her father. Vera viewed this trip as a chance to reconnect with her old friends—RD, Lars, and me.

This is a 1992 photo of Vera with her three Minnesota friends that captures our spirit when we're together. From left to right: Vera, Leslie, RD, and Lars.

It was a miracle come true thirteen years after our first meeting. None of us could have imagined that life would change so much in the Soviet Union, that one day Vera could cross that impenetrable barrier and come to the United States. There were lots of tears and laughter that day. Vera stayed with my family and accompanied me through daily life her first week in the United States.

In the middle of the largest and most fashionable supermarket in the Upper Midwest, Vera bitterly realized the deprivation of the Soviet people. I assured her that this was not a typical grocery but a high-end food emporium. Under the huge chandeliers in the carpeted aisles, Vera cried as she surveyed the many brands of every food imaginable. *Fresh fruits and vegetables of every kind. Prices were not so high.* I explained that these same fruits were available in the winter, as well, though prices were a bit higher. *Strawberries in the winter? Unthinkable! The displays were beautiful. There were no lines.* She understood at that moment what she had always suspected; that she lived in an underdeveloped country in terms of the manufacturing and distribution of basic consumer items. If she needed additional proof, she had only to visit the Target store, where she sank into utter misery. *Everything was available and at such low prices. Anyone could shop here. Svyazi (connections) were not necessary. No need for bribes. No lines. The cashiers were so friendly!* Again and again Vera was brought to tears as she tried to complete her shopping list. *How do people make choices in a country where there are so many kinds of toothpaste, cereal, and deodorant?* She was used to only one brand available, that is, if you were lucky and there was still a supply. She thought of all the time her grandmother, mother, she, and every other Soviet citizen wasted in line.

There were other wonders. Waiters at restaurants were gracious and cared about providing good service and a high-quality meal. Everything on the menu was actually available. Salt and pepper shakers, silverware, even crystal vases were set out on unattended tables, and nobody stole them. There were towels and soap in clean, public restrooms. *This was civilized.* She came from a country where people would steal light bulbs from their own apartment staircases to sell them *na levo* (illegally).

American salespeople did not scowl or yell at Vera. They did not rush people along or get angry at questions or requests. Shopping was not complicated as in her homeland by having to stand in one line to pay for an item and a second line to hand over the receipt to obtain the purchase. She was learning about a new level of customer service and business etiquette never before experienced in the Soviet Union.

I was preoccupied and harried in those days, working part-time as a psychologist and parenting a two-year-old. Vera was surprised no grandmothers lived close by to help out and that I would choose to live away from parents. She felt sorry that my son had to trudge to daycare until she accompanied me to the cozy church play area.

"Isaac had a difficult night last night, and he is a little crabby today," I related to the teacher.

"We'll take good care of him," said the teacher. She gave him a hug, smiled, and took his hand to escort him to his favorite friend and his favorite activity, playing with a ball. In Russia, the parents took orders from the teachers, who did not have time to record meals, naps, and diaper changes. It was understood that the child would perform according to plan. *Could it really be possible that there was a teacher who held Isaac's hand until he fell asleep?* Vera didn't notice any planned group activities, but rather she saw each child engaged in his or her own activity of interest. *Very strange.*

Vera returned to Minneapolis in 1990, this time with Alexei. Alexei, who didn't speak a word of English, enchanted Leslie's son, Isaac.

I think Vera was underwhelmed by my house. It was nice but could be nicer. To be exact, *uyutni* (cozy) was Vera's term. Not only did I lack attention to the details of my home and drive a car with a slight dent in it, but I didn't seem to care about the brand of clothing I wore. My clothes were shapeless and my shoes unfashionable, not a pair of heels to my name. In the land of choices, I was certainly not making good ones. It might be difficult to keep a husband's interest this way. *Wouldn't this compromise how people viewed me?* The irony was that before I left Russia, I had given Vera my clothes, which, at that time, seemed to her so fashionable. Now it was Vera who could teach me something about style. And what were these paper plates that I had used when I entertained a large group? Okay, that was just plain lazy.

What Vera could not realize was that the lack of pretension on my part was intentional. Many of us who matured in the late 1960s and 70s were still conflicted about flaunting wealth. In fact, material modesty was highly valued in Minnesota. My parents, who were first and second generation American Jews, worked hard to fit in. The house, clothing, and car were all impeccable. We had a country club membership and wonderful opportunities. Wealth and status held little attraction for us. To feel deserving of our uncanny Jewish luck, our compass directed us to follow our passions and do our small part to improve the world.[1]

Vera felt that it would have been a better choice to stay with RD and Lars, who had a more comfortable house and did not have to divide their attention between her and a child. Not to mention that she would like to smoke in peace instead of having to walk out of the house to have a cigarette. Lars was an architect now, and RD was writing full-time and acclaimed as a mystery writer with several novels set in the Soviet Union.

Vera recalled seeing a copy of *Psychology Today* in my guest room that referred to gay couples. She was intrigued. Never had she seen anything like that in print. The article appeared in what seemed to be, as Vera would say, a normal magazine; yet, it depicted homosexuality as if it were a completely reasonable lifestyle. To be gay in the Soviet Union was not only deviant, but a crime. It condemned a person to an unhappy and marginal life and possibly prison. One morning she came downstairs to the small, messy kitchen that was in need of a *babushka* and asked me, "Why have such desirable men like Lars and RD not found good women to marry?"

I responded brusquely, "They are fine the way they are."

Vera slyly smiled and reasoned that the magazine article had been placed there to prepare her, and she had figured out this puzzle. "Are they homosexual?" I was hesitant to get into this topic for many reasons, including the fact that I had been told only recently, after trying to fix up Lars with Meryll's friend. Before the revelation, I had assumed they were roommates and best friends, which was exactly what they wanted to convey. The information was theirs to tell and not something I would share with anyone, much less a Russian who was bound to have a cultural prejudice. I certainly didn't have the foresight to plant the magazine in the guest room to prepare Vera. I tried to be hypothetical in my response and tentatively asked, "How would you feel about someone that you cared about if you found out he was gay?"

Vera thought the question over.

"You're a vegetarian. I don't care how you satisfy your appetite. Why should I care about how someone else satisfies their natural appetites?" She was a bit surprised and pleased at her own open-mindedness. In addition, it put to rest any doubts she had about her own attractiveness since, of course, this explained why RD had not been seduced by her charms.

This was all new territory. With that issue resolved, she then moved into the swank quarters of Lars and RD, where the eyes of Lars's icons seemed to follow her moves. She received an elementary lesson in entrepreneurship and business as RD guided her through the city. RD had investments of his own and understood what it took to start and run a successful business. He was impressed by Vera's business acumen. He trusted her and knew he would invest in an enterprise with her if the opportunity arose. He was also thinking of contacts for her.

Before Vera's arrival, RD had noticed an article in the *Minneapolis Tribune* featuring fellow mystery writers in the Twin Cities of Minneapolis and St. Paul; then his eyes were drawn to an article below about two filmmakers planning documentaries in the Soviet Union. Bob Hazen and Sally Miller, owners of Infinity Productions, were arranging an exchange of local news anchors between a Soviet Union that was now more open and the Twin Cities.

To handle transportation, equipment, and introductions in the Soviet Union, Infinity Productions needed someone to arrange the logistics of the exchange. Systematically navigating the Soviet system every day of her life, Vera considered herself a master of logistics. A conversation and a handshake with Bob and his partner launched her first independent international venture.

A moment of awkwardness intruded into this visit after Vera was introduced to our good friends Mark and Natasha, Soviet Jewish immigrants. I saw Mark huddled in conversation with Vera and noticed her head slowly sinking, a shadow crossing her face. Vera edged to my side, whispering, "I cannot believe that you allowed Mark to read my letters. They were meant only for your eyes." *Oh, no. I never imagined the day would come that Vera would meet Mark. I had meant for Natasha, not Mark to help translate Vera's difficult prose.* Only recently did I learn more about that conversation. Mark, not known for his tact, not only joked with Vera about her letters but told her if she ever hoped to succeed in international business, she had to fix her teeth. The rough gold inlays and the poor dentistry made her look "too Russian." For Vera, this would mean a series of painful procedures in the Soviet Union to have all her teeth extracted and replaced with permanent implants.

The time in America kindled in Vera a wave of optimism that exclaimed that truly anything was possible. Traveling to the States was a fairy tale come true. Returning to the United States as a successful businesswoman would be her next challenge. Vera had found her own version of wonderland—a civilized country where the marketplace ruled, and people dealt with each other civilly and according to the law. Alice's wonderland with the hatchet-happy Queen of Hearts, the manic Mad Hatter, and the shadowy Chesire Cat couldn't have been more different from the United States. Yet, it was precisely these characters in their distorted world that she knew best. It was in this Russian "wonderland" that she would have to make her fortune.

Note

1. One of the Jewish concepts that resonated most deeply with Meryll and me was *tikkun olam*. This teaching asserts that while we are in this world, we are obligated to do our part to improve it in some way. Our Hebrew school teachers and camp counselors were well aware that this rabbinic idea meshed with the political and social activism of the 1960s and 1970s.

26

Alisa: Jewish Journey

1987–1990

Judaism is my platform.

—Alisa

Determined to be independent in Stockholm, Alisa paid all of her debts. She sold almost everything of monetary value except the paintings that she had so carefully packed and brought with her. It wasn't her intention to sell her possessions, but material links to Leningrad would not advance her life in Sweden, so she swallowed any regrets and sold them. Included in her sale was her Magen David (Star of David) necklace purchased when she was a teen. Alisa found her thumb and forefinger reaching to caress the Jewish star for reassurance, but it no longer hung from her neck. The loss was visceral. Now that she had arrived in a free country, she could have worn her Jewish star proudly without any fear. As she mourned the absence of her Magen David, Alisa remembered that for some reason she had not sold her wedding band from Boris, a gold band with small diamonds embedded in it, devoid of any emotional meaning. Why not?

While these thoughts were swirling through her mind, Alisa began to envision a new Magen David of her own design. She arranged an appointment with a Muslim jeweler known for both his expertise and his kindness. Excitedly, she showed him her design. It would not only be a Magen David but would have a small _hai_ (the two Hebrew letters that mean "life") in the center, fashioned from the diamonds from her wedding band. As an immigrant, he understood her need for the necklace and her lack of funds. Working in his spare time for a minimal charge, within a year it was ready for her. It was perfect, and Alisa was grateful to the jeweler and grateful for this new life unfolding. She fastened the clasp, placed the Magen David outside her collar, and did not remove it. She never hid it or tucked it under her blouse. At that moment she felt "truly happy."

Free of the cold constraints of her Leningrad life, Alisa proudly sports the Magen David necklace of her own design.

Back in Leningrad, Alisa's mother, Bella, could not be happy as she fretted about her daughter's future. Transforming her wedding band did not end Alisa's marriage to Boris according to Jewish law. Bella wanted to see her daughter remarry a Jewish man and knew that without a *get*, a Jewish divorce, she could never realize that dream. In a Jewish divorce, the former husband must initiate the process and hand the document to his former wife. Alisa, too, wanted to divorce according to Jewish law, the right way, just as she been married according to Jewish law.

Despite her limited finances, Alisa offered to pay for Boris's trip to Stockholm, but he refused to come. He wouldn't lift a finger to help. He didn't care. Bella tried every possible strategy she could think of to secure the document. Weekly, she visited the only rabbi in Leningrad tearfully explaining,

"My only daughter is in Sweden. My son-in-law is too lazy to travel there to give her a *get*. She needs to have this done! Please help her!"

Finally, her desperate tears persuaded the Leningrad rabbi to compose a document addressed to the Israeli rabbinate explaining Alisa's plight and Boris's stubbornness. Miraculously, after the documents arrived in Israel, they were certified by the Israeli rabbinate, returned to Boris for a signature, and then sent to Alisa. The final step to obtain the religious divorce was for Alisa to travel to a European city with a Jewish *bet din* (court) for the document to be witnessed by the rabbis. Stockholm's community was too small to support three Orthodox rabbis, the required quorum for a *bet din*, but Alisa had her choice of any major European city.

Paris! I've never been to Paris!

Paris may be a honeymoon destination for some couples, but Alisa intended to travel there to cut the final bonds to Boris. She made an appointment with the *bet din*, booked a cheap flight, and anxiously awaited the designated time.

The *bet din* was housed in a formidable building in the ninth arrondissement. Alisa rang the bell, her own nerves jangling at the same time. As she stood before the three rabbis, the conversation that ensued was unintelligible to both sides, with the rabbis speaking French and Hebrew and Alisa conversant in Russian, English, and Swedish. She understood the gist of their mumbling and nodded in the appropriate places. It was done.

Alisa is convinced that "there is a magical and spiritual connection in what happened. After 'doing it right,' with the complete *get* in hand, I met my Prince Charming." But the happy ending was still four years away.

Back in Stockholm, the question that dogged Alisa was how could she become a part of the Jewish community? In Russia this was a moot point since there was no formal community and you were Jewish by dint of the fifth line of your passport. Stockholm was home to 10,000 Jews, but no one had reached out to her. Alisa decided the most practical approach was to open the yellow pages of the telephone book and look up "Jewish community." As in most European Jewish communities, for security reasons there was only one number listed. In Stockholm the Jewish communal office was on Wahrendorffsgatan adjacent to the Great Synagogue. Alisa dialed, unsure of what to expect.

"Jewish Community Offices."

"I want to become a member of the Jewish community of Stockholm. I need help. What do I do?"

Hearing the Russian accented Swedish, the operator directed her call to the Jewish social welfare caseworker.

"I understand you're a new Russian immigrant to Sweden. What do you need?"

"I think you misunderstand me. I don't need anything like food or housing. I just want to belong to the Jewish community."

She had taken the first step and would take many more steps before she felt truly embraced by her new community. At synagogue Alisa felt she couldn't pray because she didn't know Hebrew, but she felt happy and peaceful within its walls. The

Stockholm's imposing Stora Synagoga prominently located near the harbor and Berzelii Park.

architecture of the Great Synagogue, *Stora Synagoga*, reminded her of the Leningrad Grand Choral Synagogue. *Stora Synaogoga* was a sparkling gem, not an unkempt building surrounded by a concrete garden.

By springtime, Alisa yearned to celebrate the Passover seder. Again, she called the Jewish communal offices, and they arranged for her to attend a seder with the Einhorns.[1] As soon as she met Doctors Jerzy and Nina Einhorn, she felt at home. They were Polish Jews who had survived the Holocaust. Their embrace and warmth felt familiar.

"Remember you were strangers in the land of Egypt," is the refrain in retelling the Passover story. The Einhorns understood very well about being a stranger and about starting over. At the time Alisa didn't know about the horrors of their past. She saw the gleaming table and the Einhorn family gathered around it. Alisa was the only outsider but felt drawn into the family circle immediately. Dr. Einhorn decided to conduct the seder in English so everyone could understand and Alisa would feel welcome.

"We were slaves in the land of Egypt, now we are free," Dr. Einhorn read after the Four Questions were asked.

Alisa had felt enslaved—not literally in the Gulag or in prisons like her hosts, but enslaved when her creativity and her dreams were thwarted or when she had to guard every word that passed her lips. Now she felt the freedom of Passover as if she had left Egypt with Moses, Miriam, and the Israelites.

During the seder Alisa's memory briefly flashed back to Leningrad. The familiar cooking smells reminded her of her grandmother making gefilte fish and of all the intrigue and difficulty in securing matzah in Leningrad. She sadly recalled that on Dekabristov Street, no one remembered how to chant the seder service. They would sit together at their table with the carefully prepared foods knowing it was the Jewish holiday of freedom, but they did not have the words to link them back to their ancestors. This was Alisa's "first real seder," and she treasured each moment.

Attendance at synagogue and celebrating Passover with another family did not fill the void Alisa felt, nor offer her the community she was craving. Even while learning the Swedish language and culture, Alisa made sure to attend Jewish lectures and cultural events. Her ears were always open to new opportunities. When she heard about Young Leadership, Alisa hoped it would be the way to fill up the empty space and loneliness she felt.

Young Leadership was an organization for Jews up to age forty. Part of its mission was to raise money for Russian Jews and help them emigrate to Israel.[2] During her first year in Stockholm, Alisa put herself center stage and gave interviews whenever asked to speak on the plight of the Russian Jewish community. She didn't need to lecture Swedish Jews on Soviet anti-Semitism. They knew about that. In her straightforward way, she tried to personalize the story to shake them from their apathy. She was driven to help Swedish Jews empathize with the Jews in the Soviet Union who lived behind invisible prison bars that limited their ability to develop intellectually, artistically, and spiritually. Support for the emigration of Soviet Jews was urgent. Sweden's open door was beginning to close.

Soon Alisa was not an anonymous face in the group but a key figure. Members of Young Leadership became her people, *svoi' lyudi*. Her loneliness eased. Alisa felt best as a contributor to the Jewish community, rather than as a supplicant. She began traveling across Europe to London and Paris, meeting like-minded young Jewish adults. She artfully balanced her volunteer activities with her work. At one time Alisa had dreamed of leaving Russia; now she could travel anywhere and make the same dream come true for other Russian Jews.

Within the world Jewish community, there was heated debate about the fate of Jews leaving Russia. The Soviet Union was granting visas for Israel, but not every Russian Jew who received a visa headed for the Holy Land. Russian Jews were routed first to Vienna and then onward to Israel. Vienna was a transit point and a point of decision. The Jewish Agency could not force Russian Jews to head for Israel. For some Soviet Jews, the promised land was the United States or West Germany or Italy. Should Jewish organizations help if a Russian Jew rejected Israel as the final destination?

From the pulpit, the interim rabbi of the Great Synagogue chastised the Russian Jews who were moving to Sweden. He thundered, "They are creating bad publicity for Jews already in Sweden. The Jewish community, after all, is raising millions to help Soviet Jews make aliyah to Israel, not to populate the Diaspora."

Cantor Maynard Gerber sat on the pulpit in stony silence listening to the tirade. He had traveled to the Soviet Union to meet with refuseniks and had adamantly argued for free choice. Russian Jews had no choice in Russia. *Should the rest of the Jewish world also limit their basic human right of choosing a new home? What right did Diaspora Jews have to tell Soviet Jews they had to move to Israel?* Swedish Jews were not packing their bags for Ben Gurion Airport. Alisa wrote a strong letter of protest to the rabbi with the support of Cantor Gerber. Someone had to speak up and tell the rabbi that his position was unfounded. She was that someone.

Although the Great Synagogue's interim rabbi did not warmly embrace newly arrived Russian Jews, the Swedish Jewish community had put systems in place to help new immigrants. The community had established a refugee center that housed about fifty Russian Jews at a time. A lawyer was also made available to ease the process.

Alisa tapped into these services when her brother Gera left the Soviet Union in 1990 for Sweden. Gera's wife, like Alisa's husband Boris, had no intention of leaving home. The difference was that Gera had a young son Misha. Gera left his parents, his wife, his son, and his job as a chief financial officer of a company. He requested political asylum from the Swedish government. Alisa paved the way for him by arranging for an attorney, Swedish lessons, and then a job.

Gera's absorption into Sweden was difficult in spite of Alisa's help. Gera, an aspiring poet in Russian, was tongue-tied in Swedish and eventually became a taxi driver. His estranged wife arrived a year and a half later in 1992 with Misha. Alisa arranged for Misha to enter first grade at the Hillel Academy, the Jewish Day School. Alisa couldn't push Gera along the pathway of success, but his son was thriving and that was success.

Alisa pondered her brother's slow progress adapting to Sweden. Her brow furrowed, she shook her head, *Why can't Gera make it here in Sweden?* she wondered again and again. *He is much more intelligent than I am. He is always reading; he is true intelligentsia.*

Although Alisa arranged for Gera to work with Kalle, her first benefactor in Sweden, she grew concerned by Gera's dependence on Kalle. Increasingly uncomfortable with Kalle's help, she noted that he underpaid Gera and took advantage of other Russian employees. Had she not been stubborn about living in the city, she could have ended up isolated on the estate as Inga's caretaker.

"Gera, you have to be independent of Kalle. You need to learn the Swedish way, *duktig*. Be self-reliant!! You must live in the real world," was Alisa's refrain to Gera.

Notes

1. To learn more about Nina Einhorn's wartime experience, see the film *Nina Resa*, directed by her daughter Lena, which tells the story of her improbable escape from the Warsaw Ghetto after Himmler's order to destroy the ghetto and kill all remaining Jews there. *Nina Resa*, directed by Lena Einhorn, Stockholm Sweden: East of West Film, Svensk Film Industry, 2005.

2. Young Leadership (created in 1963) began as an arm of the United Jewish Appeal in the United States. Its primary goal was to raise money for Israel. Fundraising also targeted the needs of the local and international Jewish communities. In Sweden Young Leadership devoted time and effort to assisting Soviet Jews who wanted to emigrate and Alisa became a prominent spokesperson for that cause.

27

Vera: Reaching for the Stars

1989–1991

Luchshe s umnim poteryat', chem s durakom naiti.
"It's better to be lost with intelligent people than to be found with idiots."

—Russian proverb

B ack through the rabbit hole to Leningrad. Vera was fueled with adrenaline and confidence. She had experienced capitalism firsthand, confirming her belief that only through a free market could the needs of citizens be well-served. She was ready for entrepreneurship in Russia even if Russia was not quite ready for her.

Upon her return, she was not prepared for how raw the grief felt from her father's death five months earlier. Vera's throat closed and her tears started flowing upon entering her parents' apartment with Alexei and Lev for her welcome-home dinner. Her eyes gravitated to the empty place at the table. Vera typically settled conflicts in her life by negotiation, even those within herself. Even though Vera was the second child and a daughter, she would assume the responsibility as head of the family. She could not succumb to despair, so she must succeed in this crazy changing world. Her father would expect no less of her.

Since her childhood, Papa Misha had instilled the lessons of self-reliance and pragmatism. She assessed her resources. She had raced out of the starting gate early toward entrepreneurship in the fashion business. Currently, she was responsible for International Development for a wood-processing plant and had forged the connection with her Uncle Meyer. Soon, she would be arranging logistics for the Infinity Production crew from the Twin Cities. These were opportunities on which she could build. Not a bad beginning.

The thought of being a logistics director was far more glamorous than the actual work. After Bob Hazen arrived with his film crew, her time was spent on the telephone yelling at people and running all over town to gather equipment that should have been delivered the day before. There was no customer service here. It was exhausting work. However, after so many years of absurd Cold War propaganda about the enemy, watching the American and Russian news anchors develop friendships with one another rekindled warm memories of her first encounters with Leslie and Lars. When the film project wrapped up, she hugged the crew goodbye, drove home, unplugged the phone, and fell asleep.

A few days later the phone rang the moment she reconnected it.

Slushayu vac ("I hear you"), she muttered.

Vera could detect the American accent as the caller introduced himself as Stephen Olsen, an acquaintance of Bob Hazen. He was here for just a day or two in Leningrad on a "People to People Exchange." In fact, he was standing in a phone booth outside her apartment house. Could he come in?

Strange, thought Vera. Grateful that the days were over when it was dangerous to meet with Americans, she agreed and opened her door to see a man in his thirties with dark blond hair casually striding up the stairs as if it was normal to stop by to visit a stranger out of the blue. *Physically fit and earnest—yes, he looks like a Minnesotan.*

Vera invited him to sit down and found some cake to serve him with a little tea. He pushed up his wire-rim glasses as he explained his desire to bring investors into the Soviet economy. He felt like this was the opportune time. Vera was ambivalent. *Didn't this guy read the newspaper and know about all the revolutions breaking out in the republics—Lithuania, Latvia, Estonia? It was only the beginning. On the other hand, perhaps it was all meant to be.* She liked this Stephen Olsen. He seemed intelligent and respectful of her knowledge. Later, she would notice other traits in him, such as his impulsivity and naiveté, that she had missed.

Fortunately, she could call RD in Minneapolis to vet Stephen's background. Indeed, he was well connected in the Twin Cities and knew how to structure a business deal. Vera proposed an investment in machinery to manufacture wood pallets. It seemed secure and she had a buyer. RD approved and was also willing to invest money with Olsen. RD's involvement would ease Vera through some of the rougher times with Stephen in the future.

RD and Lars visited the Soviet Union frequently.
RD served as a weekly advisor to Vera. They are
standing in front of the griffons on Bankovsky Bridge in
front of the Institute of Finance and Economics.

It was official. Vera was now the representative of a US company, an unheard-of position in Leningrad at a time when the United States did not have other registered representative offices. Vera lacked the high-level party connections of the old boys network that were so key to success in those days or tight mafia connections, but she now possessed a made-in-the-USA machete to clear an independent business path. Association with a US company differentiated her from the prevailing, corrupt Russian business culture. When an unsavory offer or threat was made, she could demur without offense, explaining her hands were tied because of her US employer. In this way, she could maintain her integrity and simultaneously play the role of insider and outsider. This was helpful when dealing with violent queens of hearts, nervous white hares, stalking Chesire cats, or mad hatters.

After Vera and Alexei ensured that Olsen & Company earned back their initial investment, they were ready to leave Genrik and Meyer to their bickering in the now unpalatable pallet business. Zahar, a supplier whom Vera respected, facilitated the transition by asking Vera and Alexei to join his construction company as partners. Zahar was getting up in years, his health was poor, and he had no one but his "worse than a criminal," no-goodnik brother to take over. A partnership was forged between Zahar and Olsen & Company.

Vera and Alexei had expected the news of Zahar's death later that year, but they had not expected to find his wife and bodyguard thrown out on the street by his "worse than a criminal" brother. Honoring Zahar's legacy meant taking care of his family. They found an apartment for Zahar's wife and retrained the bodyguard to become their driver. Business was personal.

The main enterprise of their construction company was selling processed timber. In a land rich in forests, this would have been easy had not forested lands been under government protection. Vera was creative in designating timber as a "byproduct" of road building, a function of the construction company. On that basis, they were able to get a license to export wood.

The wood, however, came from Siberia. The Siberians didn't mind bending the rules as long as they were paid in hard currency. Vera found a method. She hosted the directors on an all-expense paid trip to Sweden where they could amass the everyday goods unavailable in the Soviet Union. Ethical? The rules are different in this Wonderland.

Vera recalled. "It was a memorable trip, and I don't mean

in a good way. It was their first trip to a Western country. They were drunk all the time and completely out of control, flirting with women and generally upsetting the calm and quiet Swedish mood. I spent a lot of time either herding them to their hotels or running away from them."

This was not Vera's first trip to Sweden. Each time she stepped off the plane, she wondered about her friend Alla, but she had no way to reach her.

"I don't remember sleeping from 1989 through 1991." Vera was one of two employees at the Olsen & Company office while Alexei directed the highly profitable construction company. However, it was the star-crossed Orion Center that consumed her time and offers a glimpse into one mad hatter —Nikolai Ivanovich.

Nikolai wore two hats that, in his mind, bestowed power, access, and glory upon him. He was the director of the Leningrad office of a large lab and also an academic who headed a prestigious research institute. No matter how important a person is, being a government employee does not pay the bills. When Nikolai was allocated funds in his budget for a new building on a different site, he thought it an opportune time to assure his financial future. Moving his institute would leave his current building empty. Why not demolish this building and take possession of the empty property to build a five-star Western hotel from which he would profit? All that was missing was money and a developer for this multi-million dollar project. It didn't seem to matter that the property wasn't his. It belonged to the Soviet state. It was everybody's and nobody's.

Stephen Olsen also liked big ideas. When Vera introduced the two men, they charmed each other with their appealing smiles and mutual grandiosity. Together, they created a joint venture, branded the Orion Center. Given that there were no legal guarantees to property rights, Vera knew it would be difficult to entice investors to sink money into a parcel of land owned by the government—a small detail to Stephen. Vera was intrigued by the scope of the challenge, and her part seemed perfectly legitimate. Everyone else was dealing with the same ambiguity over property ownership or rights.

In the mind of people like Nikolai, each enterprise could

become the front for another scheme. One day he waltzed into Vera's office at Olsen & Company. She could smell the mixture of cigarette smoke and expensive imported cologne that was his trademark, and her antennae extended.

"Vera Mikhailovna, I want you to transfer six ships 'donated' by Baltic Shipping Company to our labs. Since, of course, our labs can't 'operate' these ships, I need you to transfer them to the Orion Center."

"What am I supposed to do with these ships?"

"That is not your worry," Nikolai retorted.

Well prepared for such confrontations by now, Vera looked him in the eye, smiled, and said calmly, "This contradicts our purpose. We are not in the business of stealing ships. Besides, it smells of prison."

The underlying scam was clear. He would sell the ships for scrap metal. Orion Center would collect the money for it, and Vera was supposed to transfer all the profits to Nikolai's personal account.

Not used to hearing "no," Nikolai stomped out, slammed the door, and refused to take Vera's calls. As revenge, he also refused to return Vera's international passport, which he was holding. She avenged this insult and secured her passport by appealing to his secretary. Later she secured the secretary, as well, for her own business.

"I was furious," Vera recalled. "This was a very important period. We were at the end of a lengthy procedure to get all the drawings for Orion Center approved." Too much was at stake to back down. Vera reasoned that Orion Center could still be successful without Nikolai. If the Leningrad City Council approved the idea, then the government could take the property and turn it over to Orion Center with or without Nikolai's blessing.

The exquisite color visuals and graphs held the attention of the Leningrad City Council as Vera (now a master of props) had hoped. Even the scowling, red-haired Deputy Chairman Anatoly Chubais was impressed. In time, Chubais would become one of the most powerful men in Russia, overseeing privatization in Yeltsin's administration. Following the presentation, Chubais puffed himself up to his full 5'4" height and announced that he had a question for the investor. He cleared his throat, paused, and said:

"Could you please tell us the benefit of your plan to the ordinary citizen?"

Vera almost erupted in laughter. *As if he cared about ordinary citizens.* Tempted to answer, "You would have a beautiful building instead of a junkyard, and foreigners would spend their money here, you idiot." She reined herself in, but not too much. In that period's vernacular, the standard measurement was often a sausage. Vera stated, "You can't be serious. If you're asking me how many sausages each citizen could purchase from the profits of this project, I can't answer because some of our citizens abstain from eating sausages since they are not healthy."

Insulted, Chubais jumped up and made his exit.

"It is possible that Chubais acted like a bastard not just because he was a bastard but because Nikolai had swayed his opinion," Vera reflected. Chubais had only one vote, and the majority of the City Council supported the Orion Center. This was a major success for Vera. Unfortunately, the project met an untimely death after Nikolai exhausted all the funds in his budget that had been allotted to build the new institute. The required land was never vacated.

When the Orion Center project failed, Vera still had the security of a partnership with Stephen Olsen, a thriving construction company, some key contacts, and one less headache. Vera gained an important friend—Aleksandr, head of the City Construction/Development Committee. He kept her informed of new laws and changes, and, by doing so, was instrumental in her future success.

Vera explained, "Aleksandr was sympathetic and impressed with my energy. He referred to me as a locomotive. I would never listen to 'no.' He was not annoyed but impressed by this trait."

Now, a serious contender in business, Vera would operate on her own terms. Vera had mastered the skills, but one's reputation was very important.

The best publicity for Olsen & Company, Vera concluded, was visibility in community service—a novel idea in the Soviet Union where government was expected to provide and volunteers were obtained by coercion. Pleased to be invited into the exclusive International Women's Club and proud of being one of the few women there because of her own efforts rather than those of her husband, Vera helped organize charity events.

Through this organization, she cemented her friendship with the Swedish Consul's wife Gunilla. When the Swedish Chamber of Commerce sent a delegation to Russia to consider investing, it seemed a natural fit for Vera to act as a liaison. The opportunity to work with the Swedish delegation was the final card that convinced Stephen Olsen that Vera was a "desirable asset." In 1991, he offered her a 50% partnership. Now, she could act as a principal on behalf of the company and not merely as their representative. Things were moving at lightning speed.

Olaf Lind, head of the Swedish delegation, invited Vera and Alexei to visit his lakefront estate in Göteberg, Sweden. Vera and Alexei took one look at each other and saw the exhaustion in each other's eyes. This would be their first vacation abroad together, and they gratefully accepted. Little did they know that after this vacation and a revolution, their biggest projects were in the future.

28

Vera: The Revolution
Will Be Televised

August 1991

When the beast is wounded, it might lash out.[1]
—Boris Yeltsin, August 20, 1991

Alexei and Vera had been working night and day for
months, so the invitation to stay at the Swedish estate
of their friend Olaf Lind in August 1991 sounded heavenly.
Besides, the political problems at home were increasing daily
with more in-fighting in the central government. Vera and
Alexei had always respected Gorbachev for his progressiveness
and intelligence. This was a time when many small businesses,
dubbed "cooperatives," flourished. Vera and Alexei also enjoyed
the greater freedom of the press and their ability to travel to
the West. However, a surge of protest was growing against
Gorbachev for many reasons. First, the great Soviet Union
was buckling with the various nationalities demanding a say
over their own destiny and rejecting the Kremlin's absolute
authority. Second, Gorbachev dismissed many of the old class

of *nomenklatura*—the influential hard-line Communist old guard—who, like past nobility, felt entitled to their power and privileges. Third, everything was in *defitsit*.

Because all decisions flowed outward from Moscow, small mistakes could snowball into famine or massive unemployment as edicts reverberated throughout the huge country, sparing no one except the policy-makers with private access to goods. By spring of 1990, people were hoarding food as they had during World War II. A secret CIA analysis predicted that the Soviet Union was bound for "deterioration, short of anarchy. . . . Massive consumer unrest" might tip the scales launching Russia into complete anarchy.[2]

Vera and Alexei were survivors. They took each day's news in stride and were accustomed to the Soviet Union being on the brink of collapse on a daily basis. The trip to Sweden would be a vacation where, except for their daily calls to work, they could relax on the Linds' pristine lakeside estate. The first day was wonderful and then, suddenly, the chaos of the Soviet Union interrupted.

"Two days into our vacation of excellent meals, long walks, and a dip in the cold lake, Olaf burst into our guest house, saying, 'you have a revolution back in Russia.'"

He escorted a skeptical Vera and Alexei to the main house where they watched the progress of the attempted coup on CNN. A group of eight Communist reactionaries within the government had kidnapped President Gorbachev and his family and taken them out of the city, as if this were 1917 and Gorbachev were Tsar Nicholas II. The leader of this group announced that Gorbachev had become exhausted and needed rest to regain his health. They seized control of the Russian media and declared all demonstrations and strikes illegal.

For three days, it was not clear whether Gorbachev was dead or alive. Vera called her contact in the Russian Foreign Relations office and, surprisingly, he answered. Vera tried to speak calmly asking, "What's going on? Is it true? What I see is terrifying? Are we going to lose?"

He answered, "Don't worry, we are in control, and Russia will keep moving toward democracy and freedom. Don't be scared. Everything is going to be fine."

Soon after, Vera heard from her friend Gunilla, the wife

of the Swedish consul to Russia. Gunilla warned Vera, "Are you aware that you would be one of the first who would be arrested or shot? Because you are the representative of a US company, you are the enemy."

"I realized that Alexei and our family would be under severe threat. I could be viewed as betraying my state by working for a foreign business. In just one day, all the rules had changed. This had happened too many times before in our history. How could I not have anticipated it?"

Gunilla advised Vera to stay in Sweden and let Alexei return. Gunilla's husband, the Swedish Consul, would await Alexei and Lev at the Consulate and expedite the trip back to Sweden. A visa could be provided based on Lev's medical history. Vera would still have to figure out a plan to get Mama Irina out.

Vera applied for an extension of her stay in Sweden. With Vera in jeopardy due to the political situation in Russia, the Swedes responded with compassion. During that period, they granted Russians refugee status. Vera seized this opportunity by handing over her Russian passport to Swedish authorities.

What she was seeing on TV was beyond belief. Had she been at home in Russia, she would have been watching *Swan Lake*, not the actual unfolding of events.[3] At breakfast, she learned of the coup. By dinner, there was Boris Yeltsin, President of the Russian Soviet Republic, posing atop a tank in Moscow looking more blustery and confident than ever, amid a crowd of about 20,000 people. Yeltsin challenged the right-wing government officials who had kidnapped Gorbachev, asserting that the coup was unconstitutional and that any resolutions issued by this gang were illegal. He called on the people to strike. He reminded the troops "You have taken an oath to your people, and your weapons cannot be turned against the people" and warned that the popular will toward democracy could not be stopped. Yeltsin turned out to be right. Under his charismatic leadership, an estimated 150,000 people took to the streets of Moscow, and 250,000 protested in Leningrad the next day. The preceding year, Poland, Hungary, Romania, and the German Democratic Republic had overturned the entrenched, privileged Communist Party *nomenklatura*. Finally, it was Russia's turn.

Alexei was due to leave by ferry on August 20 directly from Stockholm for Leningrad. When it was time for Alexei to embark, Vera still held the riveting image of Yeltsin rallying the public from atop a tank to protect democracy. Vera, like every Russian citizen, knew the situation was unstable and could easily turn violent. Sailing from Stockholm to Leningrad took more than two full days at sea. The passengers and crew anxiously awaited news. Many Russian veterans could remember military orders to quell protests. Would the troops follow Yeltsin's directive not to shoot their own? Would they return to anarchy, violence, or a victory of the Communist Party reactionaries? In an uncontrollable situation that could end in disaster or triumph, the logical thing to do was drink vodka so that is how Alexei and the rest of the passengers passed their time in the Gulf of Finland. It was clear by August 22 that the coup had failed. That morning, President Gorbachev and his family returned safely to Moscow. However it was Boris Yeltsin, the country's new national hero, who was in the spotlight.

Even though she was following all the events on CNN, for Vera the revolution was not over until Alexei called to tell her everyone was fine. Vera collapsed with relief when she heard his voice. That left one problem. Vera did not want to be a refugee. Unlike Alisa who was grateful for her opportunity to move to Sweden, Vera was begging Swedish officials to return her Russian passport. "The idea of Swedish citizenship made no sense. I was thinking about my mom and all the people I was responsible for."

For Vera the month of waiting for her Russian passport was one of the strangest in her life. Here she was in the middle of Sweden with nothing to do, blocked from the day-to-day business that was currently in Alexei's hands. "I was bored." This could not have been completely true because I later learned that she took this opportunity to plan her next business venture with Olaf, and they managed to fill the time together.

Curiously, Vera did not think to contact Alisa during this time. Vera was absorbed in her own troubles and assumed Alisa was, too. Their renewed relationship was still fragile, and Vera would return to see Alisa in Stockholm when she wasn't mired in such confusion.

The relative efficiency of Swedish bureaucracy thrilled Vera when her Russian passport arrived back in her hands after only a month. Alexei encouraged her to celebrate and make the best of the opportunity. Their business interests were prospering and independent of the ruble, so she purchased a Swedish souvenir—a car. The one problem was that she had never learned to drive. So it was Olaf who drove her back to Leningrad in her new Volvo 730. To Vera's shock, the dealer was so enthusiastic about the failed coup that he made her a deal Alexei couldn't refuse on an old Volvo 240 wagon. Olaf asked a friend to drive the second car. Vera was feeling very lucky until the caravan reached the ferry in Helsinki, Finland. Vera was immediately arrested because, as a Russian, she required, but did not have a Finnish visa.

"I was quite rudely taken out of my new Volvo by a Finnish officer and put in a cell with prostitutes from Thailand. I was there for fifteen hours with no food or sleep. Then, I was interrogated by very dim-witted Finnish officers who kept asking the same two questions like a broken record. 'What was your purpose in coming to Finland? Why were you stuck in Sweden?' My response was always the same."

Apparently the officers didn't watch CNN. Vera explained the circumstances over and over regarding the revolution, her separation from her husband, and her passport. She gave them Gunilla's and Olaf's phone numbers.

"Everything seemed to happen very slowly. I think the people there are frozen. Finally, they gave me a transit visa for three days explaining, 'One of your cars is not very new, so we better give you more time in case it breaks down.'"

Vera and the two Volvos were safely driven into a transformed Leningrad.

Notes

1. Cited by Hedrick Smith, *The New Russians* (New York: New York Times Books, 1983), p. 622 and attributed to Yeltsin in an interview with ABC News on that day.

2. National Intelligence Estimate [CIA] *The Deepening Crisis in the USSR: Prospects for the Next Year.*" 4: 11-18-90, November 1990. Available from https://www.cia.gov/library/center-for-the-study-of-intelligence/csi-publications/books-and-monographs/at-cold-wars-end-us-intelligence-on-the-soviet-union-and-eastern-europe-1989-1991/16526pdffiles/NIE11-18-90.pdf

3. The ballet *Swan Lake* was aired before the official announcements of the deaths of Brezhnev, Andropov, and Chernenko. On August 19, 1991, *Swan Lake* was broadcast on all channels just after the radio announcement in the morning informing the public that Gorbachev had been "ousted" due to illness and power would be in the hands of the Committee for the Emergency Situation. Available from English.ruvr.ru//2011/08/18/54859093.

29

Vera and Alisa: Sister Act Revival

1990–1993

Dlya milovo druzhka i seryozhka iz ushka.
*For a dear friend, I'm willing to take an earring out
of my own ear.*

—Russian proverb

O nly the luckiest of coincidences brought Vera and Alisa
back together in the fall of 1990, a year before the collapse
of the Soviet Union. Vera was on her way to a business meeting
in Göteburg, Sweden, with her boisterous Siberian lumber
partners, breezing through Arlanda Airport to catch her flight
from Stockholm to Göteburg. As Vera cleared customs, she
suddenly caught sight of Gera, Alisa's brother. In the blink of
an eye, Vera had Alisa's Stockholm phone number, and Gera
hurried to a phone to tell Alisa about his chance meeting.

Vera raced to her hotel, checked in, threw her coat on the
bed, and dialed Alisa's number. Breathlessly and in her little
girl voice she said, "Alla, it's me."

Tearfully, they repeated each other's name again and
again as if by doing so they could erase four years of separation.

Alisa could be Alla again. She felt she had her best friend back in her life forever. There were a lot of "sorrys." Vera told Alisa about the trials of building her business and how much she loved Alexei. Alisa broke down and recounted how hard it had been just to survive in Stockholm. She told Vera how her focus on executing her plan to check on her parents and bring them to Sweden had prevented Alisa from seeing Vera on her brief trip back to the Soviet Union. She was just trying to keep her life together and couldn't lose her focus. Now was the right time to reconnect. Vera was immersed in a business deal and would not be able to see Alisa this trip; however, business often brought her to Sweden, and she promised to schedule another business trip to Stockholm in the next month. It felt like Alisa's four-year disappearance had been only a pause in their relationship.

A month passed and Vera returned. She and Alisa arranged to meet. From a distance, they spied each other and each began to cry. Each hurried toward the other, arms opening like butterfly wings until they clasped each other and hugged. They wept for the lost years and then wept some more for the happiness of finding each other again. After a history of shared secrets, shared feelings, and so many words, there were no words this time. All the anger, the sadness, the regrets, and the longing evaporated as they came together. Alisa felt the pain disappear the tighter they held each other.

After that trip to Stockholm, Vera turned her back on Stockholm's luxurious Grand Hôtel and chose, instead, the intimacy of Alisa's tiny Söder apartment. They regained their old comfort just being side by side. Once again they felt like long lost sisters. Still, their friendship ebbed and flowed following their reunion. Alisa was absorbed in basic survival and assimilating into her new environment, while Vera was trying to keep her businesses successful in an ever-changing political and economic climate.

After Yeltsin was established as the new leader of the new Russia in 1991, Alisa began to plan a trip back to Leningrad/ St. Petersburg. In 1992 she returned with a mission—to convince her parents to leave the newly renamed St. Petersburg. Economic and political chaos hovered menacingly over Russia after the coup. Nothing was certain. This was the time to try and convince her parents and grandmother to leave and join her in Stockholm. Although Alisa's parents embraced her, through their tears they protested yet again, "We're too old to move. Rosa is too old to move. We can't leave her." True, they had survived the 900-day Nazi blockade of Leningrad, but Alisa could see the dangers lurking in the predatory post-Communist atmosphere.

Alisa made sure to call Vera to arrange a get-together—their first in St. Petersburg since she had left for Sweden. Vera invited Alisa to join Alexei and her at Krisha, one of the top restaurants in St. Petersburg. Alisa felt chills of apprehension about seeing Alexei. His barbs had hurt deeply. She had not forgotten his insults and blamed him for the distance between Vera and her. Still, it was the right thing to do for the sake of her friendship with Vera.

Appalling was the feeling Alisa had upon entering Krisha. The contrast between her parents' struggle for daily food and the overabundance of gourmet fare available to the Russian *nouveau riche* and foreign visitors was almost too much to bear. She swallowed her distaste and sat down with Vera and Alexei in their world. The food surpassed any meal in her Leningrad memory. The flavors, quality of the food, and the polite service convinced her that a new day had arrived—at least for those who could afford the astronomical prices. Of course, glasses of wine and vodka generously lubricated the conversation as well.

Dinner was almost over when Alexei placed his wine glass on the table and looked directly into Alisa's eyes. His expression seemed genuine and open. *What was going on?* Alisa wondered.

"Alisa," Alexei began without his trademark humor, "I want to apologize. My perceptions about you and Boris were wrong. I know I acted like you were beneath me because you were a hairdresser and Boris worked at a grocery. I was blinded by Communist propaganda, and I thought I had the right to judge. I'm not proud of this. I'm sorry."

Vera smiled and remained silent. Alisa had never heard Alexei speak like this before. He sounded sincere, and she sensed Vera's hand in this. Alisa was stunned into silence and shocked into instant sobriety. Alisa heard the genuineness that underscored the difficult apology. *This is like having somebody come back from another world,* Alisa thought to herself. Yet, she couldn't quite forget the past to allow herself to grant him forgiveness at that moment. The breach between Vera and Alisa was now on the mend. Alisa and Alexei would not become close, but neither would he stand as a wedge between the two friends any longer. Alisa returned to Stockholm without her family, but she had her friend back in her life for good.

Even after Alisa heard Alexei's apology, she was not yet ready to fully embrace him. The apology allowed Vera and Alisa to pursue their friendship. (Stockholm, 1992)

30

Meryll: Improvisational Governance[1]

1992–1994

Scene: Moscow 1992
Shopper: Give me 200 grams of cheese, please.
Shop assistant: You go and bring me some cheese, then
I'll cut off 200 grams.

—Russian Joke

Not even the hero of the bloodless revolution, Boris Yeltsin, who occupied the position of power in the Kremlin, could obliterate the entrenched seventy-year old Soviet mindset and substitute a smooth-running market economy. The improvisation began. The majority of Russians were pawns in a game played by novices. Given that the rules of the game were constantly in flux, the pawns were the first to be sacrificed while those with political connections and capitalist ambition amassed great wealth.

The pathway to wealth was *privatizatsiya*, the privatization system nicknamed *prikhvatitsya* (grabbing). Initially, all citizens were entitled to vouchers so that they could own a share of their country's property. But soon the privileged found an angle and, at a stunningly deep discount, favored bidders could purchase their stake of Russia's state-owned natural resources. Thus, the national wealth was soon distributed among a few individuals, who had been the first to establish banks and companies, leveraging their power to function as Yeltsin's brain when the alcohol clouded his thinking.

Not only was unleashing property from State ownership on Yeltsin's improvisational agenda but so was dismantling the central planning system and normalizing the propped-up ruble. When the Soviet flag was finally lowered from the Kremlin on Christmas Day, 1991, there was an urgency to dismantle the Soviet system so that it could never reemerge.

Egor Gaidar stepped up to assume the position no one wanted—devising a way to create value for the monetary system. The method, referred to by Yeltsin's economic advisers as "shock therapy," certainly caused Russians to feel shock as the ruble went into free-fall; however, one would have been hard-pressed to find a Russian who would endorse its therapeutic value. By the end of 1992, allowing the market to determine the value of the ruble created an inflation rate of 2500%. Most Russians, especially women, were impoverished and were without the safety net of healthcare, education, subsidized food, subsidized apartments, or even childcare that the Soviet government had previously provided.[1]

There were some winners. Some saw the *likhiye godi*, the years with no law, as an opportunity. One had to be bold, ready to move assets on a moment's notice, well-connected, and a skilled improviser. Ironically, the era of *glasnost* (transparency) mutated to an era of the shell game and obfuscation with profits hidden offshore. Eventually, the rules of the new order evolved and were described by Professor Alena Ledeneva.[2] "The central principle of financial scheming, to misrepresent the state of affairs, is founded on a basic imperative—'If you have money you should pretend that it does not really belong to you or that you owe it to somebody.'"[2] She summarized the new business rules as follows:

1. All firms work without profit.
2. All firms keep double books.
3. One has to share profits through payouts.

4. One has to respect the informal order.
5. One has to make and keep friends.
6. One should avoid dealing with formal institutions.[3]

Russian laws did not make it possible to succeed honestly nor was there a reliable judicial system. What was the informal order? Businessmen paid bribes and deployed private mafia gangs to negotiate the chaos and preserve their wealth.

The intellgentsia lost their hope for real democracy as they watched the coverage of the war in Chechnya in late 1994. Slowly, the awareness hit that this government lied like the old one—the Russian military had staged the so-called anti-government "coups" in Chechnya only to rush in to eradicate any resistance to Soviet power. The government considered itself *nezakanoye* (above the law).

Like Americans in the 1960s watching newsfeed from Vietnam, ordinary Russians were seeing live war telecasts for the first time. As Soviet citizens Russians had been "protected" from any bad news including car crashes or train wrecks by heavy censorship and propaganda until this moment.

As the gulf between rich and poor increased, social problems intensified in the 1990s. The Russian government exploited the resurgence of ethnic violence propagated by skinhead gangs. Scapegoating minorities like Jews deflected criticism of the government. *Pamyat'*,[4] the nationalist political party embraced the rhetoric: "Russia for the Russians." At the same time, ethnic groups such as the Chechens were committing their own acts of terrorism to strike back against the repressive measures of this new Russia. Journalists who dared to tell the truth feared reprisal from hit men hired by government agents.

Russia was imploding.

Notes

1. A short summary of the economic woes of the 1990s can be found in Stephen F. Cohen, *The Victims Return: Survivors of the Gulag after Stalin* (Exeter, NH: Publishing Works, 2010), p. 169. For a fuller account, see Cohen's *Failed Crusade: America and the Tragedy of Post-Communist Russia* (New York: WW Norton, 2000).

2. Alena Ledeneva, *How Russia Really Works: The Informal Practices That Shaped Post-Soviet Politics and Business* (Ithaca, NY: Cornell University Press, 2006), p.148. Ledeneva, a student of Tatyana Zaslavskaya (who originated the theory of *perestroika*), is Professor of Politics and Society at University College of London.

3. Ledeneva, *How Russia Really Works*, p. 116.

4. *Pamyat'* is the Russian word for memory.

31

Vera: Thank-You for Smoking

1991–1993

Volkov boyat'sa—v les ne khodit.
"If you're afraid of wolves, don't go into the woods."
—Russian proverb

When Vera rolled her Volvos home from Sweden in 1991, she was not contemplating democracy but, rather, entrepreneurial opportunities. Vera's month in Sweden had not been spent merely watching the revolution on CNN and strolling around the estate. She and her host, Olaf, planned a partnership for a boutique in central Leningrad. While awaiting the return of her Russian passport, she was researching the trendiest Swedish boutiques and choosing designers. Through the brother of a trusted employee, she located a perfect corner building on Nevsky Prospekt, right by the Kazan Cathedral. By late fall 1991, the renovation was almost complete and the clothes were ordered.

"This was a time when thugs were everywhere," Vera announced over Skype more than twenty years later. When asked to describe a thug, Vera smiled and said, "It depended on the year and the current thug fashion. But they all dressed alike. They could be wearing a burgundy jacket one year or an expensive tracksuit the next year. They accessorized with a gold chain bearing a crucifix hung around the neck. We called the crucifix a 'gymnast' because these guys were usually trained as boxers or wrestlers. It seemed ludicrous to us that they had taken on religion."

But Vera wasn't worried about thug fashion or security at this time. She was delighted to be opening the boutique at such a prestigious address on Nevsky Prospekt. Everything was moving along fine. Thinking back, she can now recall the nervousness in her landlord's voice when he phoned to summon Alexei and her to the store, but she was not anticipating danger.

"Alexei and I arrived to see a group of thugs greeting us, who fit the precise description I gave you. One had an overgrown head, meat-cleaver fists, and a tree-trunk neck adorned with the 'gymnast' crucifix. They told us that if we wanted to walk out alive, we needed to give them ownership. I don't know what got into me. Whenever someone wants to take away what we have built ourselves without recognizing our investment, I get enraged. This overtook any fear I had. I told them that we had paid for this renovation, and if they wanted the business so much they could fucking pay for it. They could kill us, but what would they do with our bodies and what would they actually gain. Alexei was watching me with a smile on his face. I think these are the times when Alexei is proudest of me. The thugs began to negotiate with us, and we left with our lives intact and about half the money which we had invested. There was no more store. We took security very seriously after that."

To do business in Russia, you need some kind of *krisha* or "roof." A *krisha* refers to protection or security from an association with a group that will protect you from bandits just like themselves. Vera never had to worry about security at the construction firm since her old partner, Zahar, was surrounded by a cadre of loyal ex-cons who had worked with him years ago in the gold-mining business, but she would have to consider security if she planned to branch out now.

Vera turned her energy back to Olsen & Company and, perhaps, it was "Jewish luck" again that as Russia's economy was drowning, Vera was given her biggest opportunity to date. The month in Sweden had heightened Vera's craving for sleek, modern, and clean interiors—nonexistent in her home city. She was now able to design an elegant office for Olsen & Company near the Yusupov Palace. She was aware that the space would reflect her business persona.

Vera was finally able to create a sleek, modern dream office for her company – the perfect set design for her business productions.

"I've always been in the business of creating, organizing, and building my own environment. It's like a theater and I have to find my role in this theater and act accordingly. I have to perform."

Soon she would have an opportunity to test her theories. Stephen Olsen had told her that a humanitarian relief project was being organized and they stood a good chance of winning the contract. Although Vera credits their success in signing the contract for logistics to the impeccable interior design of her office and her professionalism, connections also played a role. Coincidentally, a member of the Joint Distribution Committee (JDC)[1] was from Minneapolis and could vet Vera through her Minneapolis contacts.

The 1992 project, overseen by the JDC, was ambitious in scope. A total of 4,000 tons of rice, beans, vegetable oil, and powdered milk would be shipped from New York City to Russia. Russia was sorely in need of these supplies, and the United States had a strong interest in stabilizing the Russian government. For Vera, this period provided an intense education in defining and meeting Western management expectations.

The first step was hiring three hundred people. Since the Russian government was bankrupt and, therefore, had stopped paying salaries, workers were readily available, but locating those with a good work ethic was challenging. Even when Vera and Alexei hired employees who prided themselves on exceeding productivity demands, they had to teach them to think beyond their own task in the logistical supply chain. Loading more trucks in one day was a liability if no one was there to unload the food supplies.

Vera and Alexei directed the distribution of 4000 tons of humanitarian food aid in Russia during the shortage. It would have been easy for a box to go missing.

Her American mentors expected timely and honest communication. This meant Vera had to retrain her workers to believe they would not be punished if they informed their managers of problems. This broke the cultural norm every Soviet citizen knew. If you make a mistake, sweep it under the rug, deny the accusation, make excuses, or blame a scapegoat. Vera explained, "We grew up afraid to admit 'I don't know.' Instead, we pretended we knew or we'd come up with a story. It was upsetting to admit you failed because you would be instantly shamed by teachers, parents, or other students."

In Russia, the old or the new, business was anything but

transparent. When Gorbachev introduced the term *glasnost* (transparency), it was a novelty. In Russian businesses, numbers could change; people could be paid off—not so on this project. Vera and Alexei were operating under a microscope. The Swiss certification firm SGS was hired by the US government to validate delivery. Israelis hovered over security. A former Citibank executive ensured the efficiency of the operation and supervised Vera on a daily basis. This experience of transparency and accountability gave Vera a decisive advantage when she later presented proposals to international companies. She distinguished herself from other Russians by not having the attitude of "Give us your money and leave it to us to worry about the details." In the future, Vera was prepared to account for her time and efforts in a way that would satisfy not only SGS but any Western corporation. She and Alexei also refined their style of working together, with Vera taking over the big picture and Alexei focusing on the details.

As much as she learned from the Americans involved, there were a few lessons that Vera could teach. At one point, the longshoremen in St. Petersburg refused to unload the ships unless they received a pay increase. Vera would have been liable for hefty fines if the freight was not removed by deadline. Her tactic was to call a meeting with the four top officials of the St. Petersburg Port Authority.

"I always tried to research the history, personality, and goals of the people I was going to deal with in order to create my script." Three out of four of these men were traditional, middle-aged Soviet directors. "The most important part was a good first impression."

First, to reduce their aggression, she would have her attractive blonde receptionist Natalya serve them coffee in her comfortable reception area for ten minutes. Vera's outfit, an ensemble of feminine allure and military formality, consisted of a nearly transparent gold-trimmed Escada skirt and a double-breasted jacket with gold buttons and epaulets. As she made her delayed entrance, the effect was just as she had hoped. The men stood at attention, almost as if saluting a superior.

Vera smiled and repeated her practiced lines. "You can take your seats and let's talk about our problem." It was clear who was in charge. Vera had worked out the strategy and had a *quid pro quo* in her pocket to help the longshoremen save face. She suggested appealing to the workers by reminding them that they were part of the effort to help Russia's neediest. To express appreciation for the longshoremen's efforts, she could offer them products (damaged cans) to take home. Success.

During the four months of this relief project in 1992, Vera, Alexei, and the newly expanded labor force worked practically around the clock. The work was exhausting but exhilarating for Vera and Alexei. Vera's right-hand woman Svetlana fondly recalls these days as the most rewarding of all. It was meaningful and important.

Vera proudly states, "We were able to deliver almost 100% of the food. We were the only relief effort that achieved that percentage."

Vera had just accomplished the execution of a large-scale humanitarian project without black market involvement. It would not be so easy in other enterprises. Just as Vera was about to take a short break from the months of nonstop work, she received a call from an SGS executive in Switzerland inquiring whether Vera could locate warehouse space for its client, a huge tobacco firm.

Vera was stunned but not daunted. "I am sure I could do that. Tell me the specifics."

This meant entering a new industry in a big way for Olsen & Company. The supplier was eager to expand into the Russian market, an opportunity not to be missed. She ran out of her office, reined in her enthusiasm, and moved into executive mode as she announced, "Okay, people, we need to find a warehouse. Check your contacts to find out who knows about space."

There is nothing so valuable as *svyazi* (connections). Perhaps the only efficient system in Russia is the communication network among acquaintances. One of the women in the office located warehouse space in an empty hangar belonging to the firm of an acquaintance. This enabled Vera to sign the contract with SGS.

Just like the old Soviet Union increased the ante each time a quota was met, the SGS representative called her again with a greater requirement. "Now that I know you can arrange warehouse space, this time we need a space to accommodate

9,000 tons of leaf tobacco." In addition, he specified that it be close to the main highway, a seaport, an airport, and have railroad access.

Vera took a deep breath and said, "I will give you a call back within the next two weeks."

In her head, she was saying something very similar to what Alisa, in negotiating her early years in Sweden, had said. *It's impossible, but it can be done.* Vera had never promised something she couldn't deliver. She unfolded a map of St. Petersburg and found one specific area that met the need. She marched into her office to tap her most valuable resource, her staff, and once again announced that she needed them to comb through their contacts for space in that area. As always, her staff came through for her.

Vera researched the general manager of the desired site, Sergei Ivanov, who was recommended by an employee, and the tap-dancing began. Alexei made the first contact and set up the relationship—one Soviet manager to another. When it was time for negotiating details, Vera was brought in. The negotiations had to be quick, or they could lose the opportunity. It wasn't surprising that to close the deal, she had to agree to take Sergei Ivanov's son into the business and clear out tons of old equipment. They now had the right to use the existing warehouse and had access to the property.

"If any other Russian had gotten hold of $700,000 in 1993 as we did from SGS, he would have taken the money and run. However, we used this money to remove the old equipment."

Vera heard from a contact that property rights were about to change and she would be in a favorable position if she could quickly erect her own building. How to construct a large warehouse quickly in Russia was a puzzle and one the United States military had already solved for Desert Storm. At an international exposition, Vera and Alexei discovered hangars that could be constructed in one month. They continued to expand the following year. In this way, they escaped the offer to join Sergei Ivanov in privatization.

Vera proudly said, "I never privatized anything because I didn't believe it was fair. Everything I had, I built from scratch."

Vera described the *zeitgeist* of Russia in the 90s. "If I was in a public restroom, I could think I had the right to privatize the toilet as my own. I was here. No one else was claiming possession, so I could. It was horrible. Privatization made people vulnerable to being destroyed by government officials or others who were jealous."

The founding of her warehouses had two significant implications. First, it put Vera and Alexei in an industry with the "Big Boys,"[2] many of whom were unsavory and dangerous. From its inception, this new business involved the Customs Agency, now privatized and infiltrated by organized crime. Second, it brought a major deal to Olsen & Company and provided more evidence to Stephen Olsen that Vera and Alexei were major players.

"We were providing a facility for others who were importing or exporting. Nobody wanted to deal with a 'dirty' commodity like tobacco—an agricultural export with potential infestation by insects and a lot of liability. We had to fumigate. It was dangerous, dirty work and always a fire hazard. Everyone else wanted to be in consumer goods. Tobacco is what SGS brought us. We might never have gone into the business if tobacco hadn't been the first commodity offered. However, I would not have chosen to be in the customs business with another product."

Consumer goods were highly susceptible to the criminal market. Unbeknownst to the importer, invoice prices or item names would be altered so that lower customs were paid with the difference going into the pockets of the customs officer, the distributor, and any other middlemen. This was not the environment that Vera would have chosen, but she wouldn't back down now.

Profits were important, but Vera's core value was taking care of her employees. Vera and Alexei gathered people they trusted. Vera nurtured her staff and was aware of their personal issues. Employees depended on Vera and Alexei for more than a salary in dollars. If they needed something and Vera could provide it, she would. This included medical care, clothing, enrollment in select schools, tuition, or security. It was a delicate symbiotic balance.

Practically, there were other reasons to carefully invest in the loyalty and satisfaction of their staff. Disgruntled employees could cause a lot of damage. An unhappy ex-worker could give a false tip to the tax police or seek revenge through more violent means. Some employees, like Svetlana, whose mother was Lev's nanny, had been with them from the beginning. Others were brought in, based not only on their résumé but on the connections they offered. Her employees were "family," and many of her family were employees including Alexei's sister, Vera's brother, Grisha, and nieces.

Vera recognized that everyone had their strengths and weaknesses and considered it her job to match people properly to their job. She was not always successful. One fellow named Dima, whose father was KGB and whose wife worked for Customs, seemed like a perfect hire. When Alexei and Vera heard that his infant was sick, they readily "lent" him money to obtain the best medical care. One month later, Vera sent Dima to Moscow on a mission to "facilitate requests," a process of handing over envelopes stuffed with cash to strategically positioned bureaucrats. Vera's voice starts to rise in anger as she tells the story.

"When Dima returned from Moscow, there were no results at all, so we requested the four thousand dollars back. He was angry and insulted, claiming it was not his fault. Eventually, we found out that none of our connections in Moscow ever received their payments. Instead, he pocketed all the money. We fired him. Right or wrong, Alexei reminded him that he owed us money for his child's medical care. We apparently made an enemy of Dima."

It could happen so easily, and now the question was whether their *krisha* was sufficient. It would turn out that it was not. The sum total of their security force was a former KGB colonel, who spent a lot of his time drinking on the job. For now, that had to be enough. Vera wanted to stay away from association with the well-dressed and well-armed gangsters who would gladly provide additional protection.

Notes

1. The Joint Distribution Committee (JDC) is a Jewish organization that was established in 1914 to provide aid to Jews in the Diaspora. It extended its mission to provide relief to those who were in need during the crisis in Russia.

2. "The Big Boys" is our term for referring to people with key mafia connections. It was extremely unusual for a woman like Vera to be in this industry.

32

Alisa: Finding Home

1990–1993

Den som väntar på något gott, väntar aldrig för länge.
"When you are waiting for something good, you can never wait too long."

—Swedish proverb

As Alisa struggled to learn the complex jargon, customs, and principles of Western business in her government-sponsored program, she continued to sweep floors and dust the office for Kalle, her first benefactor in Stockholm. While she closed the blinds before grabbing her dust cloth, she muttered, "*duktig* (self-reliant), *duktig*. The need for self-reliance felt as primal as hunger.

After her business studies were complete, Alisa breathed a sigh of relief as she readied herself for an internship at ISS Clorius in 1990 and was able to end her dependence on Kalle. ISS Clorius was a large, international facility management company. The Swedish branch concentrated on logistics, together with selling and servicing energy meters.

To anyone else, logistics and energy meters might sound ho-hum and boring, but Alisa focused on the international scope of the business and the potential opportunities. She presumed if she could be successful in her internship, a full-time job would await her. Hired for the Finance Department, Alisa uncovered the advantages of this ten-person office as she gained experience in every area, frequently filling in for others.

"If the telephone rang and the receptionist was gone, I answered the phone. We needed everyone to help load products, so everyone went out to load the van."

Alisa's cooperative spirit and quality work led to a permanent position as she had hoped.

Alisa was attuned to the nuances of the business culture. Clorius embodied Swedish business values — egalitarianism, solidarity, and maintaining a spirit of consensus at work. Bosses were addressed by first names; meetings were held to ensure everyone was on board for all decisions. Despite Alisa's energy and her studied attempts to fit in, she could not bridge the distance between her and the nine Swedes in the office.

"My Swedish was still not perfect. It was clear I was a foreigner, but it took the others a long time to simply ask me where I was from. In the United States someone would have asked that question within the first five minutes of meeting me."

As she had learned in her Swedish culture class, the Swedes were demonstrating good manners, respecting Alisa's privacy. Despite her objective understanding, it hurt. It seemed as if they didn't care about her as a person.

Alisa was reminded of her foreignness not only within her company but also when she traveled. Alisa was scheduled to fly with her colleagues to London for a business trip. When she submitted her Russian passport for a visa application, she was refused. The company wrote a letter guaranteeing it was a business trip, assuring the British authorities that Alisa had a permanent green card. Alisa's embarrassment didn't end with the visa process. She arrived at British passport control and greeted the agent.

He looked up and asked, "Why is your English so good? You hold a Russian passport and you're traveling on behalf of a Swedish company."

Alisa made a silly face in response, "I went to a special English school."

"Wait here."

The agent assumed that any Russian fluent in English must be KGB. Alisa waited, her face now strained, as the agent spent thirty minutes checking computer files before stamping her entry visa. No more joking with passport control or customs agents for Alisa. Her fellow employees made no mention of the delay in order not to embarrass her further. Alisa couldn't wait for the day she would travel on her own Swedish passport.

By 1991 Alisa could apply for her Swedish citizenship and passport. There was no ceremony like the drama of immigrants in the United States gathering before a judge with hands raised to pledge allegiance to their new country. Still, a Swedish passport meant freedom from association with that red Russian passport and all the suspicions it aroused. Prepared with the necessary documentation, including her official divorce papers from Sven, she happily renounced her Russian citizenship. In exchange, she received the document with the bold "SVERIGE" across the top and the Swedish crest emblazoned on its blue cover. Even this treasured passport could not magically transform her into a Swede.

Alisa ticked off her achievements since her arrival in Sweden, but she still felt isolated and restless. By 1993 she was earning enough to save for her parents' eventual arrival and now had enough money to realize her dream of traveling to Israel. She remembered how strong her desire to move to Israel had been when she was in her teens and her twenties. She wasn't sure how she would feel when she landed on Israeli soil.

As she flew south to Ben Gurion Airport, she remembered how hard it had been to survive in Sweden. She had struggled to learn Swedish, to get a job, to learn new business practices, and to acclimate to a new culture. She had been so lonely she ached. Proud of all she had achieved in Sweden, she still felt pangs of regret that she hadn't realized her original dream—a home in Israel. *How hard it would be to start over again. No, even the thought of immigrating again was a fantasy she could not entertain.* She had made her choice.

The plane glided over the Mediterranean and minutes later landed. Applause echoed through the plane. The blue and white Israeli flag with the Magen David was visible as the wheels touched the runway.* *Like the Magen David necklace I had in Leningrad, like the new Magen David I'm wearing now.*

Collecting her thoughts and her bags, she strode proudly down the jetway. As she entered the long hallway leading to baggage claim, the bright sunshine warmed her right side. Alisa raised her hand to shield her eyes from the tropical sun. She turned to look out the picture window and saw the bank of plantings that read in Hebrew and English, *brukhim habaim*, "welcome home," and she wept. Her tears became sobs, her body looked like it was wracked with grief. It wasn't grief; these were the words she had craved to hear all these years. *Welcome home. You are home. You belong here.*

Seeing her collapse in tears and concerned for her welfare, a crowd gathered around her, but she couldn't verbalize her feelings. The very fact that so many people huddled around her in concern heightened the emotion. Never could she imagine this in Stockholm or Leningrad where passers-by would avert their eyes and hurry past a crying stranger.

Like any Jew from the Diaspora, she toured the land and soaked up the history and the sights. However, Alisa was not really like any Jew from the Diaspora. The everyday activities of the trip such as visiting a kibbutz, touching the Western Wall, dipping her toes in the Mediterranean were extraordinary for her. Israel was no longer a dream or an idea, but a real place pulsing with life. Regretfully, she reminded herself on the return flight, *I can't immigrate again. I can't begin again.* But Israel would remain her spiritual homeland.

Once Alisa made peace with remaining in Sweden, "good luck arrived" when Kalle announced that a penthouse apartment was available in the center of Stockholm in his Södermalm building if she wanted it. Of course she wanted it! Söder was the made-to-order neighborhood for Alisa, a Bohemian area brimming with artists, theaters, bars, and restaurants. Its funky old buildings and creative mix of people were a welcome change from the uniform tidiness of Sundyberg.

"I was single and independent and that was the right place for me. I am a city girl, and it felt right to move from the suburbs."

Hanging the Potapenko painting she had brought from

Russia in her new urban apartment overlooking the rooftops of Söder was a milestone. Friends visited and marveled at the view and the hip decor. Now Alisa had a home of her own design that fit her perfectly.

Alisa proudly stands in front of her new apartment building in Söder.

Note

* "Blue and White" (in Hebrew, *kaḥol velavan*), is the title of a simple song written by Yisrael Rashal (b. 1948) of Minsk. It became an anthem for Soviet Jews who wanted to make aliyah to Israel or identify positively as Jews. The melody in minor key is reminiscent of Russian folksongs. In the eyes of the Soviet regime, the simple lyrics represented treason.

33

Alisa: A Foot in the Door

1993–1994

Den beskedlige får ingenting.
"The modest one gets nothing."
—Swedish proverb

A lthough Alisa had settled into her dream apartment in Söder after her journey to Israel, it soon seemed her luck had soured. Following a process of financial liberalization, the Swedish banking crisis hit. Recession rolled across the global economy as well in the early 1990s. In these dire circumstances, Sweden was forced to restructure its vaunted welfare state. Joblessness soared to over 9% in a country that was accustomed to a 1–2% rate of unemployment. Companies had to rethink their strategic plans. Many cut back on hiring. Sweden's immigrants (12% of the population) faced discrimination in the hiring office and intimidation on the street, where skinhead groups chanted "*Sverige år svenskarna,*" "Sweden for the Swedes."

Alisa's ecstatic mood collapsed once she discovered she lost her job and had to find a way to pay her rent to keep her dream apartment in Söder.

When ISS Clorius shuttered its Stockholm office in 1993, Alisa was a casualty. She refused to surrender to encroaching despair. Action was her antidote. She vowed not to slip down the ladder of success she had so painstakingly climbed. Frantically, she networked and pieced together a steady income with two part-time jobs. Alisa became a photographer at a friend's photo agency specializing in passport and ID photos. At lunch she waited on tables at another friend's café. This was her frenetic survival package for a year while she job hunted relentlessly to further her career, not just to survive.

After responding to countless want ads and talking to her network of friends, Alisa wasn't making any inroads in her search. She decided to take a bolder approach when friends alerted her that Ericsson was hiring, but their job postings were internal. Alisa researched Ericsson and discovered that the telecommunications giant with 60,000 employees in over 140 countries had been founded in 1876. Known as one of the "genius firms" in Sweden, its success was rooted in engineering innovation. She learned Ericsson was a leading supplier of mobile systems, applications, and service. Moreover, the Board of Directors had faced crises much more drastic than a recession in the past 118 years. Besides, Alisa suspected mobile phones were not just a passing fad, but on the cutting edge of technology.

Dressed for success, Alisa headed for the main office of Ericsson in suburban Kista without a clear action plan. Conscious of the echoing click of her heels, she walked confidently to the reception desk. She noticed a yellow book lying near the counter. Her heart raced as she glanced at the title of the thick volume. It was the listing of all the internal postings in the corporation, information not intended for public consumption. Now a plan instantly formed in her mind.

"Do you mind if I take this book?" Alisa politely asked the receptionist.

"Go ahead, please," she replied without looking up from her work.

"Thanks."

Alisa managed her thanks in an even tone, trying not to show her astonishment as she left with her treasure. A Swede would not have been so bold, but there were times when hutzpah was her greatest asset. She pored over the tome and applied for every job that seemed suitable. Her persistence led to an interim project-based assignment. Alisa's foot was in the door, and she would not allow the door to close.

Within a few months, she surpassed expectations. By 1994 she was hired as a manager—the first female manager of twenty male telecom engineers on a production line. Her assignment was to create the technical repair center and, in doing so, she had to constantly challenge the engineers. This was a job unlike any other she had ever had or dreamed she could have.

"To be a woman, to be an immigrant, to be a new hire, to have an economics degree rather than an engineering degree were all handicaps. All the guys were from an engineering background."

Alisa had already learned from her experience at ISS Clorius. "You can't just tell a Swede to do something different. It's a process of consensus all the time. You had to be creative to push change to get around the Swedish attitude of *lagom*, in between is best."

It may not have been the sexiest sector of Ericsson, but Alisa relished problem-solving. Without formal management training, Alisa relied on her "brains and logic" to challenge the existing system and improve it. She was balancing precariously between creating consensus for change among the staid men while gently guiding them in new directions. At first Alisa's determination to change the system resulted in pushback from her staff and many sleepless nights. By day, she applied her make-up and presented a positive face persisting until she created a cooperative, working team that delivered results, rather than "a bunch of engineers" wrangling over every detail. Eventually a team ethos emerged.

As her understanding of the Swedish way deepened, Alisa prodded the metamorphosis by providing training for her team. She saw her job as "people development," and her guiding principle was to trust her employees. She allowed them to think about solutions and treated them as part of a team rather than imposing her own solutions and slipping into the hierarchical pattern that pervaded Ericsson's top-down management style. Although most Swedish companies had adopted the consensus model of management, Alisa discovered that Ericsson still operated as it had 100 years ago. The innovations at Ericsson had been in technology, not management techniques. Alisa felt successful each time one of "her people" was promoted. This was taking care of her staff.

The engineers' attitudes toward their enthusiastic and driven boss softened over time. By her third year as Repair Center manager, the men finally dared to ask a personal question, "No one can match you! Is your energetic attitude a Russian trait?"

Alisa laughed to herself thinking of the Soviet "tradition" of obfuscation and delay tactics to avoid accepting responsibility. She thought of Russians more as sleepy bears than energizer bunnies. She turned to them and replied, "I am not Russian. My attitude, brains, and spirit are a cocktail of a Jewish-Russian-Swedish mix."

Alisa had been trained as a finance expert, examining profit and loss figures, but she was a natural manager by intuition. She buttressed her intuition with coursework, enrolling in every management and leadership course available at "Ericsson University."* By the time she ended her career at Ericsson, Alisa carried with her a well-stocked toolbox of management strategies.

Just as no one at Ericsson suspected Alisa's sleepless nights as she began her work in the Repair Center, no one there had an inkling of the personal crises that she faced in 1994, which Alisa dubbed the year of ketchup.

Note

*Courses available within the company.

34
Alisa: The Year of Ketchup
1994

Kerplop.

—Alisa

You know how you have a hamburger and try to get the ketchup to come out of the bottle? You hit the side of the bottle again and again. Nothing happens. You tip the bottle and look inside. There's the ketchup—why won't it pour out? Then, kerplop, it seems like half the bottle lands on your small burger. That's what happened in my life in 1994."

Alisa had been hammering hard on many fronts to achieve her personal and professional goals. It was her first year working as a manager at Ericsson. Finally, after years of pressuring her parents to leave Russia, they packed and turned their backs on St. Petersburg. It was also the year she met her husband-to-be, Rolf. Life changes were furiously pouring out on top of Alisa.

Alisa faced two roadblocks trying to facilitate her parents' emigration: her parents' stubbornness and a change in policy by the Swedish government. With Gorbachev in power and *glasnost* in the air, the Swedish government no longer believed the need for asylum was pressing. So a more restrictive asylum policy was initiated in December 1989 for all Russian refugees. The upsurge of xenophobia that began in the mid-1980s continued as some Swedes feared the influx of Russians, as well as immigrants from Africa and Asia, who could dilute their culture and drain their coffers.

While the Swedish government raised barriers to immigration in December 1989, Alisa's parents built their own wall refusing to consider a new life in Sweden. Not trusting that Gorbachev's policies would lead to a better life in the Soviet Union, Alisa urged her family to emigrate before the political and economic situation deteriorated. "We don't want to move. We're old. We can't leave your grandmother."

Alisa persisted, "But you'll come when Rosa dies?"

"We'll be all right as long as we're working."

After the collapse of the Soviet Union in 1991, few people were all right anymore. At one time, life in the Soviet Union promised financial security through old age along with free medical care. This was no longer true. Naum and Bella were forced to sell their dacha and car, but their rubles bought less and less. Rationing returned in 1990. All those years of working from early morning until late at night — for nothing. By 1992, the minimal rate of inflation was estimated at 2500–3000%. Most worrisome to Alisa was that her father was ill; without ready cash, how would he afford medical care? She sent what she could to help her parents and hired a lawyer to locate any loopholes in the law.

In desperation, Alisa traveled to St. Petersburg to see her parents. Watching their savings erode was like watching the sands of an hourglass slip away. She continued to plead with her parents to leave. Rosa's death at the age of 87 in 1994 freed her parents from staying on Bella's mother's account. Only when Naum and Bella realized that they could no longer support themselves in Russia and Boris Yeltsin could not fix the Russian economy, did they agree to leave.

One obstacle was removed, but Alisa still had to concoct a plan to circumvent the new Swedish immigration law. She secured guest visas for her parents in May 1994 and informed her parents that once they arrived in Sweden as tourists, they would stay. In other words, they would defect. It was a brazen plan, but it worked. Naum and Bella remained in Sweden the rest of their lives.

By 1994 Alisa was finally surrounded by family in Sweden. Once Alisa's parents arrived in Stockholm, family that had scattered in the 1920s began to convene. Her father's cousin Fred Plain and his wife Tilly came for a visit from South Africa, and now Alisa met Uncle Aaron's descendants. Alisa's dream of another world had begun with the princess-like dresses sent by Uncle Aaron. *Who would believe that these cousins could visit her now in her new world?*

Her parents' arrival did not completely fill the emptiness. At thirty-seven, Alisa "just didn't feel like a woman." She longed for a loving relationship. She had tried to understand Swedish men. They respected her at work and were polite at social gatherings but where was the romance? Alisa felt she had entered an Amazonian world where feminism had demolished all notions of chivalry. *A date didn't mean the guy would pay. Want to enter a movie theater with a date? Open the door yourself. Pay your way. As you put on your coat, a guy looks the other way. "It's not my coat," his gestures seem to say.*

Young Leadership meetings for Jewish adults in their twenties and thirties offered Alisa the possibility of meeting an eligible Jewish man. However, when Alisa attended these meetings across Europe, she was laser-focused on the organizations's primary goal of fundraising. Of course, she went to the "Let's Meet Meat Market" and did meet a series of suitable men—Italian, French, and Swiss. For a time she debated whether or not to move to London where there were more Jewish singles, but she had resolved that moving again was too difficult. She refused to settle for a man who met her criteria without making her heart leap. Alisa was waiting for the man who would take her breath away.

On a crisp October afternoon, Alisa methodically examined the designer dresses at her favorite boutique, Prêt à Porter in Biblioteksgatan. She meant to impress the pool of eligible Jewish bachelors from across Europe who would be among the 300 guests at the Annual Young Leadership Ball to be held this year in Stockholm. Finally she found her perfect dress—a magnificently cut, black Alaïa designer gown.

"Too expensive," she fretted when she first glanced at her image in the mirror.

One more look in the mirror and Alisa knew it was her dress. "Pragmatism—who cares? Somehow I'll manage the cost. I look like a princess-warrior in this dress, ready to face international Jewish society!" After years of monitoring every expense and saving from each paycheck so her parents could buy an apartment when they arrived, it was time to splurge.

A view of Stockholm's Grand Hôtel where Alisa and Rolf met.

As a member of the Steering Committee, Alisa was responsible for greeting the guests when they arrived at the imposing Grand Hôtel Stockholm. Built in 1874, it stretches its wings along the water opposite the Royal Palace. In the ballroom, aptly called the Vinterträdgården, Alisa felt she entered a charmed fairy tale world with sparkling chandeliers and elegant people whirling around the parquet floor to the music. For Alisa it was "almost a decadent atmosphere." Clad in her "fancy, sexy dress," she felt confident. She belonged in this venue. She began to "work the room." With her natural charm, she easily conversed with acquaintances and friends. Richard, a friend from the Steering Committee, approached Alisa with a good-looking man beside him.

"Alisa, meet Rolf Bornstein, my brother-in-law."

Rolf smiled broadly. Seeing this handsome man with the sparkling eyes and warm smile, Alisa drew in a deep breath. Suddenly the air felt charged. She quickly established that he was single. What Alisa did not know at the time was that Richard had mounted a full-scale campaign to drag his wife's brother Rolf to the ball. Rolf's first response to Richard had been, "boring and I know all the locals." Rolf had been the only European attending Young Leadership meetings in Washington and was reputed to be the most involved Young Leader on the international scene. Stockholm gatherings were ho-hum for Rolf. Still, it was easier for Rolf to capitulate than listen to Richard's persistent nagging. So, Rolf donned his evening dress and his cavalier attitude.

Once in the Vinterträdgården, Rolf avoided the "Jewish Swedish princesses." To amuse himself, he sought out the Russian women. The first one he approached was depressed, the second was on the hunt for a wealthy spouse. Then he spotted a mysterious, lovely woman. Her energy and warmth captivated him. The mirrored ballroom seemed designed to magnify her allure. Rolf remembers thinking she was "refreshing." He asked Richard who she was. When Richard replied she was an émigrée from Russia, Rolf's stereotype of Russian women crumbled. She was not a snobbish princess with a stone face and cold handshake—his image of a Russian woman.

Once introduced, Alisa and Rolf began to talk. Initially, Rolf's tone was didactic and formal, but as Alisa cocked her head to listen and began to rest her chin on her hand, his Swedish formality melted, and his playful and earnest character emerged. As they discussed their shared passion to raise awareness of the plight of Soviet Jews, magic bubbled below the surface. Right here in the Winter Garden a fairy tale was unfolding. The crowd of 300 became background scenery and the orchestral music their score. Time passed and Alisa watched as a humorous and charming man emerged. Heads bent ever closer to each other as they talked, Rolf revealed his profession to Alisa—he was a dentist. She had to smile. *It was Jewish luck! Bashert (fated)!*

"My father is a dentist, my mother a dental technician."

Rolf returned the smile and enthusiastically offered to Alisa, "I'll show your parents the medical school where I teach."

Why was Rolf so different from other Swedish men? True, he was born in Sweden, but his mother decided from his birth that he would be cosmopolitan. There would always be a Plan B. Born in Poland, his mother suffered through the Nazi death camp and, for her, an escape plan was as essential as a toothbrush.[1] His Swedish-born father was the head of the of the Jewish National Fund office in Sweden.[2] His parents wanted to ensure that he would grow up to be a proud, knowledgeable Jew and enrolled him in the Stockholm Jewish day school, Hillel Academy. At age seventeen, he went to Israel to work on a kibbutz and returned there summer after summer. Raised in the shadow of the Holocaust, his compassion for all refugees was boundless. He could differentiate a Chilean refugee from a Ukrainian by dental work. His innovative campaign urging the Swedish government to initiate preventive dental care for immigrants was only one example of his compassion.

In 1977 while Alisa and Vera were students at the Institute for Finance and Economics, Rolf traveled to the Soviet Union with a group briefed by the Stockholm Jewish leadership and the Israeli Embassy.[3] Their mission was to distribute books and salable goods like jeans to designated refuseniks in Leningrad and Moscow. Despite some glitches, he accomplished his mission in Leningrad quickly with a nighttime visit to a dreary suburban apartment.

In Moscow, Rolf attended Shabbat services in the masssive Choral Synagogue. Saddened by the scant congregation comprised exclusively of old men and a KGB minder, he stepped outside the synagogue where he encountered a group of refuseniks. Refuseniks felt safe in front of the Moscow synagogue because foreigners gathered there. In the late 1970s the Soviets were sensitive to Westerners publicizing human rights violations in the USSR and would not dare arrest refuseniks in front of Western eyes.

One man approached and introduced himself to Rolf by name and profession—Dr. Akselrod—a psychiatrist. When Rolf indicated he was a dental student, Dr. Akselrod brightened and launched into a wrenching account of desperately ill Jews who lived beyond Moscow and Leningrad and the eyes of foreigners. They were routinely denied life-saving medicines simply because they were Jews. Rolf sat down with Dr. Akselrod and laboriously wrote down the case histories Dr. Akselrod had compiled.

When Rolf returned to Stockholm, he wrote a scathing article and secured the agreement of a famous Swedish scientist to claim authorship, so the article would appear prominently in the Stockholm daily paper *Dagens Nyheter*. The result—all the necessary medicines reached Dr. Akselrod for distribution thanks to both the British and Swedish governments. Rolf couldn't stand idly by if there was any way to help.[4]

On the night of the ball, comfortably situated in one of Kalle's apartments, Alisa's parents anxiously awaited a report of the ball from their daughter. When Naum and Bella saw Alisa, she was transformed—softer, somehow. They didn't really understand what this Young Leaders organization was, but whatever it was, their daughter was absolutely joyous. Alisa was not yet divulging the whole story. She was waiting to see if Rolf would really call. She was no longer the naive eighteen-year-old falling in love at first sight, but even at thirty-seven, she wanted her life to mirror the fairy tales she had heard growing up—the princess finds a prince and lives happily ever after. But first, they needed a real date.

Rolf had to travel to Germany after the dance and promised he would get in touch when he returned. Thinking Rolf was "a little slow" with his follow-up, Alisa decided that she had nothing to lose if she pursued Rolf. So she employed the most up-to-date 1994 technology—she sent a fax. After a series of faxes and phone calls, Rolf did invite her parents to the Karolinska Institute and, despite the language barrier, Bella and Naum could discern this was more than sightseeing.

Finally, Alisa and Rolf had a real date after Alisa once again faxed Rolf at work. Her boldness compensated for his hesitation. Rolf wasn't just dating Alisa. He was also courting her parents, especially Naum. Their conversations, just like the dinner conversations of Alisa's childhood, were "teeth, teeth, teeth." This time Alisa truly reveled in dentist talk, watching how it drew together the two men she loved most. Naum regaled Rolf with the details of the mobile drill he had jerry rigged in their apartment. Rolf was impressed and explained that he, too, had worked on a mobile drill in his research and development company. Most of the time Naum and Rolf were mirror images as they sat in armchairs talking to each other and nodding in agreement about dental practices until the day Rolf excitedly explained one of his new developments.

"Naum, we've invented a process we're calling Carisolv®. You can eliminate cavities without drilling the dentin. It's a three-step process: apply, scoop, and repair. It's revolutionary. I've finished a paper and will be presenting on this process."

"What!? No drilling? In Russia we were drilling, we always drill. We drill and we love to drill!" Naum's voice reached a crescendo, and his arms waved in the air as he professed his attachment to drilling. Alisa could almost hear the whir of the machine as a backdrop to his ode to drilling. Despite the dispute over the merits of drilling, Naum was also in love with Rolf.

After dating for six months, Rolf asked Alisa to marry him. Without a second's hesitation, she responded, "Yes!" Later that evening Alisa thought she probably should have hesitated and perhaps taken a day to think about it, but "yes" was the right answer. Or was it? Doubts lapped at her definitive yes. Rolf was so kind, but was there enough passion? Was he the right man for the rest of her life? Time to talk to Vera. Vera cataloged all of Alisa's past relationships. In Vera's mind, Alisa always seemed to fall for the "bad boy," and it led to some disaster or another. Vera persuaded her it was time to put an end to "bad boys." Instead, she needed a good man and a man who shared her values and her dreams. Vera was certain Rolf was Alisa's prince.

Alisa and Rolf certainly didn't need parental consent, but Alisa could hardly hold back her tears of joy when Rolf suggested that he ask Naum for Alisa's hand in marriage. "Alisa, it's *kavod*. I want to give him the *kavod* of asking."

Alisa nodded her head, and they embraced. Rolf understood her and understood what her parents needed. *Kavod*, the Hebrew and Yiddish word for "honor," would return Naum to a world where he was in control.

One evening, Rolf invited Naum, Bella, and Alisa to dinner. The wine was poured, the atmosphere was warm and comfortable. Rolf turned to Naum and gallantly asked his permission to marry Alisa. Naum puffed with pride.

This is how a proposal should be made, he thought. Here is a very good man.

Naum gave his blessing. Naum was under no illusion that he still presided as the patriarch. He was well aware that his daughter was the actual head of the family now that they were in Sweden. Still, it was nice to be asked and it proved Rolf was a real mensch.[5] Naum beamed his happiness around the room. Bella watched the romantic scene unfolding. Her daughter's happiness amplified her own.

Alisa later met all of Rolf's family who warmly embraced her. She felt she belonged when she was with them. Alisa was Rolf's first serious Jewish girlfriend, and it made his mother, Halle, feel she was on the "march of the living." She would fight her cancer with all her strength to remain alive for the wedding. But in the warmth of Halle's embrace, there was a chill for Alisa as she glimpsed the numbers tattooed on Halle's arm. In the Soviet Union, one heard about the Holocaust only in whispers.

Alisa and Rolf's parents anticipated the wedding with great joy and hope for grandchildren. Although Alisa was already past thirty-five and had not yet had children, they were praying for a little luck.

Notes

1. Rolf's mother and sister escaped Ravensbruck and the Death March in April 1945 thanks to the Swedish Red Cross operation: White Buses. That operation is documented in the film, *Harbour of Hope (Hoppets Hamn)*, directed by Magnus Gertten (Sweden: Magnus Gortten and Lennart Ström for Auto Images, 2011). A video clip with English subtitles is available from http://vimeo.com/29373070. This Swedish documentary is featured in Jewish film festivals. It should not be confused with another documentary called *Harbor of Hope*, which is set in Lisbon, not Malmo, Sweden.

2. Founded in 1901, the Jewish National Fund (JNF) is an international fundraising organization whose mission until 1948 was to purchase land in Israel, reforest the land, and provide education. Once Israel became a state in 1948, JNF added immigrant absorption to its mission.

3. International Jewish organizations, concerned with the plight of Soviet Jews, compiled lists of dissident Jews in the Soviet Union who would be open to foreigners and welcome their visits and their gifts. Lists of names were smuggled out of the Soviet Union with trustworthy foreigners and gathered from known dissidents like Ida Nudel.

4. One might question the ethics of Rolf asking another to lend his name as the author of Rolf's article. Rolf knew that his plea would have the most impact on page three of *Dagens Nyheter*. This is analogous to having one's opinion on the op-ed page of the *New York Times*. For the Swedish scientist, the greater good was ensuring that medicine reached the Jews on Dr. Akselrod's list.

5. In Yiddish, mensch literally means a man. It is used to mean a good, decent, and ethical person, either male or female.

35

Vera: The Roof Caves In

1996

Ne boisya sobak, shto layet, a boisya toi, shto molchit, da khvostom vilyayet.
"Don't fear the dog who barks but the one who is quiet and wags its tail."

—Russian proverb

This time when the anxiety struck, Vera felt the usual signs of her shallow breathing, the shakiness, and the sweat, but there was something else—a pulling and a voice, perhaps. Like a little old man tugging her skirt insisting that she listen, refusing to give up, whining again and again, "Be careful. You need to pay attention." She named her inner advisor *Zhidonik Isya* (the little Jew Isya) and embraced him as an opinionated and fearful piece of her soul that guided her toward survival.

"Isya sometimes tortures me with his doubts, but he's also the source of my success. I picture him with stereotypic Jewish features. He insists 'you have to deal with this issue,' even when I would prefer to ignore it." Isya tends to push Vera to adopt an ethical solution that will bear fruit in the long run rather than to adopt a short-sighted solution that might be more pragmatic.

Isya is Vera's own creation. He is not a psychiatric disorder. He is not an echo of Papa Misha or her grandparents. For Vera, Isya seems to be a piece of the Jewish collective unconscious that she carries within her soul. Isya helps Vera recognize risk and leads her to make hard decisions. When I commented on her bravado during the confrontation with the thugs at the boutique on Nevsky Prospekt, she said "Yes, but Isya was terrified. He's not brave like me."

By 1996, there was no safety. During this critical year, Vera and Alexei reconsidered the wisdom of remaining in Russia. This was the year that Isya became extremely agitated. Everything Vera and Alexei treasured most deeply was in jeopardy. Someone was trying to intimidate them and was succeeding.

The First Disaster

Vera's voice is shaky as she recounts the experience. By this time Vera and Alexei had a house outside of St. Petersburg in Razliv and an apartment in the city for weekdays. On this particular work day, Mama Irina was in Razliv with Lev and the general manager's daughter. Irina didn't call Vera at the office unless something was wrong but that day, her voice was unrecognizable when Vera answered the phone. Irina choked on her words—the neighbor's house was in flames. Fortunately, no one was home. Vera and Alexei had Irina and the children driven to their city apartment immediately. Vera received another unusual call the next day from a neighbor telling her that it was Vera's house on fire this time. Vera didn't assume this was a personal threat. "This seemed to confirm our initial theory that somebody had a scheme to destroy the houses in that area to usurp the property. We thought it was bad luck."

Vera had not considered that her son and mother would be pawns in a criminal game. It was painful to go out and investigate the damage to their house. The house was completely burned, and the fire seemed to have originated in Lev's bedroom and the living room where Irina slept. A canister of petroleum was left on the scene. It was clearly the work of a mafia gang.

After the fire Vera and Alexei needed to replace their Razliv refuge twenty miles northwest of St. Petersburg and devised the most efficient way to replace their home—a Finnish prefab house constructed in six months complete with security cameras.

The Second Disaster

A few weeks later, a bomb was planted on the steps of the Olsen & Company office. Fortunately, a neighbor noticed the fuse before it ignited and called the fire department.

"A brave fireman destroyed it with his boot and, thank God, it didn't explode or I would be in jail. The victim of a bombing was responsible for any collateral damage. We were lucky."

The Third Disaster

Just a couple of weeks later, Alexei was prodding a pokey, nine-year-old Lev to get ready for school. They were already running late. Just as they were about to leave, they heard the sound of an explosion down the street. A moment later Mama Irina phoned and breathlessly described how chunks of their car were flying past her third-floor window. Alexei and Lev rushed down the block to Mama Irina's courtyard, where their car had been parked for security reasons. In its spot, only a heap of scrap remained. Across from Mama Irina's building, windows were shattered, which Vera and Alexei had to replace. Later they learned that a bomb had been planted under the wheel of their car.

These were not coincidences, but acts of terror. Vera, Alexei, Mama Irina, and Lev were being targeted. But why? Vera and Alexei racked their brains to think of anyone with a motive to hurt them. They came up with no one. Vera decided to consult an expert.

"I approached Uncle Meyer to please ask around and find out who was behind all of this. Meyer reported that none of the "serious people" (major mafia guys) knew anything about us. 'Look inside your group,' he said.

Our house number was 25, and the neighbor's house number was 25A. The intention had been to burn our house down that first day with my family in it. We didn't know what would be next. We felt so insecure. We didn't even know who our enemy was. We didn't owe money. We weren't taking anyone's business. We had no idea. Our official *krisha*, our one former KGB agent, told us that the next act might be kidnapping, and the safest strategy would be to remove ourselves and Lev."

Vera and Alexei couldn't imagine abandoning work at this critical time and decided to send Mama Irina and Lev to Baltiysk Resort thirty miles away. They created a top secret plan and didn't tell anybody where they were going, except for one man, the mechanic who had repaired all their cars. This mechanic who drove Mama Irina and Lev to their secret hideout turned out to be a member of the gang targeting the family.

Mama Irina was not passive. She had her own solution to the terror. Becoming a "true believer"[1] might protect the family against future danger.[2] Lev remembers Mama Irina interrupting his play at the resort and bringing him to a priest.

"The priest put some water on my head and said some words in a strange language. He also gave me a necklace like Mama Irina's with a cross."

He and Mama Irina were wearing those crosses when Vera and Alexei came to visit them at the Baltiysk. Vera rarely got angry at her mother, but when she spotted the cross around Lev's neck, she felt betrayed. The Russian Orthodox religion had fomented anti-Semitism in Vera's mind, and it was like joining the enemy. She understood that Irina was spiritual and not particular about denomination, but she was furious that Lev was converted without even a word to her. She grabbed the cross from him and scolded Mama Irina. Mama Irina could choose her own religion, but leave Lev out of this craziness. The whole world was turning upside down, and this was yet another example.

Notes

1. "True believers" are those who adhere to the tenets of the Russian Orthodox Church.

2. There are two different accounts of this story. Lev believes his grandmother was influenced by his Uncle Grisha's wife who thought that conversion would protect the family. Vera believes that it was Irina's way of appeasing Alexei's mother, who was Russian Orthodox.

36

Vera: The Man in the Red Ferrari

1996

I volki syty, i ovtsy tsely.
"The wolves are sated and the sheep are intact."
—Russian proverb

The aftermath from the trifecta of threats played out like a "black comedy." Vera's intuitive Isya suspected that whoever showed up offering security would be the very people responsible for the terror. It was a mystery, and Isya was growing more nervous each day.

In summer 1996, out of the shadows emerged Tolya—tall, handsome, and fashionably dressed—playing the knight in shining armor. Instead of riding a horse, this Jewish knight drove a red Ferrari. With just a slight hint of regret in his voice, he reminded Vera and Alexei of their meeting the previous year when he wanted to "invest" with them. In return for being a partner, he offered security. What a shame that they had declined his invitation. But, good news. He was giving them another chance to use his services. Isya was watchful. Then

Vera could feel him pointing the finger at Tolya and jumping up and down.

Tolya instructed Vera and Alexei to remain visible and go about their normal activities. A few weeks later Tolya, their new security representative, informed Vera and Alexei that the call for a meeting had come. He would attend on Vera and Alexei's behalf. Vera now understood the game. The party that called the meeting was the one responsible for the violence.

Tolya reported, "They were serious people, but I told them that you're under my protection. So, now we have to do business together in order for me to protect you." Vera knew the big prize for Tolya and his bosses would be partnership in the customs business. Vera suspected Tolya was setting them up. Isya was certain of it. Vera expected that the moment when she and Alexei were most vulnerable, Tolya would strike, "suggesting" a transfer of shares in the warehouse to his name.

Vera said, "In the end, I outsmarted the gang, but it took five to six years to finish this business."

What she did not realize at the time was that Tolya, Dima (the employee fired for lying about his trip to Moscow), and the mechanic that they had trusted to drive Irina and Lev to the Baltiysk Resort were in cahoots. The three collaborated in a lucrative business—fencing stolen cars. Dima used his contacts with Customs to import the stolen cars from Europe and then changed the VIN numbers. No doubt, employment at Olsen & Company provided Dima with a good cover. Dima might have wanted revenge for being fired or for Alexei's final jab reminding him of the money owed for his child's surgery. Vera imagined Dima saying to his gang: *Here are the sheep, Alexei and Vera; here is the grass where they graze; and here is an opportunity to shear their wool.*

Now that Tolya and his red Ferrari were part of their lives, Vera accepted the investment money cautiously. Her objective was never to lose the money but also not to make a substantial profit with him.

First Vera had to tend to her swollen, aching jaw. As a result of the insertion of implants years ago, inspired by a critique of her Russian smile, her gums had become infected. After intense research, Alexei found an Israeli dentist practicing in St. Petersburg, who completed a *remont* (reconstruction) of

Vera's mouth. Sitting in the dental chair, it occurred to Vera that she could solve two problems at once: her bad teeth and the need to invest with Tolya. *Perhaps this dentist might be interested in starting a new dental clinic.* Vera had no trouble enticing the dentist. The next step—Vera would lead a dental mission to Israel with the dentist, Tolya, and Alexei to purchase modern dental equipment. For Alisa, Israel was a climactic journey. For Alexei, Vera, and their new associate Tolya, it harkened back to travel to a 1980s Soviet Black Sea resort. Their nights were spent drinking vodka, overeating, and dancing at Russian restaurants with people they didn't like. Their days were spent trying to reverse the damage from Aunt Lena's sabotage. She discouraged the dentist they had interviewed from joining Vera. Vera, Alexei and Tolya returned home without their Israeli dentist.

Nevertheless, the dental clinic was established and survived several dentists. It provided high-quality dental care but little profit. Tolya truly tried to protect Vera, but his criminal bosses recognized that investing in the dental clinic would bring them no closer to the customs business.

Relationships are woven together in strange ways. Tolya, once considered their enemy, was trying to separate himself from his gang. Slowly, he was winning Vera and Alexei's trust and becoming family. When Vera and Alexei were trying to rebuild their home after the fire, pay Vera's private dental bill, invest in the dental clinic, and deal with a tax issue, they ran out of cash from their private accounts. Although business was good, it was not generating enough profit to cover all these unforeseen expenses. It was Tolya who came to the rescue by buying Baba Lyuba's old apartment and Vera and Alexei's renovated apartment. Tolya allowed them to remain in their apartment until the Razliv house was rebuilt. Recently, I asked Vera why she didn't just sell her Lexus if she was short of money. She replied, "And how would we get around?"

Stephen Olsen understood the important role of "protection" that Tolya played and, with Vera's encouragement, invited him to the States in 1998. A trip to the United States would be a thrill for Tolya and further cement the relationship with Vera and Alexei. Unfortunately, his visa application was rejected when he was discovered to be on a list of individuals associated with organized crime. This proved what Vera and Alexei had already suspected.

"I wasn't surprised," Vera said. "Tolya was angry and very upset. We continued to make him feel like a part of the company although we kept him away from the warehouse business." Eventually, Tolya's bosses started to scrutinize their investments with Vera and Alexei more closely, and their patience wore thin. "Tolya's bosses called for a meeting with us at our office. They were clearly irritated and got to the point 'Where is the protection money? Why are we not part of the customs business?'"

"You never invested. Why should I share profits with you?" Vera retorted. Isya shuddered.

Tolya's superiors were fed up. Vera and Alexei were not cooperating. The gang leaders began spreading information that Vera and Alexei were "by themselves" and nobody would "say a word on their behalf." In other words, they were announcing open season for extortion on Vera and Alexei. Now they were prey to "less civilized" thugs. It was not long before the next predator emerged.

The next bandit's tactic of attempting to steal Vera and Alexei's outrageously expensive Lexus seemed mild in comparison to the bombings. Following the first attempt to steal their car, Vera and Alexei were casually approached by a man stalking the car. After normal pleasantries, he introduced himself and handed them his card. He stroked their car with admiration, shook his head, and said that a lot of cars were being stolen and they should feel comfortable contacting him in case of a problem. He knew the "right people." Vera told Alexei that she was 100% sure that he was the thief who wanted to "find and return" our car. Then he would "befriend" them, which would obligate them to share profits with this gang.

Vera and Alexei refused to to be sitting ducks any longer. By 2000, "we were strong enough to play our own game. So, my idea was to stage a 'performance.' Through contacts, we hired two men from the Special Anti-Organized Crime Department, who personally knew most of the gang leaders and sometimes even did business with them, to explain to our new thug and his superiors that we were not 'by ourselves,' but with *militsia* and the FSB (the new KGB)." Therefore, it could be assumed that Vera and Alexei had protection from the highest places. Vera and Alexei paid $5,000 for this performance that lasted less than an hour. It was successful in that this gang never approached them again. Meanwhile, inside the other gang, Tolya dealt with the wrath of his superiors. Tolya had provided information that Vera and Alexei were unprotected. When word spread that Vera and Alexei were under high-level protection, Tolya's group lost face. As a result, Tolya was kicked out. He would later be grateful for this twist of fate.

Tolya, who once was part of the plot to ruin Vera and Alexei, grew closer to the family. Tolya loved Mama Irina. He lived nearby, and he stayed in touch with the family over the years. Until recently, they never spoke about his role in the arson at Vera's home, the bomb outside the office, and the intended car-bombing death of Alexei and Lev. According to Lev's account, he may have been their "white angel." He may have given the wrong address for the first arson and made sure the house was vacant. He may not have let his superiors know that the family was at the Baltiysk Resort even though he had access to the information.

Long after all this, in spring 2008, when Vera's cash flow was far better, after not hearing from Tolya for a while, he called, saying, "I need your help. I need to borrow money. Custom duties are more than I expected, and I am building a house and need $50,000."

Vera replied, "For you, anytime."

Tolya said he would repay the money in six months, but this promise came prior to another financial collapse. Tolya brought Vera and Alexei $10,000 and said "I'll pay you the rest in a couple of months." Vera responded, "Relax, whenever you can," which, to a former gangster, was a phrase in a foreign language.

"During that visit, he spoke more openly about the past intrigue. He confirmed that all my suspicions were right. He was so thankful that he was kicked out of the gang. He was so happy to be a shareholder of a legitimate business. The gang was smashed after 2003, and those who weren't killed went to prison. He was saved from their fate because he failed to deliver the prey, us, to the predator."

Just recently, Tolya returned the favor. When Lev needed to renew his passport quickly, Tolya helped expedite it. Lev was amazed how they bypassed all the lines. When they stood face-to-face with a typical humorless bureaucrat, one smile from Tolya, and she warmed up, flirted with him, and couldn't do enough to help Lev.

The man who once drove a red Ferrari was now riding a white steed.

37

Alisa: Not Everything Goes According to Plan

1995–1996

Det blir aldrig som man tänkt sig.
"Things never turn out the way you imagine."
—Swedish proverb

Through their phone conversations, Alisa couldn't keep up with all the drama in Vera's life, but she understood that the so-called New Russia wasn't any more secure than the old Russia. She urged Vera to leave for a safer haven. Vera wasn't interested, but at least Alisa knew that no matter how chaotic Vera's life, she would not miss Alisa's wedding day in September 1995.

Fifteen years later when we (Leslie and Meryll) visited Alisa in Stockholm, she sat at their dining room table with Rolf and reflected on their wedding. Her cheeks flushed and her voice softened, she tilted her head toward Rolf. Rolf leaned toward Alisa, drawing her close as he wrapped his arm around her shoulders.

Alisa and Rolf reminisce with Leslie and Meryll at the dining room table in their Stockholm apartment.

Privately, Alisa had told us that before she could plan her wedding, she had a task to complete alone—expunging her history of past boyfriends. Alisa collected all their photographs, cut them up, and let the shredded images of the "bad boys" float into the trash bin and out of her memory.

The wedding was small, and the preparations hastily completed in hopes that Rolf's mother would be well enough to attend. This time the ḥuppah would be public in the elegant Stora Synagoga, not hidden in a small Leningrad apartment. The reception would be at the Diplomat Hotel's restaurant, close to the synagogue. Alisa returned to her favorite boutique Prêt à Porter on Biblioteksgatan and selected the "perfect, most beautiful bronze, tiered dress." As the seamstress circled Alisa to tailor the dress to her slim figure, she recalled her boastfulness in kindergarten, showing off her Western dress from Uncle Aaron. Now, she glanced in the mirror at the light bronze silk dress, its bodice bejeweled with beads and pearls. A smile crossed her face. A princess at last.

Two weeks before the wedding, Alisa returned to the seamstress for her final fitting. She was so physically tired from juggling wedding plans, her work, her parents, her brother, and Rolf. She lifted her arms to try on the dress as the seamstress walked behind her to zip it up. But, it wouldn't fit. It was too tight. Alisa had put on weight. She cried and fumed, her beautiful dream of a dress—gone. Businesslike, the seamstress assured Alisa she could alter it.

"This happens to brides. No need for sadness."

"Not to me," responded Alisa. "I'm a planner. I did not plan to be fat."

Hurrying out of the boutique, Alisa's brain began to whirl. *I'm fat. I'm tired.* Pause. *I could be pregnant.* She was. This was not in the plans—yet. Alisa's moods were volatile. On good days she was grateful for the miracle of being pregnant at thirty-eight. She warmed at the thought of her mother-in-law and parents' joy in becoming grandparents. Other days she brooded about her beautiful dress.

The wedding day arrived tinged with sadness that Rolf's mother Halle was too ill to attend and accompany him down the aisle. Alisa's thoughts about her mother-in-law's absence were interrupted by the late arrival of one of Halle's effusive friends. She rushed up to Alisa, chattering that she had always wanted Alisa to marry her son. Like a noisy squirrel, she squawked on and on, oblivious to Alisa's impending procession down the aisle. Finally, when Alisa tried to gracefully exit the conversation, the woman's heel caught on Alisa's delicate dress, and she heard a r-r-r-r-rip. Alisa's heart momentarily sank, but what could she do? Hopefully no one would notice.

Naum and Bella took her arms and positioned themselves behind Rolf and his sister. The organ music began, Rolf reached for the door, but it wouldn't open. He pulled harder, but no luck—it was most definitely locked. The organist's fingers danced along the keyboard as she peered down into the synagogue. Faces were turned to the door, where was the groom? The organist detected the puzzlement on Cantor Gerber's face as he awaited the couple under the ḥuppah.

Cantor Gerber relieved the tension by asking, "Does anybody else want to get married while we're waiting?"

Suddenly the organ music stopped and heads turned upwards. The organist was also in charge of unlocking the doors to the sanctuary and she had forgotten! The bride and groom were stranded on the other side. She hurriedly unlocked the double wooden doors and scrambled back upstairs to the organ so the ceremony could finally begin.

Despite the tear in her dress and the delayed procession, Alisa beamed as she walked the length of the red carpet of the Stora Synagoga on the arms of her parents. The happiness of clasping her parents' arms en route to Rolf in this magnificent synagogue lifted her heart to the heavens. Underneath the velvet ḥuppah stood Rolf and Cantor Gerber. For Cantor Gerber a marriage between a Russian Jew and a fellow Jew was "fantastic." As he watched them approach, he thought, *They tried to kill us but we won—another Russian Jew is reconnecting and building a Jewish family.* The cantor joyfully chanted the *sheva berakhot*, the seven blessings, of the wedding ceremony. At the conclusion, he placed the glass on the carpet, and Rolf's shoe smashed the glass to choruses of *mazal tov*.[1]

Alisa savored the moment as she gazed at the faces of their family and their closest friends including Vera. Despite Vera's temporary paralysis, she was there to witness and share Alisa's happiness. Alisa could feel her parents' absolute joy. It was as if they had entered the Paradise of Hope Fulfilled. Their rebellious and eccentric daughter was married to a mensch, and a child was on the way. The entire family was together, thanks to Alisa's indomitable will.

The pre-ceremony glitches forgotten, Alisa and Rolf savor the moment under the ḥuppah. Alisa's pregnancy is invisible to the onlookers. Only her glow hints of their future daughter.

Now that the wedding festivities were over and the videocassette shared with Rolf's mother, Alisa allowed herself time to enjoy her pregnancy. She was stunned when she stopped to think about her good luck. Although she was thirty-eight, she voiced no worries about her pregnancy. She had faith that both she and her baby would be healthy, and she continued working at Ericsson up to her labor and delivery.

Halle grew weaker as Alisa's pregnancy progressed. There was no longer any way to slow her cancer, so Rolf and Alisa were quick to bring an ultrasound photo to show Halle. She smiled her biggest smile looking at the swirls in black and white that would grow to be her granddaughter. Six weeks before her granddaughter's birth, Halle died. Rolf and Alisa agreed that the baby would bear Halle's Hebrew name, Hadassah.

Throughout the winter, Rolf and Alisa curled up together on the couch at night discussing the choices for the little girl's middle name and Swedish name. The middle name Gita, was an easy choice to honor the memory of both of their grandmothers who coincidentally bore the same name. Alisa pondered the best choice for her daughter's first name in Swedish. She turned to numerology.[2] The right name would confer the most desirable qualities that Alisa could bequeath to her daughter. The name required a double "l" because that conveyed strength. Strength was Alisa's number one priority. As Alisa continued to add qualities—independent, ambitious, artistic, systematic, organized, honest, loyal, successful, she uncovered the name. She would be Daniella Gita Bornstein. Rolf laughed heartily at the nonsense of numerology, but why dispel Alisa's belief in the power of the name to mold the child?

Swedish health care was a marvel for a Russian emigrant. Rolf joined Alisa in the birthing room. Between contractions, Alisa saw Rolf grow pale. Holding her hand, he reminded her "I will manage. I'm a dentist, almost a doctor." Daniella Gita was born healthy and strong, and the new family returned to their hospital room. Soon Bella and Naum arrived. Naum's eyes opened wide with wonder. He, too, was a dentist, almost a doctor, but he had never before seen a newborn infant. When Gera and Alla were born, he was stationed in Pilau, and Bella traveled to Leningrad without him for their births.

Alisa and Rolf had rented a small apartment for Bella and Naum, not far from their own. Alisa and Rolf's Östermalm penthouse apartment in a 1939 Bauhaus building boasted a fireplace, ample rooms, and a view of the green space below and the harbor. The terrace wrapped around the apartment, providing their own dacha at home in the summer. At first Alisa had felt embarrassed by the reputation of Östermalm as the home of the rich and famous and cultural elite of Sweden, but she grew to love its elegance. After Rolf affixed the mezuzah to their door and intoned the blessing, Alisa embraced him and then her parents. She was at home. Bella and Naum would now also feel at home and live only a few blocks away. Daniella's arrival in the apartment banished any doubt for Alisa that Östermalm was home.

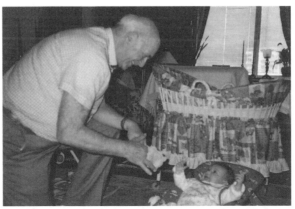

Naum readies the baby equipment for Daniella. He and Babulla Bella will care for her when Alisa returns to work.

Each time Naum told Alisa, "I've finally found paradise!" she warmed not just with joy but also with anger.

"I could have brought them earlier. Why didn't I push harder?" In a flash, she banished the anger and smiled in acknowledgement of her father's happiness. Regrets were a waste of time.

A much gentler Naum than Alisa remembered drew her close and softly said, "Alla, it seems you are the head of the family now. It's a new country. I can't do what I did before. I am very happy to give you the job. Take the Prometheus clock for your apartment. It will remind you of your family and be the symbol that you're in charge."

The strong figure of Prometheus, creator of fire, propped up the gold clock face. The chimes on the quarter hour were the sights and sounds of her Leningrad home. Long ago she watched her father lovingly repaint the naked Prometheus figure and the clock face. Where others might have seen decay and tossed the nineteenth-century piece on the scrapheap, Naum saw the potential for beauty. Alisa accepted the clock and accepted her new, official role in the family. Naum had lit the fire in Alisa that fueled her determination to find freedom and create a meaningful life. Pride mingled with sadness as Alisa acknowledged Naum's faith in her but also his deteriorating physical state. She placed the clock on the table in the living room but, in deference to Rolf, she silenced the chimes so he could sleep.

Alisa remained at home with baby Daniella; however, a few months after the birth, Alisa began to receive phone calls from the higher-ups at Ericsson. "Alisa, we need you. When will you return? No pressure, of course, you are entitled to *mammaledighet*."[3]

Alisa reveled in her new baby girl, but she also was eager to return to work. She knew that if she availed herself of the full two-year leave, she might be slotted into a less desirable position upon her return. Rolf and Alisa discussed how she could smoothly transition back to work while having Bella and Naum babysit Daniella, just as Rosa had done for little Alla. When Daniella was eight months old, Naum and Bella had a new job. Until her second birthday when she could enter Swedish daycare, Daniella would remain at home showered with love and kisses and Russian endearments.

Alisa opens her arms wide to embrace three-year-old Daniella on Scheveningen Beach.

Notes

1. A Jewish wedding ceremony includes seven blessings ending with the smashing of a glass. Before the public ceremony, the bride and groom along with two witnesses sign a *ketubbah*, a legal document that testifies to the marriage of the couple. Before the signing, an officiant (usually a rabbi) must certify that the bride and groom are Jewish and that if either had been married before, he or she could provide a *get*.

The bride and groom are married under a canopy or ḥuppah symbolizing the new Jewish home they will build. It is customary for both mother and father to walk down the aisle with their child and then stand on the side of the ḥuppah during the ceremony. Although the guests typically shout *mazal tov* ("Congratulations") at the sound of the groom's shoe smashing the glass, the intention is to interject a somber note even to the most joyous of all celebrations to commemorate the destruction of the Temple in 70 CE.

2. Numerology has a Jewish parallel—*gematria*. Each Hebrew letter is equivalent to a letter and the letters are often added up. For example, Daniella equals ninety. Alisa had a Swedish book on numerology that she consulted to discover the "right" name.

3. *Mammaledighet*, Swedish maternity leave, allows mothers to remain home one year after birth with full salary, another six months on half salary, and another six months with no salary. Workplaces must guarantee a position to a new mother upon her return.

38

Vera: The Crows Are Circling

1996

Nobody ever went broke paying taxes.
—Grandma Rae Levine

Perhaps in the United States, people did not go broke paying taxes, but in Russia they did—broke, bankrupt, dead, or imprisoned. Vera would soon discover that observing all the precautions wasn't enough. After all, Russian laws served the whim of bureaucrats, not the needs of citizens. Thus, successful business people could find themselves broke, if not in jail, once the tax police begin circling their prey.

In 1996, Vera was concerned about internal matters. "I was coping with bombs and fires." Vera thought perhaps she hadn't paid enough attention to the business and how to cut costs. She needed to consolidate inventory so that she wouldn't have to rent as much space. Yet, day after day, her general manager sabotaged her orders. Finally, she and Alexei began opening every box themselves to catalog the contents before moving the crates. What they discovered was that half of their inventory was missing. Apparently, the general manager had been filling railroad cars with the cigarettes, sugar, and olive oil owned by their clients. Vera and Alexei fired him for stealing, but it's arguable that the ex-employee got the better end of the deal, having already reaped a considerable profit. He also filed a complaint to keep the apartment that the company had provided him. This was the moment when Vera called in her brother, Grisha, to take over as the general manager.

The problems within the company had been solved for now. But the threats from outside precluded any complacency. In summer 1996, on their way to work, Vera and Alexei received a call from their secretary Natalya. In a hushed and shaky voice, she warned them that the *voroni* (tax police) had arrived at the company. [1] A minute later, Vera heard a male voice ordering Natalya to hang up the phone. Masked men with machine guns had muscled their way into the office. As the men in black told everyone to turn their face to the wall and not touch anything, they grabbed every document in sight and emptied the file cabinets, pitching documents randomly into paper bags. The tax police confiscated sixteen bags of documents and all the computers.

When Vera arrived on the scene with Alexei, she felt "like I was in the middle of an American action movie. They were acting like an American SWAT team. They had badges like Americans and were flashing them. Alexei's first reaction was to be calm, charming, and hospitable, offering tea and coffee." Vera added, "I knew this was all about money. They just wanted to humiliate and threaten us to make us soft and cooperative. But, I wasn't terrified."

By this time, I knew to ask about Isya. Vera softened and looked much younger as she answered, "Isya was so scared. He couldn't say a word."

Who was responsible for the raid? Vera knew it was usually the result of a grudge. Was it connected to the house fire and the other bombings, or could it be freelance racketeering? It usually sufficed to offer a bribe, but Vera refused. Oddly, the tax police requested that Vera and Alexei send someone over to organize the confiscated documents. Vera's most trusted associate Svetlana sorted the papers as Vera had advised, and she was able to leave the tax office with the potentially incriminating documents stowed in her large purse. At stake were the profits received from the humanitarian relief effort and an additional 20% surtax on unpaid profits, adding up to six million dollars. Vera now had the leverage of knowing which documents were in the hands of the tax police.

"I was going to fight it," Vera stated fiercely. "The investigator was threatening me with a criminal case, claiming that we had avoided paying taxes by hiding revenues overseas, which, by the way, was what every business in Russia was doing. Legally, we were absolutely clean. Because our warehouse business was a joint venture between the United States and Russia, we were covered by reciprocity and, therefore, not subject to double taxation. We had proof that taxes had been paid in the United States."

Unfortunately, in Russia, facts are not enough to win a lawsuit. The investigator was pressuring Vera to plead guilty and then apply for a pardon on the basis of having a child under sixteen. "I felt like this was a trick. Funny enough, I turned to the yellow pages for legal advice. I called a free telephone number and explained the situation to a woman, who listened closely. Then, with classic Jewish intonation, she said 'So, are you guilty?'"

"No."

"Then my little girl, why should you admit it?"

"Okay, but what are the risks if I do?"

"If you admit guilt, they will drop the criminal charges, but the State can still pursue a civil case and claim damages of unpaid taxes."

She didn't have to remind Vera that there was no such thing as a fair trial in Russia. Vera is still amazed how helpful this free legal advice was. It inspired her to prepare her role for the next day when she was due to report to the tax investigator and a representative from the prosecutor's office.

Having not yet received the correct diagnosis or a treatment for the herpes virus that was causing her paralysis, Vera exaggerated her limp from her most recent bout by dragging her right leg behind her as she entered the office.

The tax investigator said, "Are you going to plead guilty?"

Vera furrowed her brow and responded gravely, "I'm so sorry. I can't make a deal with you. My American employer guaranteed me that if you put me in prison, he would provide my family with a great deal of money for the rest of my life as compensation for my suffering. You will also give him the opportunity to announce to the international press the games modern Russia plays with foreign investors."

The woman from the prosecutor's office sneered at Vera and said "I can't stand it. She's nuts!" and walked out.

The investigator understood Vera's game. "Vera Mikhailovna, don't be stupid. You know that we can't open the criminal case because there are not enough grounds."

Vera whined, "Can you please try to arrange a prison sentence?"

He said "Fuck you," turned to exit, and slammed the door behind him.

It worked. Ten days later the computers and documents were returned to her office. Five years and $35,000 later, the case was finally put to rest. As Vera intended, not a penny of that was paid to the Russian government although $25,000 was paid as a bribe to the tax police. Her lawyers swallowed up the rest as they followed up in Arbitration Court to fight the original claim of $500,000. Throughout her ordeals, Vera was calling RD every week. RD's advice was consistent—"Get the hell out of Russia." Vera insisted that she wasn't ready yet. She did not think she could be financially successful elsewhere. Isya, her inner Jew, agreed wholeheartedly with RD and was urging her at least to get Lev out. Vera asked RD to sponsor Lev for summer camp the following year, and RD was delighted to do so. Lev flew to the United States for the first of three summers in Minnesota. This prepared him to be fluent enough in English and American culture to attend three years of boarding school in Minnesota. "You are our vanguard," Vera told him. "We will follow."

Where was Stephen Olsen during the tax fiasco? "He handled it the exact same way as the fire and the bombings. He said, 'So you're dealing with it, right? You're great. You're fantastic; and, by the way, do we still have money in Sweden?'"

Vera found comfort cuddling with her German Shepherd puppy, Pavla I.

Note

1. *Voroni* is a slang term for the tax police. The literal meaning is "crows." In Stalinist times, *voroni* referred to the black KGB cars that arrived by night to arrest Russians in their homes.

39

Vera: Independence Day

1998

Druzhba druzhboi, a sluzhba sluzboi
"Friendship is one thing, business another."
—Russian proverb

Vera hung up the phone in disgust. Even though Alexei did not understand English, he could guess what Stephen Olsen was proposing based on the widening of Vera's eyes, the raising of her eyebrows, and the deliberation of her speech as she enunciated each word, baring her teeth. Alexei used an arsenal of expletives as they debriefed. Stephen wanted to invest in the Russian stock market, and what would his collateral be? Their business. *Insane!* It was as if Stephen decided to gamble their business at a poker table in Las Vegas, but the Vegas odds would have been far better. She had been questioning Stephen's judgment lately. She could not have asked for a more supportive partner in the early years. He valued her input and respected her. That respect had earned her distinction in the St. Petersburg business community.

That synergistic relationship with Stephen now seemed

like ancient history. For two miserable years Vera and Alexei were under siege—bombings, fires, tax police. Now the relationship with Stephen felt parasitic. Stephen did not appreciate the daily risk they faced nor the sweat that went into maintaining the business. Besides, she sensed Stephen's life was out of control and he was desperate. She and Alexei could not afford the $25,0000-dollar monthly allowance that Stephen demanded as part of the deal that sustained his luxurious lifestyle, including a fancy downtown office in a Minneapolis skyscraper, golf club membership, travel, and who knew what else. Vera and Alexei had reached a point where Stephen's participation could spell bankruptcy. She and Alexei would not be able to recover from that.

How stupid did you have to be to invest in the Russian stock market at the time? Enormously stupid and enormously greedy, according to Vera. Vera and Alexei were never fans of making money by speculation. Investors were promised returns of up to 150%, and Stephen was falling for this nonsense. It did not take a genius to understand that Russia's finances were in worse shape than Stephen's. Stephen would never understand the fragility of the Russian economy. A perfect storm of catastrophe was brewing. Money could not be printed fast enough to pay for the five-billion-dollar war in Chechnya. Cash reserves were being liquidated. Foreign loans would rarely reach their destination. Changes in the price of oil could land the whole country into further debt.

Isya's voice whined constantly urging her to cut the cord with Stephen and protect her businesses. By the time Vera's flight touched down in Amsterdam en route to Minneapolis in April 1998, Yeltsin had dismissed his entire cabinet. It was time for her to dismiss Stephen. Business was personal, and Stephen had been there from the beginning. She might say she built everything on her own, but she knew that he provided the credibility, funding, and connections to get her started. He had always believed in her.

She paced around Lars and RD's house as she prepared herself to confront Stephen after her arrival in April. She would have to play a role, and this one required nerves of steel because it involved ending a partnership that was also a friendship. Indignation fortified her.

She met with Stephen, and they hugged as usual. Stephen was congenial and happy to see her. Vera could not disguise her mood of irritation and disappointment. In a serious tone, she stated that she could no longer support his lifestyle or his risk-taking. She offered a six-month timeline and then requested that he sign over all the shares in the business that she and Alexei had built. She wanted to incorporate separately from Olsen & Company in the Cayman Islands, so her investments would be safe.

Stephen seemed deflated. His usual energy and charm were absent. He was passive and agreed to all her terms. Vera suspected this wasn't the only area of his life where he was feeling defeated. Despite a strong front, Vera felt sorry for Stephen. She entered Lars and RD's house exhausted and in tears. This day had required her to reach deeply inside herself for toughness. She knew she was right, but from Mama Irina she had learned that friendships were supposed to last forever.

RD empathized with Vera's conflict and was prepared for her. He drew her a a bubble bath, gave her a glass of wine, sat down on the edge of the bathtub, and talked quietly. He asked Vera in what way Stephen had helped her plan her future. "Did he set up a bank account in your name in the United States? Did he help you get a green card? Did he ever help you plan out a secure future?"

Vera softly answered "no" to each of these questions. As Vera reflected, she realized it was RD, not Stephen, who had been her major support. When Vera couldn't meet her payroll, it was RD who provided the loan from his personal funds. It was RD's advice and support she sought on a weekly basis, not Stephen's. It was RD whom she trusted completely and for good reason; he was always there to lend his heart and hand. Everything they did was by verbal agreement with no written contract, and both profited emotionally and financially from their relationship.

The following day was Vera's independence day. RD escorted her to his bank and helped her to establish a bank account and apply for an American Express card. Despite years of being a successful businesswoman, this was the first time she had credit in dollars in her own name. She was ecstatic and hugged and kissed RD throughout the day. From here on,

Vera could plan her own future. It was a great relief to finalize her "divorce" from Olsen & Company. The next step was to travel to the Cayman Islands for the incorporation under sole ownership of Alexei and herself. As Vera traveled there, she imagined a new life someday—of openness, ocean views, and freedom.

Her timing could not have been better. Once again, Isya was right. All investments in rubles flowed down the drain. On August 13, 1998, the Russian markets collapsed. Four days later, the Russian government devalued the ruble. Russia defaulted on domestic debt and stopped payment to foreign creditors as well. Had she followed Stephen's lead, her business would have been liquidated. In fact, yielding to Isya's advice had ensured their safety.

"There was a financial crisis, and, once again, we were among the few who benefited because our contracts were in dollars." This was a time when they could expand their operations and eventually become one of the largest independent customs and warehouse business in Russia. They had their own railroad, thirty transporters (car carriers), and continued to own the construction firm as well.

Vera and Alexei found the perfect site for their fresh start. Now, life was going to be on her terms, she hoped. Once again, she would create office space that would be like none other in Russia—clean, comfortable, and civilized. This is how all Russia should be. What was particularly special was that from Vera's window, she could view her beloved Neva River flowing in the distance and a cityscape of the Winter Palace and the Admiralty. What made her smile especially was that in the foreground, just across the street and close to her childhood home, she could see the corner where she had met Lars and Leslie.

From Vera's office, she could see the Winter Palace in the background and in the foreground – the corner where she met Lars and Leslie, now occupied by a new building. The few cars that would have dotted the street at that time would have been black Soviet-made sedans. (2011)

40
Alisa: Swimming through *Lagom*[1]
1997–2011

Den som vill ha något gott får söka där det finns.
"Whoever wants to have something good, has to seek it out."

—Swedish proverb

Alisa pushed open the door at Ericsson with brio as she returned triumphantly from maternity leave. She felt trim and fit and enthusiastically wanted to show Ericsson colleagues just how well she could lead them to new heights. Ideas had been percolating while she enjoyed her leave. Time to press the accelerator and rev upward and onward. In Alisa's mind, there should be no roadblocks. She remembered first becoming a manager in the Repair Center in 1994, knowing full well that she was on the lowest rung of the hierarchy. Telecommunications was hot and trendy in the 1990s, but repair centers and production lines were not where one advanced a career. Alisa beat the odds. Ready to meet her new challenge, she set her sights even higher, confident that her ambition, coupled with creativity, could dispel the cloud of *lagom*.[1]

In 1998, as the Russian economy was collapsing, Alisa was ascending the corporate ladder and, with each rung she climbed, her self-assurance also rose. By 2000 she could update her nameplate from Manager to Director of Procurement.[2] In 2004, another new title and position—Manager for Global Travel and Group Sourcing, supporting 85,000 employees. She was proud of her innovations, but she kept butting up against the company's stodgy culture, a feature of most Swedish corporations. She was restless, feeling mired in the Swedish *lagom*. The Swedish corporate mindset made Alisa want to scream.

It was time for Alisa to extend her reach beyond Ericsson. She focused on her professional organization ACTE, the Association of Corporate Travel Executives, eventually becoming a director. There, too, she helped initiate new technology like video streaming. She now felt like a world citizen, working with professionals across the globe.

Alisa embraced the opportunity to moderate a panel on business travel to Russia at the March 2007 ACTE Conference. All the key industry leaders would be there, and she knew she could present a stunning and memorable introduction. She enjoyed the freedom of creating a slide show about Russia without the old constraints of Soviet censorship. Or so she thought.

Laughing to herself, she assembled a photo montage of "Russia 2007" with images culled from Google. Featured were Russian leaders from Brezhnev to Putin, scenes from current Russian life, and photographs of two controversial oligarchs—Khodorovsky and Abramovich, both out of favor at the moment. Click, she sent the slide show off in an e-mail message to the panel. Not long afterward, the Russian presenter Yuri called. President of the Russian Business Travel Association, he was ten years older than Alisa. Yuri had worked abroad, was fluent in several languages, and had no sense of humor. To Alisa, those credentials meant former KGB.[3] No question.

Alisa culled these images from the Internet for her ACTE presentation. Note Putin in the upper right hand corner and the imprisoned oligarchs, Khodorovsky in the lower left corner and Abramovich in the lower right corner.

Yuri began in an even tone. "Alisa, you know how I respect you and appreciate all your work. You opened the door to Russia to business travelers. This is a great opportunity for Russian development. But, these pictures, we don't like them." Before Alisa could ask who is "we," Yuri continued his monologue. "This picture of Putin on the same page as Khodorovsky behind bars is not appropriate. Our president would not appreciate that. Why don't you just take out the photos of Khodorovsky and Abramovich? It will be better."

Alisa slammed down the phone. She was fuming. He was threatening her. Putin wasn't her president! *Damn*, she thought, *now I have the KGB after me*. She did not change her photo montage. When it flashed onscreen, she felt a small victory as she observed Yuri's stony silence. She was no longer a Russian citizen, and she would not be intimidated or bullied.

Involvement in ACTE did not eradicate Alisa's restlessness. She acknowledged to herself that Ericsson was a prestigious workplace and, once hired, most people never leave.

But, unlike her fellow workers, Alisa feared stagnation more than change. She knew Ericsson's profits were healthy, and it was going to remain true to the system in place—closed-door management from the top down.

Fortunately, at the same time that Alisa began to feel trapped by the company culture, she was working on a project with an outside consultancy, Travelogica. Alisa collaborated well with the company's head. When Alisa confided she was dissatisfied and felt stuck at Ericsson, he suggested she become his partner.

Alisa sought the advice of the human resources manager at Ericsson. She voiced her ambivalence. "I want a change. On the one hand, I want to leave. On the other hand, why should I give up everything I have?" Alisa thought about all the people dependent on her now—could she even afford to take such a risk? Was it a personal indulgence?

Alisa was surprised by the HR manager's sympathetic response. He encouraged her to talk to a job coach for a few sessions at the company's expense and then decide what to do. What a great country! In Russia, nobody cared about personal fulfillment in the workplace. There were no job counselors to advise you. If you were dissatisfied, no one would pay to help you find a better option. Leaving a secure, comfortable job would have been considered crazy. Alisa eagerly took advantage of the coach's services. His gentle questions and intent listening helped her decide by the third session. She concluded, "I do need to leave."

Alisa became a managing partner in Travelogica. She had never thought of herself as an entrepreneur. Now she was expected to bring in her own clients, which meant developing marketing and sales skills, capabilities she had not learned at the Leningrad Institute of Finance and Economics. She could tap into her network of friends for leads, but that did not feel right. Employing *svyazi* (connections) in Russia had been normal everyday behavior necessary for survival, but in Sweden doing so felt exploitative. She needed to think creatively to find another way to attract clients.

Realizing that companies without a travel and logistics

department frequently turned to temp services like Manpower to fill requirements, Alisa devised a plan mutually beneficial to both Manpower and herself. Manpower referred customers seeking personnel for travel and logistics to Alisa. Manpower received finder's fees for positions notoriously difficult to fill; Alisa's client roster grew, and the customers were satisfied.

Soon Alisa was ready to expand, but her partner was stuck in the *lagom* mindset. A British company seemed like the perfect solution—a *lagom*-free zone. When she had consulted at British Telecom (BT), Alisa had liked the energetic feel of the company. Why not apply? Secure in the knowledge that BT would remember her, she submitted her résumé. As she expected, she was hired as Head of Procurement for the Nordic and Baltic Region. Purchasing anything from travel services to desk chairs to hiring external custodial services was under her purview.

Alisa's thirst for innovation was welcomed at BT. The corporate culture set high targets and encouraged competition. Alisa savored the challenge and met the goals. She proudly remembers reducing BT travel costs by 35% in her first year. Following a series of profitable innovations spearheaded by Alisa, BT offered her an executive position in the London headquarters. Alisa declined. She enjoyed climbing the corporate ladder but not when it meant uprooting

Alisa strolling at home in Stockholm.

her family from Stockholm or commuting to her family on weekends.

Again, Alisa was ready to search for a new job. In April 2010 she made a lateral move to TeliaSonera's Stockholm headquarters where she holds the same position as she had at BT. The corporate ladder was set aside. There were other heights to scale at home.

Notes

1. *Lagom* means just right, just enough, with moderation. It refers more to interpersonal relations and corporate culture than to innovation. A company can be technologically innovative, but the culture can be stuck in old patterns. This was the source of Alisa's frustration with Swedish firms.

2. Procurement: In US firms, this would be the job of the purchasing agent. In her Linked In profile, Alisa describes the job this way:"category management, strategic, tactical, operational sourcing and organisational developments, transformations and start-ups, building-up cross-functional and cross-border collaboration and relationships with key 'stakeholders.'"

3. Russia's security police are now called the FSB, not the KGB, but old habits die hard. Alisa still calls them KGB, believing only the initials have changed.

41

Vera: VeraLex

1998–2007

More powerful than a locomotive
—from the introduction to *Superman*

Vera and Alexei were now independent of Olsen & Company, but they were still hamstrung by the chaos in Russia. As always, almost all of Vera and Alexei's waking hours were spent at the office. Fortunately, Vera was surrounded by her family of employees. None was more trustworthy than Svetlana. Svetlana is tall, striking, smart, and slim. Vera takes credit for Svetlana's figure, saying Svetlana had been chubby before joining Vera in a diet in the early 1990s. Vera credits Svetlana for standing by her through the most difficult years of her life.

Their story captures the roller coaster life in Russia. Svetlana's mother started babysitting Lev when he was three. Intimate with the details of her nanny's family, Vera suggested that Svetlana, whom she deemed "sensible," come work for her. Olsen & Company paid for typing and English lessons to prepare Svetlana to work as Vera's secretary and receptionist starting in 1991.

Svetlana said, "We developed together. There was no structure in the business, and nobody knew what to do. Vera was a locomotive. I tried to help, and it evolved that I took on more and more responsibility." When asked what made her boss successful, Svetlana said, "Her absence of fear, her energy, and her ability to arrange a team of diverse people well. Vera has a lot of intuition and readiness to work hard. I have known 'VeraLex' since they began from nothing. They created a big business from the ground up, and they didn't lose themselves in the process. This is rare." Svetlana said her happiest days with Vera were during the days of the JDC food distribution project. It was a very exciting time. "Vera spread her charisma to everyone." Svetlana served as Vera's junior partner until 2000.

Vera's face contorts in pain as she described the day of the brutal attack. Svetlana's responsiblities had grown, and Vera could depend on her for anything. She was in charge of picking up payroll, which, on this particular day, was $50,000. She stashed the cash discreetly in her purse overnight. The following morning, as always, a security guard was supposed to escort Svetlana from her apartment door to the car. This time, he waited out front. Svetlana locked her apartment door and turned to walk down her dark hallway when she noticed an electrician. *Strange.* Suddenly, he grabbed her with one arm and with his other arm, beat her with brass knuckles, ravaging her beautiful face.

"He was a professional. He knew what he was doing. He was trying to hurt her, but not kill her," Vera said.

The assailant was never caught. While Svetlana suspected the security guard's involvement, Vera found no incriminating evidence. To Vera, it seemed more logical that Svetlana's abusive partner set her up. Compelled to talk through the details of the attack and resolve the issues, Vera visited a weakened and depressed Svetlana almost daily. Svetlana, a much more private person, was not ready. Driven to protect her friend and the company, Vera gave her friend this choice, "Leave this horrible man and return to work. If not, then I must ask you to leave the company." Svetlana had already decided to leave her partner but did not want to do it as a result of an ultimatum. She needed more time to heal. Svetlana spent six months recovering from her physical injuries. It would take far longer to recover from the emotional trauma, which Vera did not understand until years later.

When I touched on the delicate topic of guilt, Vera quickly answered, "I did everything I could for her. The business paid for everything." I asked about the amount of cash Svetlana carried. "Wouldn't that make her an easy target?" Vera is patient with my naiveté.

"Carrying cash is very dangerous, but until recently we could not use any bank transfers, checks, credit cards, or debit cards." In Vera's eyes, Svetlana made the wrong decision. Had Svetlana given up this man, who eventually left her, she would still have her business family and she would have had a million dollars in profit-sharing from the sale of the company.

Meryll and I heard this story when visiting Vera and Alexei at their home outside of St. Petersburg in September 2010. Vera had invited Svetlana to join us. The two women shared their perspectives on the assault of years ago and looked at each other, their eyes welling with tears. We observed moments of silence while their thoughts and feelings traveled the distance from the past to the present. Dining at Vera's house, we could see strong emotions pass between Vera and Svetlana. Svetlana credited Vera with reaching out to repair the friendship a few years earlier. By that time, Svetlana was ready. They resumed their friendship and, eventually, their business collaboration. Today, Svetlana supervises Vera's remaining businesses in Russia.

Just before the assault on Svetlana, Mama Irina, who had suffered for some time with high blood pressure and poorly controlled diabetes, became ill. When Irina was admitted to the hospital, Vera observed the warm and competent attention that a nurse named Zoya bestowed on her mother. Vera's goal was to provide the best care she could at home. She had a knack for recognizing talented and skilled people, finding the perfect position for them, and providing an incentive for them to join her "family." She found the right caregiver in Zoya and also hired her husband to take care of the house, offering them an apartment. Fortunately, she also located a physician she could trust, Dr. Arkady, who lovingly provided palliative care to Mama Irina until her death in 2000. Along with Vera, Dr. Arkady took care of Zoya after she became ill until her death in 2009. Zoya's husband and Dr. Arkady were among the guests Vera brought to the Caymans for her son's wedding. She trusted Dr. Arkady completely until 2011 when he wagered her life for money.

Vera's antidote for emotional pain from losing Svetlana and her mother was hard work. During these years, Vera would continue coming to the States at least once or twice a year. Seeing Caribou and Starbucks coffee stores in Minnesota inspired Vera to imagine a Russian version. Purchasing espresso machines in Minnesota, she trained a staff and set up a coffee cart at the Hermitage Museum and the Moscow airport. The main problems she encountered were price and culture. She said, "We were too early. Why would someone spend that much money for a cup of coffee when they could buy a bottle of vodka?" However, she enjoyed the venture; and, as of 2012, there is still one espresso bar and restaurant in St. Petersburg. The restaurant has the mark of Vera's international style with a menu created by a Minneapolis chef, furniture purchased from Italy, and graphics from a contemporary Russian artist. When in St. Petersburg, Vera conducts her business from the comfort of a booth, glass of wine in hand.

There was still one desire that nagged at Vera. Customs and warehouse work was grueling and sometimes dirty. To be perceived as truly legitimate by the public, Vera had flirted with the idea of owning a publishing house. When a friend approached her with the idea, Vera was ready. "We had extra money and we agreed that a publishing venture would be a good investment and good public relations for the company." She founded a publishing house in 2004, which printed two beautiful, glossy magazines filled with articles from worldwide experts on the topics of business etiquette and human resources, two novel areas for Russian business culture. Vera took pride in the work, and her eyes were the last to edit the copy. Publishing was enjoyable but time-consuming. The magazines were breaking even. It was a labor of love rather than for profit.

Vera's scored a personal victory in late November 2006 when she entered the elite St. Petersburg State University, the same university that had once rejected her, as the sponsor of a conference on business communication. Following the opening address by the vice-president of research at the university, Vera welcomed everyone and participated in a panel. This was exactly the type of opportunity she relished. She had a lot to share from her own experience. She remained visible in the nonacademic business world as well. When an expert panel was formed to select a business executive of the year from St. Petersburg, Vera participated. She was gaining prestige.

Isya finally won the battle to send Lev to a safe haven, which meant that Vera felt split between Minneapolis and Russia. She was relieved Lev was away from the "hooliganism" in Russia, attending boarding school in Minnesota, and parented in abstentia by RD, Lars, my husband, and me. Vera was still involved, talking with Lev daily and visiting a couple of times a year.

Lev and his grandmother had a tender bond.
He left for the US after she died in 2000.

After spending Thanksgiving of 2003 in Minneapolis, Vera and Alexei took Lev on what should have been a dream trip to Hawaii. Vera felt like she was in paradise until she couldn't stop bleeding. She went to the hospital in Hawaii and was told that a hysterectomy was required. Her instinct was to be in Dr. Arkady's care. He would arrange everything. She asked to be patched up enough to make it home. She followed through with the surgery at the end of January 2004.

One week after the surgery, as she was driving into the city for a follow-up visit, she talked Alexei into stopping by the office to check on things before her appointment. She was catching up with her secretary when her brother, Grisha, called from the warehouse to report a fire. Vera's first thought was that she had to be on the scene at the warehouse so that she could handle the questions from the fire inspector. Stitches still intact, wobbling on heels on the icy cobble-stoned St. Petersburg street, she hurried to the warehouse to inspect the damage for herself. The fire affected 200 square meters of the warehouse and destroyed 2,000 tons of leaf tobacco worth three to four million dollars.

Vera and Alexei had just spent three weeks developing and installing new technology. The worst scenario was that the fire might have occurred during the installation, and they might be found negligent, which could cost them two million dollars and bankrupt the company. However, Vera was suspicious of the timing, which coincided with SJS's scheduled inspection. She suspected arson but to prove it, they could not leave the investigation up to the police or the insurance company. Vera and Alexei hired a technical expert. It took four months before the case was settled. The investigation confirmed their suspicion that a competitor had started the blaze, and their insurance reimbursed the business for losses.

Isya, the inner voice of that cautious old Jewish man, was fed up. He was now constantly nagging Vera as were all her friends. "It's time to think about leaving." But she wasn't ready. There was no doubt Isya was right, as always. Her days in Russia were numbered, and she and Alexei should leave before the next disaster, but where would that leave her staff?

Russia was not liberalizing. Putin was elected in 2000 and then re-elected in 2004 on a platform that seemed more Soviet than European. The message was a familiar one. Vera felt that time had gone backward in terms of the limited individual freedoms and the centralization of power. We were afraid she was habituated to a crisis-driven life. She answered that she was just waiting for the right opportunity to leave, and she thought she had found it.

Pavla I was diagnosed with a "false pregnancy," but gave birth to five pups. Once again Russian medicine failed. Alexei was disappointed that his well-bred Pavla could be such a floozy.

42

Vera: The End of an Era

2007–2010

Kuy zhelezo, poka goryacho.
"Strike while the iron is hot."

—Russian proverb

By summer 2007, Vera was finally able to calm Isya, the whiney, inner Jew who accompanied her through life. A newspaper article she was reading mentioned that one of their clients was planning to build a customs terminal. This particular client, a multibillion-dollar firm, was an international leader in supplying auto parts. After verifying the facts, Vera staged a meeting, tantalizing the representative of the firm with a money-saving proposal.

"Why build? Just buy our business," she offered.

"Is it for sale?" the representative asked.

"It depends on the price," Vera countered with a smile.

In April 2008, the deal was closed. According to the Russian business press, the estimated value was $15 million at the time of the sale. After all her effort, all the resources invested, and all of the years of hard work, she now felt validated. Vera whispered to Isya, "See, it was worth waiting," but he reminded her that she was not out of Russia yet.

Vera and Alexei were not yet free. The buyer required that six key employees including Alexei, Vera, and her brother, Grisha, stay for two years. To Vera, receiving a salary as the director and having Alexei paid as operating director sounded good. The deal was great. The work was not. They were used to being entrepreneurs. They already were "VeraLex." No matter how prestigious her title, the job was too reminiscent of the old Soviet work machine. "Working in the corporation, we dealt with exactly the same rubbish as we had twenty years ago before we ran away to create our own company. I could never be a corporate person because I don't want to play by somebody else's rules."

In February 2009, when they were told they would be commuting between the Moscow and St. Petersburg offices, they were not pleased. Like many St. Petersburg residents, they loathed Moscow. They also hated working for bosses who were inaccessible. Vera glowers as she remembers, "It seemed absolutely crazy to us that we would live in a rented apartment in Moscow, a city we both hated, get up at 6:00 a.m., drive an hour to a smelly office, and have nothing to do there." Vera got her way and they returned home, serving the rest of their "sentence" in St. Petersburg. However, they already had their sights set on the faraway islands in the Caribbean, the Caymans.

With their pockets full and the first profits generously dispersed to their employees, Vera and Alexei set up their retirement. The next trip to the United States consisted of a shopping spree that included buying a townhouse for themselves, coincidentally a central location close to Meryll, RD, Lars, and Leslie. This was followed by a trip to the Caymans where they purchased condominiums at the Ritz-Carlton. Living under a Russian economy had taught them that investment in real estate and jewelry made sense and leaving money in banks or the stock market did not. One foot now was in Minneapolis with Lev and one in the Caymans. Vera was on her way out.

43

Alisa: How to Be a Jewish Mother in a Swedish Culture

1996–2011

Enda barn, kärt barn.
"Only child, dear child."

—Swedish proverb

Watching Daniella Gita grow from infancy to adolescence, Alisa repeated the lessons she learned from Naum and Bella.

"My parents taught me values and also to question, analyze the society, read 'in between the lines' of what was published in the Soviet newspaper *Pravda* (Truth) where only a few facts were printed. They taught me by their own example to work hard and take care of family and friends. They taught me to be proud of being Jewish and the importance of remaining Jewish and passing it on to other generations." Alisa summarizes her own philosophy in one simple desire: "I want Daniella to be a good person." The strategic plan was in place for rearing a child, and the primary tactic was clear: be an example for Daniella to emulate. Tactics and strategy may work well in business, but Alisa was to discover that childrearing does not always yield to reason and logic. Alisa's memories of her own rebelliousness may have gone underground.

Rolf and Alisa lavish their love on Daniella while trying to implement their strategic plan. A good person has the strength to stand up for her beliefs, trusts her own instincts, and feels connected to her past. Alisa also wants Daniella to be successful and insists that she study hard enough to earn all A's. The Soviet system didn't apply pressure to students to excel, only to comply. No argument or debate, Daniella must be at the top academically. As a Swedish-born child, Daniella is steeped in the idea of *lagom*, just enough. *Lagom* just won't do in Alisa's eyes.

"*Lagom*. I hate it. It's typical Swedish. *Lagom är bäst*. In between is the best. That's how the Swedish raise kids. Work at your own tempo. You don't need the best scores. You're good at what you're doing. It's the Swedish credo." Alisa is clear; Daniella will be the best.

Naum's categorical imperatives seep into Alisa's consciousness as she lays down the law for Daniella: "Study first, play later."

Daniella has been raised among Swedes, and she is not about to accept categorical imperatives.

"Why can't I study later?"

"Because I said so," responds Alisa in her Naum parenting posture.

When Daniella questions and analyzes, Alisa smiles to herself and at Rolf. They are raising a child who knows how to question, to think for herself. It may create Alpine highs and Death Valley lows in her teen years, but Rolf and Alisa plan to enjoy the roller coaster journey so that Daniella can emerge an independent and strong woman.

"Daniella, never give up—everything is possible, the impossible only takes longer." How many times did Alisa repeat her motto to Daniella? When she was ten, Daniella found a way to load the phrase as ammunition against parental arguments. Daniella wanted pierced ears. Among her girlfriends, everyone had pierced ears and a startling array of earrings. She took the measure of her parents and decided her dad was less likely to issue an unqualified "no." Daddy was the weak link. Daniella approached him and in her sweetest voice asked, "May I get my ears pierced?" She held her arguments in reserve.

Rolf peered up from his reading and with kindness replied, "No, Daniella."

Before she could marshal her arguments, Rolf continued as if addressing a dental seminar. "Daniella, you have a serious skin allergy. The most recent academic studies show that ear piercing will aggravate your condition. It is not recommended." Rolf did not spare her the scientific details. These did not convince Daniella. She pleaded, cried, lobbied, and wheedled, but Rolf was not moved.

Exhausted, Daniella turned away from Rolf and asked Alisa the question. Alisa, well-schooled in the divide and conquer tactic of making demands of parents, responded with, "What did Daddy say?"

Daniella reported the negative response and Alla advised her daughter, "Crying, demanding, and carrying on won't work with Daddy. You have to think about what arguments Daddy will respond to. Your arguments are all emotional, but Daddy isn't persuaded by emotion."

Daniella said nothing and retreated to the computer. She returned to Rolf thirty minutes later waving a sheaf of papers. "Daddy, I found new research that says there is a safe way to pierce the ears of girls who have allergies like mine." Rolf scanned the article, assessed that the study was valid, but still said no. Alisa watched the scene unfold. Daniella had discovered precisely how to counter her father's academic protests—find an academic argument. Alisa now knew how it felt to be confronted by her own motto, "never give up" and a daughter's indomitable will. Alisa said to Daniella, "Let's find a time to get your ears pierced safely." In the end, Daniella had divided and conquered.

Like most twenty-first century parents, Alisa wants to avoid mistakes her parents made. Remembering her lack of sex education, Alisa determined to do better with Daniella. Swedish schools include sex education in their curriculum, but in a society where teens as young as fourteen are sexually active, Alisa decided better too much than too little. Neither Rolf nor Alisa felt comfortable with "the talk." They agreed

Alisa would set up an appointment for the "full briefing" with a physician friend who headed the children's clinic. Alisa and Rolf hope she won't be swayed by peer pressure or hormones now that she knows the facts of life.

Raising Daniella as a committed and knowledgeable Jew is a priority for both Rolf and Alisa. Even without much intellectual grounding in Judaism, Alisa kept an emotional connection to her people and religion throughout her life. Daniella could learn and be part of the community from her earliest years. Like her father, Daniella attended the Hillel Academy, the Jewish Day School until sixth grade. When Daniella began first grade at Hillel Academy, she was flush with excitement. "It's the best, look what I know! Why didn't you send me there for pre-K instead of sending me to Swedish daycare?" This was the best possible reaction Alisa could have hoped for.

By the time Daniella was in second grade, Alisa began hearing rumors from other Hillel parents that the school was slipping. There was talk that the Jewish Studies principal wasn't maintaining the expected academic rigor. Hillel Academy was not on par with Swedish public schools. Alisa wanted the best for Daniella and for her community. No *lagom* here. It was time for action. Alisa was moving up at Ericsson, but there was no question for Alisa—there had to be enough time for her career and for Daniella. She brought her formidable business skills and energy to the board of the school.

Besides developing an approach to upgrade the school's academic program, Alisa had to face her fear of being labeled an outsider in the insular Stockholm Jewish community. Alisa brushed away her apprehension as well as the resurgence of lonely memories and plunged into the work of bringing immigrant students into the mainstream and weaving them into the community. She dubbed herself the "integration minister of Hillel Academy" and told the board, "You have to teach the new immigrants, you can't just treat them as second-class students."

Daniella did complete sixth grade at the vastly improved Hillel Academy and along with most of her classmates moved into the Swedish school system for junior high school. Although there were 1,000 students in the junior high Daniella attended, the Hillel graduates remained a cohort thanks to the Swedish school system, which provided Hebrew and Judaica teachers for them along with a kosher kitchen and eating area.

Alisa's dream of moving to Israel was diverted, but she and Rolf have traveled to Israel with their daughter so that Daniella can feel the connection with her Jewish homeland and meet Rolf's Israeli relatives who live in a comfortable suburb of Tel Aviv, as well as Alisa's relatives who immigrated to Israel and live in a hardscrabble settlement outside Jerusalem. Daniella complains to Alisa about her Russian roots; they embarrass her. Alisa is confident "she will get over not liking her roots. She needs a solid base to know her heritage, to know who she is."

While Rolf and Alisa can accept some of the typical teen angst, Alisa laid down the law about Daniella visiting her ailing grandmother. Naum's death in 2006 left Bella bereft, and subsequent strokes robbed her of her vitality. Until fourth grade, Daniella spent all her after-school time with her grandparents, painting and chattering away in Russian with them. By 2010 she refused to speak Russian and refused to visit Bella.

"Daniella, it's not a choice. This is serious. You are going to see your grandmother, or you are grounded." Alisa assumed her "no excuses allowed posture" each time she repeated this.

Daniella would grumble as they walked the three blocks to Bella's apartment. Alisa carried chicken soup to her mother remembering how many times Bella walked with soup over thirty-five years ago for Alisa when she was a new bride in Leningrad. Seeing both her daughter and granddaughter, Bella would smile, her light green eyes would sparkle, and she would straighten her back. It pained Alisa to see her mother suffer, and she guesses that Daniella also suffered witnessing her grandmother's decline. But, no excuses, she had to visit Babulla Bella. In February 2012 at the time of Bella's final hospitalization, Alisa again stood, arms akimbo with her feet planted firmly and told Daniella there was no choice—she was going to visit Babulla in the hospital.

*Six months before her death, Bella's eyes lit up
when she saw Alisa's childhood photos.*

Not only does Alisa push Daniella, she expects to keep
her close. "The Swedish way is to expect independence."
Statistics show most Swedish children leave home by age
eighteen. Some leave sooner.[1] They are expected to make it
on their own. The Russian way is to "take a whip" but then
continue to embrace your children and care for them well into
their adulthood.

Daniella, a striking beauty and avid soccer fan, is now
in high school. Alisa looks ahead to the future. Where will
Daniella study? What will she study? Will she marry under a
ḥuppah? Alisa announces, "I need to put some effort in that. I
need to have a plan."

Fifteen years ago, Alisa proclaimed she would never
move again. She is comfortable almost anywhere in the world,
but she has built a life in Stockholm. Now she wavers as she
thinks ahead. "If Daniella decides to study elsewhere, I'll
move." She can remember the feeling of waving good-bye to

her own parents in Leningrad in 1986. She said a final good-bye in 2006 to Naum and in 2012 to Bella. No more good-byes.

The Bornstein family in 2013.

Note

1. Robinson and Carr, *Modern Day Viking*, p. 59.

44

Vera: VeraLex in the Caymans

Spring 2011

I want to be driven.

—Ivan, the chauffeur

Whenever I skype Vera at her island home, I am interrupting. She is about to stroll on the beach, go out on the boat, exercise at the Ritz Spa, grocery shop, or dig in her garden. If I call in the evening, she and Alexei will no doubt be breaking open an expensive bottle of wine at dinner with friends. Vera pursues these pleasures with the same vigor with which she attended to business. Vera is on a diet and exercise regimen. She announces her weight loss during each call to me. She recommends that I do the same. She poses for me over Skype to show her toned figure.

These days I see an expression of relaxation and mirth on Vera's face. What Alisa would call the "soft Vera." Only a few topics challenge that happiness. The first subject—the garden—represents a mixture of victory and defeat recalculated on a daily basis. For the first time since she was thirteen, Vera is gardening. To her surprise, she is joyful at rediscovering the wonder of playing in the dirt and creating something. She cares for her flowers much as she cares for her employees, tending to their every need and making sure they are happy. They are not. A war has developed. Vera is the battle commander in this war of the flowers against the iguanas. So far, the iguanas reign victorious. She thought she chose iguana-proof flowers; she planted them in the front, then transplanted them all carefully into the backyard, but alas, the iguanas invaded with their stealth troops. Recently, a new battalion of enemies strutted through her gardens—the wild chickens that populate the island, digging wherever they please.

Whenever Vera turns her camera on her home, it looks immaculate, light with brilliant greens and blues flooding in. I imagine the fragrance of the greenery and feel the humidity as I peer through the glass doors toward the water.

Vera is learning to balance. No matter how wonderful and loving she is, and how true a friend she would like to be, her life has been consumed with work to the exclusion of nearly any other interest. Vera was center-stage, and the rest of us were supporting actors or audience members. This past year, Vera has had time to sit back and listen, and to share her experiences in a much deeper way than in the past. Vera and I are getting to know each other anew much as we did over thirty years ago by long and frequent exchanges of the most personal information and viewpoints. We are trying to make our lives less foreign to each other. At one time I seemed exotic to Vera. Now I probably strike her as boring—I drive the same car, live in the same house, am married to the same husband, and have the same job. It is not easy to convey to Vera the nuances of growth in my life, the joy that Meryll and I have shared in reviewing our lives together, and planning the upcoming trip to St. Petersburg and Stockholm, our first sister adventure together. There is a delicate balance of power between Vera and me. Vera is not an easy critic, and I am sensitive to her need to be understood and respected.

Vera can't let go of business yet so our conversation always gravitates to that topic. Vera is running her remaining businesses from afar, with a total of fifty-six employees spread among a restaurant, dental clinic, security company, and construction business. She thinks for a moment and then tells me she forgot to include the temp agency that she also owns. The evolution from a hands-on director to a long-distance owner/investor, who cannot monitor her employees' moods and desires has not been a natural one for Vera.

Vera describes the typical dynamic between employer and employee with an anecdote. There was a boss who for years had a chauffer named Ivan in his employment. Ivan was an excellent driver but chronically unhappy. Feeling responsible, the boss said, "Ivan, let me help you put your children through a good school." Ivan agreed, but he remained morose. The boss then suggested, "Ivan, let me buy you an apartment." Ivan let his boss buy him a nice apartment, but still he was sad. The boss gave Ivan a very nice raise, but Ivan continued to be despondent. Finally, the boss said, "Ivan, I have tried my best to help you solve your problems. What more do you need to be happy?" Ivan looked wistfully at his boss and said, "I want to be driven."

This sums up the irony. Employees want the perks of being the boss but not the responsibility for doing the hard work, making personal sacrifices, or making decisions according to Vera.

"If you read Russian fairy tales, you will see that they are all about getting the best effortlessly. It's the self-cooking stove, the self-serving tablecloth, the golden fish. It is about miracles providing the outcome, not hard work."

Most Russians find the concept of private ownership befuddling according to Vera. Accountability does not translate. That a manager is accountable to a director, accountable to a CEO, accountable to a board, or accountable to stockholders is an unwieldy and inconvenient arrangement. Vera feared that their businesses would be untenable now unless she could entice Svetlana to take charge. The idea that Svetlana would gain financial security and that Vera and Alexei would gain a trustworthy manager was her favorite kind of win-win solution.

Vera's inner voice Isya has been subdued in the Caymans. Traveling back to Russia induces anxiety. Vera doesn't need Isya to warn her of possible attacks. Even though the sale of their business was conducted aboveboard, blackmail is widespread and easy. "There is no doubt that we are safer in the Cayman Islands than in Russia."

If you could choose your citizenship, where would you go? For Vera and Alexei, this question is neither sentimental nor idealistic. It is practical. She chose a country I had never heard of—the West Indies islands of St. Kitts and Nevis. With no criminal record, referrals, and a donation of $200,000 to a government fund, citizenship could be theirs without even a visit to the island. Until then, they remain at the mercy of the Russian government. It is striking that Vera and Alexei, who were born in a country of 8.6 million square miles chose citizenship on an island of 65 square miles, about the size of Lake Ladoga outside St. Petersburg. To us, this is a strange way to choose a new homeland. Vera and Alexei have had enough of this homeland idea, and it's worn them down. They just want to live the rest of their lives in freedom with a minimal tax burden. Lev can pay US taxes. Perhaps when there are grandchildren, they will reconsider.

Meanwhile, Vera has not retired. She and Alexei have five holding companies, three apartments, one house, and a candy store. RD wants to tear his hair out that Vera invested so much on one Caribbean island. She's not concerned. Hurricanes don't scare her. I ask Vera when she will learn how to drive. She shakes her head and dismisses the idea. That's Alexei's job. She likes to be driven.

Vera and Alexei entertain RD and Lars aboard their yacht,
their favorite pastime.

45

All of Us: St. Petersburg Summit

September 2011

The Soviet Union is dead and communism long-buried. But Mr. Putin wants you to know that the Russian bear is back—wearing a snarl with designer sunglasses.

—The Economist[1]

September 9, 2011

As Meryll and I entered St. Petersburg, I felt like I was stepping into a revolving door, rotating me between the gray, hard-pressed city of 1977 and the seemingly prosperous European metropolis of 2011. The country had moved from the regime of the old Soviet cadre to the rule of Medvedev and Putin. For Meryll, the iron curtain was rising to unveil an enchanting city familiar from books and photographs. Meryll had met Vera a few times, but this would be her first meeting with Alisa, who had shared her secrets with Meryll over the past fifteen months via Skype and already felt like a friend.

The apartment telephone rang. Meryll looked to me to answer. In rusty Russian, I said *Slushayu vac* ("I hear you"). Vera announced her presence outside our courtyard. We hurried through many doors and down the dark stairwell with its lingering odor of urine. I ran ahead to open the wrought-iron gate protecting the apartment complex's courtyard. My first words tumbled out to an unappreciative Vera, "I can't believe we are meeting on a street corner in St. Petersburg after thirty-five years!" Vera's expression burst my exuberance.

Vera warned, "I am not the happy Vera today."

With each tap of her burgundy heels on the broken cobblestones, we heard Vera's recitation of the to-do list. In the next few weeks she would be closing her office and businesses, selling her house, distributing her belongings, saying her goodbyes, finding a home for her dog, and undergoing minor surgery. We had been so enthusiastic about the book project that we had forgotten the imposition we were placing on Vera. Just driving into the city from her Razliv home was a one-hour enterprise, and Vera wasn't sure she had time for all this sentimentality.

We were soon seated at Roma — Vera and Alexei's restaurant, just outside the city center. Vera and Alexei simultaneously checked on quality control and greeted customers and associates. Vera revealed the itinerary.

"Logistics is everything," she told us more than once.

First stop on Friday after Alisa's arrival from Stockholm, Vera told us, would be the Jewish cemetery.

September 10, 2011

Through the drizzle we rode in a taxi for miles, following the banks of the Neva River until we reached St. Petersburg's biggest Jewish suburb—the Preobrazhensky Cemetery. This swampy, remote location alongside the railroad tracks has been the final address of St. Petersburg's Jews since 1874. In front of our cab, a shiny, black SUV was parked. From the back emerged curly-haired Alisa, petite and fashionable. She smiled. Meryll recognized her and ran to embrace her. After all, Meryll and Alisa, whose intimacy was forged by modern technology, felt like long-lost friends. Uncensored e-mail messages and Skype would have been science fiction to Vera and me thirty-five years ago.

I faced the bearish gray-haired man standing next to Vera.

"Do you recognize me?" he asked in Russian.

I squinted to try to make the face young again. I shook my head no.

"It's Grisha, my brother," Vera said.

I drew a deep breath and shouted, "Grisha," while I fast forwarded from the thiry-one-year-old Grisha to Grisha today at sixty-five. As he smiled, I remembered him as gentler and warmer than Vera's recollections had conjured up.

Vera led us into the densely packed cemetery with markers poking above the ground like unruly teeth. Some of the dead occupied front row spots along the street behind the wobbly wrought-iron fences, but most were shoved to the back rows forcing a grieving relative to step on the neighbors and climb through overgrown hedges just to check the "addresses." Vera and Alisa had business to attend to. They were hunting for the graves of their family. We first came across the gravesite of Mama Irina and her childless sister, Lusya, who died in her twenties. Even in death Mama Irina was caring for others.

Alisa found her grandparents' grave and gently placed stones atop the monuments stroking the curve of the marble.[2] A tear escaped her eye. We have spent hours listening to tales of Mattus and Rosa and felt their presence, too. The moment was recorded with a click.

"Bella will want to see a picture of this. Did I tell you I used to come here with my dad on Sundays and play with my brother like it was a park? It's been thirty-five years since I was here."

*Alisa fulfills a promise to her mother
to visit the graves of Bella's parents.*

Vera finally found Papa Misha's grave through the overgrowth. A scream pierced the sound of the soft pattering rain.

"Grisha! The marble is ruined." He rushed over. "How could you let this happen?" Grisha was used to this berating tone from his younger sister.

In a distraught voice he responded, "It wasn't like this in April."

She stated emphatically to all of us, "My job is to take care of the living, and Grisha's job is to take care of the dead. I cannot leave this cemetery until I know exactly who will fix this and when."

Noticing Grisha's stooped shoulders, we sensed his embarrassment as the two returned with the timid caretaker. The drizzle became a downpour. We flipped our hoods over our heads and watched Vera instruct the caretaker shaking her index finger. Even at 5'3" Vera was formidable. Alisa empathized with Vera about her responsibility to her parents, given her plan to leave Russia permanently.

Alisa thought she had left Russia permanently, handkerchief in hand, blowing her nose and feeling wet to the core. She had nearly cancelled because she was so sick. Rolf's persistent urging had pushed Alisa forward. Absolutely, this was her last visit to St. Petersburg, she told us decisively.

Within fifteen minutes, everything was arranged. The gravesite would be cleared, and the stone would be repaired. Grisha would check up on everything after Vera returned home to the Caymans. We walked behind Vera and Alisa wending our way out of the dismal cemetery. The two friends strolled arm-in-arm, heads tilted toward each other, earnestly conversing. In the next two days, we would follow their story, retrace their steps, and listen to them chart their hopes for the future. The first piece of business was done.

September 11, 2011

When Saturday came, our feet hit the pavement. From every possible angle, Vera had questioned to see if we could be driven instead. "No. Meryll keeps Shabbat," I told her. She had appealed to RD by phone, who echoed, "No, Meryll keeps Shabbat."[3] We agreed to meet at synagogue on Saturday morning at 11:00 a.m.

I had last been in this building when it was dark and held just barely a *minyan* of older men murmuring,[4] a few *babushki* chattering, and a KGB minder observing.[5] That morning, children raced around our legs as we headed upstairs to the balcony. From the women's balcony, we had a full view of the renovation that transformed the previously decaying space into one alive with spirited chanting and illuminated by golden light.

Alisa and Vera slipped into our pew. Meryll and I glanced at them, checking their footwear. Flat shoes, good. They were not used to being pedestrians in St. Petersburg. Once seated, tears filled Alisa's eyes as she absorbed the changes in the Grand Choral Synagogue. Vera's silver sneaker began tapping faster and faster as she glanced repeatedly at her watch and asked, "How long do we have to be here?"

Alisa admonished her friend, "You should be more appreciative of the role Judaism has played in your success. Can you deny that everything you did in life came from being Jewish? It's part of your DNA."

Vera defended herself. "I just need to prepare myself to know how long we'll be here. I don't feel anything. I don't deny my Judaism. I'm not religious." The hushed voices and gesticulations flew fast. Ignoring the shushing around us, Vera turned to me and, with a glimmer in her eye, said, "I just realized that I don't need to think about whether I deny or accept being Jewish. Maybe I just need to be thankful for this Jewish part of me."

Despite her newfound gratitude, Vera was still eager to leave. Vera's wish was granted, and we left to explore Alisa's old neighborhood. Vera's mood remained somber while Alisa became more animated, throwing her arms from side to side

as she pointed at windows and doorways which opened into recollections. As we entered the once elegant vestibule at #54 Dekabristov, Alisa pointed to signs of deterioration in the hall. Alisa scurried up the stairs stopping on the landing to admire the view through the tall French windows. Here was the courtyard scene of her childhood antics.

When we reached the third floor and apartment #16, I rang the bell three times. We had come a long way, and we

Alisa and Vera standing with the synagogue off to their right. Vera and Alisa point out the window across the street where the KGB set up surveillance during Simḥat Torah.

The once elegant building is now marked by graffiti along the marble staircase and broken windows. Common areas are neglected now as they were in Soviet times.

were eager to see the interior. Vera and Alisa held back. I had forgotten that despite the Russian graciousness with friends, even in the new Russia, knocking on anyone's door could be viewed as reckless. A fortyish Russian man opened the door cautiously while his five-year-old daughter peeked between his legs. He shook his head at Alisa as she explained, "I grew up in this apartment."

"You must be mistaken because I have been here since I was a young boy."

They did the math and realized that it was his father who bought the apartment from Naum and Bella. He warmed to us and ushered us in. "This is just half of the original apartment. My brother lives on the other side." We entered a high-ceilinged room filled with light. Alisa pointed to the outlines of the swans on the ceiling, now barely visible, and to the shelves Naum had built into the closet. Alisa laughed and gestured with delight as she narrated the scenes that unfolded within these walls.

Inside, the apartment is airy, spacious and filled with light.

As we left the building, Vera voiced the reason for her melancholy. "My environment was gloomier—the apartment, the street. The first time I went to your house, Alisa, I felt like I was visiting a museum. Mine was like a poor *intelligentsia* house."

Vera enters her old apartment house with dread.
She is flooded with sad memories.

*For the first time Leslie understood how imprisoned
Vera felt during her years on Blokhina.*

Vera's comments hung in the air. After Alisa flew home, we would walk through Vera's old neighborhood to her apartment building on Blokhina. The contrast was stark, and we began to understand the lack of nostalgia. Vera had no interest in seeing her old apartment. She slumped and shrank back after walked into the building, pointing out the decay. She begged me not to knock on the door. Once she was at a safe distance, she said, "My life was not fun." Like a festering open wound, her anger against the system seeped out. "It was so hard to have dignity." For Vera, this visit elicited despair from the deep well of grief over the grueling hardships that shortened her parents' lives.

*After visiting Alisa's apartment,
Vera's mood was somber.*

Our foursome continued the Saturday walk over the canal to Alisa's English language school, identical to Vera's on the other side of town. Following lunch at the posh Astoria Hotel, where Alisa could finally have Russian mushroom soup, we trekked to the Institute of Finance and Economics still well protected by the two golden griffons on each side of the bridge and a drunken guard inside the door. Vera and Alisa laughed and reminisced, Alisa scowling at a poster announcing a dance for first year students. "A dance! Oy, we were sent out to the countryside to dig up potatoes."

By 4:30 the rain convinced Vera it was time to go to one of her favorite spots, a bubble in the midst of St. Petersburg, the café at the Grand Hotel Europa. Before entering the café, we stopped to view the art deco, formal dining room where Vera and Alexei held their wedding reception. As we mounted the stairs to the balcony, Alisa

Poster from the Institute for Finance and Economics advertising a freshman dance with DJ in 2011.

reminded Vera, "I don't remember being invited." They recalled the tensions that arose the year before Alisa "disappeared." Alisa and Vera were discussing the Alexei factor. Alisa had been afraid to tell Vera about her plan to escape from Russia, fearing that Alexei would divulge the information to others. Vera explained Alexei's ideological evolution and assured Alisa that his apology at the St. Petersburg dinner twenty years ago was completely his own initiative. Alisa's curls bounced as she absorbed this startling new insight.

We adjourned to the atrium café with its murals of St. Petersburg's Italianate pastel buildings while we sipped our ten-dollar tea. By now, we looked and sounded like four sisters: our hands in motion, our conversation revealing an outpouring of our hearts. The morning conversation resumed with me lecturing Vera that she could not remove her Jewish identity like an unfashionable coat. Alisa joined the offense—"Don't you feel your Jewishness?"

Alisa and Vera are outraged in 2011 when they see how current Institute students are babied with a party heralding the new school year. They remember mandatory work harvesting potatoes on a collective farm.

Perhaps in revenge for the one time I was treating, Vera added a $100-shot of Jack Daniels to the bill. She was irritated. Three against one. She was tired, so tired of having to explain that she didn't feel Jewish. Culturally, she was Russian *intelligentsia*. Spirituality had never gotten her anywhere as far as she was concerned. She was suspicious of all religion. She didn't need a community, just her family and good friends. She wanted to change the subject, but she didn't want to be rude. Vera folded her arms, sighed, and explained. "There is a huge gap in my understanding. I don't feel part of a Jewish collective or of Jewish spirituality. Maybe my family was too underground. There was no tradition passed on. But I feel comfortable inside of myself and quite happy to have just one Jew inside me."

Alisa's head snapped up as she removed the cookie from her mouth. "This is new?"

"Yes, the one Jew inside me is Isya, my inner voice. For some reason, he is male, very afraid, and whiny. He protects me. That voice has been there all along. I just didn't know how to represent it until recently when Leslie asked me about it."

Alisa nodded, fascinated about this newly revealed Jewish part of Vera.

Vera succeeded in changing the conversation by remarking that she just noticed that I was the fattest of the four of us. Sarcastically, I thanked Vera for bringing this to my attention and assured her that I would be on the lookout for fatter friends. Six months later on a trip to Minneapolis, Vera apologized for the remark. She had replayed the conversation and realized that she had felt attacked and I was the easiest target for retaliation. I loved Vera for her honesty and self-reflection.

Back to our little table at the overpriced café in St. Petersburg. *What about the future?*

Alisa presented her ten-year plan—ten more years of work and then, if Daniella stays in Sweden, she and Rolf will remain. If not, they will follow Daniella. In addition, she would like an apartment in Israel. Alisa turned abruptly to Vera and predicted, "I don't see you in the Caymans in ten years. You'll get bored."

"We cannot be bored with the joy we have there." Her voice softened as she explained how she and Alexei are learning to do tasks for themselves that they had previously delegated. If they are bored, they can pursue business partnerships as they already have with their island candy store and real estate investments.

Alisa was still not convinced and repeated a phrase Vera had heard before. "You're living in a bubble on a pirate island." Vera reminded her friend that Alexei likes to be in a bubble. The Lexus, the four-star hotels, their St. Petersburg restaurant, and the Razliv and Cayman homes were all part of the bubble.

She didn't deny it. She agreed that Alexei and she created a private, comfortable world and operate best this way. Alisa admitted, "I forgot about Alexei. He might enjoy being there 'in nowhere.' As for me, I will not grow old in Sweden. Both the community and weather are too cold. Enough of being an outsider."

Vera returned to their earlier discussion. She felt like an outsider also. "That's what drove me to the Cayman Islands where there are no distinct identities. All the population consists of outsiders."

"Bubble island and pirates," Alisa remarked carefully rearranging the silverware on her saucer.

Vera retorted that she's looking forward to returning to her beautiful bubble island after her minor medical procedure. Alisa touched Vera's hand and anxiously questioned why she would have any medical procedure in Russia. Vera reassured her she had ultimate faith in her Russian doctors and felt comfortable. It was nothing to worry about. Alisa gave her the familiar look, peering skeptically over the top of her glasses with pursed lips, indicating she could not change Vera's mind, but she did not approve.

September 12, 2011

Our weekend together ended on Sunday. Alexei chauffeured us to Pulkovo Airport to drop off Alisa, and the conversation switched to Russian. Now that Vera was leaving, she no longer defended Russia. She sadly agreed with Alisa, "It will never be better here," she says. "The country has lost its track forever. There is no civil society, no people's will. Putin holds all the cards."

Alexei added that he, too, felt strange here now. "I don't even know who to bribe anymore." Alisa sighed with relief. The argument about leaving Russia was over.

Alexei pulled into the parking lot at Pulkovo. We hugged Alisa and then Vera and Alisa clung to each other before posing for photos. They agreed—they will never ever meet again in St. Petersburg.

Notes

1. "Putin's People," *The Economist* (August 25, 2007): http://www.economist.com/node/9687285.

2. Placing a stone on a grave is a symbolic act indicating the deceased has not been forgotten.

3. One aspect of Shabbat observance means no driving or riding in vehicles from sundown Friday to after sundown on Saturday.

4. A minyan is the quorum (ten men) required for a Jewish prayer service. In some synagogues women can be counted as part of the quorum but not in this synagogue.

5. As a matter of course, every synagogue had a KGB operative lurking inside during the services. It was not a secret to congregants because his presence would deter many Jews from participating in religious services.

46

Leslie: Rupture in St. Petersburg

October 16–November 14, 2011

Prishla beda, otvorya i vorota.
"Trouble is coming. Open wide the gates."
— Russian proverb

Just a month after our return from St. Petersburg, I found myself staring at the autumn sunset over Lake Calhoun through the windows of RD and Lars's penthouse. This was my first visit with RD since my trip to Russia with Meryll, and our mood was grim. Now he paced the parquet floors repeating, "I can't believe it . . . I can't believe it." *Vera brought us together again,* I thought, waiting for RD to settle in one spot. Lars was working late as usual across the street at his architecture firm. But for the last few days, he and RD had talked of almost nothing else but Vera.

"A minor cosmetic surgery," she had assured us when RD, Alisa, and I separately questioned the wisdom of undergoing any medical procedure in Russia because the system was rife with incompetence. As in all other aspects of Russian life, *vranya* (deception) pervaded the hospital. Vera believed that her special relationship with Dr. Arkady exempted her from danger. After all, she had trusted Dr. Arkady with her family's health for years and provided perks to seal his loyalty, such as flying him to the Caymans for her son's wedding.

However, days after the original surgery, Vera's condition was grave. She was unresponsive on a ventilator, in the second day of a coma. She had survived four subsequent surgeries, each leading to another set of serious complications.

"Vera would be so angry if she died in Russia!" I said to RD. He was used to my lack of logic and heard the love, fear, and anger in my voice. "She can't—not now, not at the brink of finally getting out of the damned country. Meryll and I are her biographers and this is not the way the story is supposed to end."

RD and Lars had already reached the same conclusion. "Lev needs to fly home now. Don't wait. Tell him to fly home even if Alexei doesn't agree." Alexei was under siege. We guessed he couldn't think beyond the tunnel vision of Vera's daily care. Frantically trying to save Vera, he had little patience for anyone who could not provide concrete help in the form of muscle or scarce medicine. Phone calls were strained and e-mails were not answered. Vera was the engine of Alexei's life; they had functioned as VeraLex for years, but now their son needed to join them.

RD phoned Lev. He was awaiting directives. Usually, those came from his mother, but in this case, RD filled the parental role. Through all these years of separation from his parents, Lev had talked to his mother almost nightly. Last week had been unbearable with no contact and no clear idea of her prognosis. What he heard from Alexei were heavy sighs and terse medical reports alternating with combat tactics against the doctors.

Lev despised traveling on a Russian passport, but this time it enabled him immediate entry to St. Petersburg. The rest of us would have been delayed for days or weeks waiting for a visa.

Leaving RD's home, I drove the half mile from Lake Calhoun to Cedar Lake to reach the townhouse purchased by Vera and Alexei for their son and daughter-in-law. I had a good excuse to stop over. I was late for Lev's twenty-fifth birthday and had collected some gifts for him over the last few months: a bottle of wine, a miniature golden-edged picture book of cars purchased at St. Petersburg's *Dom Knigi* (House of Books), a print-out of an online conversation from five years ago, detailing how his life was over because he had not been accepted to Macalester College. The most precious items I delivered were family pictures and Vera's childhood sketchbooks, produced at the command of her grandmother at the dacha. Vera had given these treasures to me for safe-keeping since she would be packing everything up in Russia and arrive in Minneapolis soon. Soon? Lauren and Lev paged through the drawings, smiling at her "bourgeois" sense of style even then, as she dressed Dickens characters elegantly during the fashion-phobic Soviet era.

Lev called Dr. Arkady for the latest medical report. Rather than a fatherly, loving tone, which one would have expected from their family friend, Arkady sounded defensive and nervous on the speaker. *Slozhno* ("it's complicated"), he repeated throughout the conversation. Dr. Arkady lamented "Your mother had lost so much weight, and I told her not to have the surgery, but she insisted. She has the best doctors, the best care," Arkady intoned. "Your mother had diverticulitis. The colon had ruptured itself. A colostomy had to be performed. Now she has peritonitis."

When he hung up, we stared at each other in disbelief. Vera did not force the surgeon's hand. Nor did we believe Dr. Arkady had diagnosed diverticulitis. If she had diverticulitis, shouldn't Dr. Arkady have prevented the surgery. A clear case of *vranya* (deception). Did he expect us to pretend that we believed him? We agreed he was covering up. That much was clear. "The colon ruptured itself." Doubtful. Our bet was that the surgeon had nicked it.

In Stockholm, Alisa, geographically the closest to Vera, was the most in the dark. I had been e-mailing her. She had just telephoned a pessimistic Alexei and was informed of vague details but heard Alexei's anger clearly. I texted her that Lev was on his way.

"If he were my son, I would have sent him yesterday. Will Vera make it?" she typed.

"It will take a miracle," I typed back. "I hope Lev will be that miracle."

Alisa had also contemplated visiting Vera, but with a new job, a teenage daughter, and a dying mother, she was pulled in so many directions. She, too, would need a visa, requiring precious time.

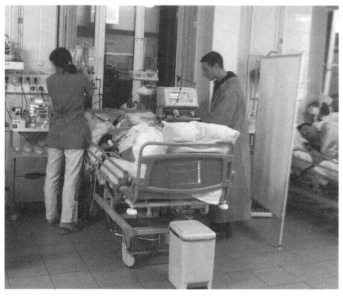

When Lev saw his mom just three weeks earlier in St. Petersburg, she was healthy. Now she was in a coma. "Just pray," the doctor told him.

Once Lev arrived in St. Petersburg, we received specific information from Lauren. Lev described an "awful, dirty, public clinic" in need of *remont* (repair). In fact, they were renovating right next to Vera's room in Intensive Care, and the paint fumes were suffocating. She shared a room with three others, one of whom was still intoxicated and moaning loudly. Alexei informed Lev that Vera was barely responsive over the last few days. Lev walked in cautiously and spoke gently to his mother, who looked so pale and small. Vera squeezed Lev's hand and tears welled in her eyes. The nurse ordered Lev to leave so she would not be further upset.

Lev guardedly reported improvement day by day, but the doctors refused to be hopeful. Then, on October 21, Vera's fifty-fifth birthday, the ventilator was removed and she breathed on her own. Coincidentally, that year, her birthday fell on Sim<u>h</u>at Torah, the one holiday when Jews had felt free to dance in the streets in the Soviet Union. Vera wouldn't have been interested in that. But perhaps Isya, her internal Jewish man, was. Then, there was Meryll who prayed for Vera's recovery in morning services. Vera would have hated that.

After we heard that Vera was questioning Lev about his job and whether he could take so much time off, we were convinced of real improvement. The best news—she was hungry. No doubt Alexei would make the broth himself. He would not trust anyone else to cook food for Vera. After she ate, we all breathed a sign of relief, except Dr. Arkady, who refused to confirm the positive prognosis saying these were just "subjective indicators."

On Sunday the twenty-third, Vera resurrected herself. We knew first by Lev's message that she was sitting up, eating more, and talking on the phone. She was also moody, a good sign. Disgust and anger fuel Vera. After spending a week grieving his imminent loss, RD received a text with an order from Vera: "Call me." Vera's voice was raspy from the tubes, and her thinking was not as clear as usual, but her words rang out "Never again." We hoped that meant no more medical procedures in Russia. From that moment, Vera, appalled by her surroundings, took charge, demanding a private room. She contacted each of us, one by one, to tell us that contrary to Dr. Arkady's wishes, she survived.

On November 14, after five weeks of hospitalization, we received good and bad news. Vera was being discharged. However, Vera would not be leaving Russia soon because in four months she would undergo one more surgery—to repair the colostomy. She assured us she trusted her new surgeon completely. RD,

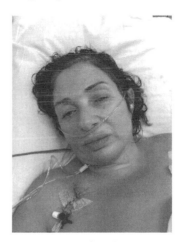

Vera emerging from her coma on her fifty-fifth birthday.

Lars, Alisa, and I wanted to scream, but Vera was back in the director's chair.

"This is what I dreamed," Vera recounted.

47

Vera and Alisa: Epilogue

March 22, 2012

Elämä on epävarmaa, syö jälkiruoka ensin.
"Life is uncertain so eat your dessert first."
—Finnish proverb

As they had vowed in September 2011, Alisa and Vera were not meeting in St. Petersburg. They were fortunate to be meeting at all. Life had derailed the women with plans. Both were in pain. On this cloudy March morning, reuniting in Helsinki, even for five hours, would be healing.

This time, Alisa took charge of logistics, arranging to meet Vera at Helsinki Central Railroad Station on platform eight at 1:00 p.m. sharp. Nervous about seeing her old friend in fragile health, Alisa managed her agitation by attending to details, the same coping strategy that sustained her through her mother's final months. Alisa's morning arrival at Helsinki Airport gave her time to busy herself in planning the day. She ensured her hotel room would be available if Vera needed to rest following her journey. No doubt the luxurious Hotel Kämp was the right place for lunch. With its commanding view of the Esplanade Park and neoclassical brick facade, it resembled their usual haunts.

Vera looked back just once as she left St. Petersburg after her six-month long nightmare. As she and Alexei pulled out of the drive from their Razliv home, her dog Pavla's ears stood up as if this were her final departure. Once aboard the Allegro train to Helsinki, Vera could feel her hands tense as she thought about how she would narrate the story of her brush with death. All these months she had listened to Alexei's version, stifling her own feelings. It would be a relief to unburden herself to Alisa.

When Alisa saw Vera emerge from car number two, she burst into tears. Vera's eyes mirrored her friend's, but this time the tears were equal parts joy and sorrow. Since their last meeting, both women had confronted mortality. Alisa's mother had died. Vera had battled for her life. They needed to hold each other. Talking was not enough. Before embracing, they stepped back to take the measure of each other. Vera saw Alisa in gray tones. All the vibrant color had drained from her. Alisa saw "soft Vera" before her, a frail Vera. But, thank God, she was alive.

Arms linked in their usual fashion, the women unwrapped their sorrows to each other. Alisa's pain is common to all children who have lost their last beloved parent—the escalating medical crises before one watches helplessly as one's parent slips away in a hospital room. Only forty-four days had passed since Bella's funeral, and the wound was raw. Vera had seen her own mother suffer through her last years and understood. She said the right things. "There is no more suffering. Now Bella and Naum are again together."

When she added, "Perhaps they are with Misha and Irina," Alisa smiled, thinking that Bella wouldn't be so keen on that reunion. Vera knew what it was to feel orphaned. Both women had lovingly shouldered the responsibility for their parents for so many years and death brought loneliness rather than relief.

They moved to their table at the Hotel Kämp and pushed their chairs closer together. Alisa leaned over to Vera and asked, "I thought this was minor surgery. How did it all go so wrong?"

Vera's face turned ashen. "It was awful. You can't imagine."

For almost four hours sitting in the subdued quiet of the restaurant, she walked Alisa through the horror. Vera felt she had been in good hands with a surgeon she trusted. But the family physician, Arkady Nikolaevich, referred her to a different doctor, one they now understood provided a kickback to him. Alisa remembered her first impression of Dr. Arkady at Lev and Lauren's wedding—*a bizarre man!*

"When I went under for surgery, I was sure that I'd be out of the hospital in less than a week. But I awoke in a filthy ICU room in pain next to a screaming drunk. I developed a fever, and the doctors just kept telling me 'This is normal.' Then the most disgusting thing, my colon 'ruptured itself,' and I was back in surgery. Four surgeries in one week. Imagine, my poor body. The final blow was that I developed sepsis and lapsed into a coma. The doctor said my chances were slim. As you can imagine, Alexei was beside himself. He was standing outside the ICU unit saying 'Verochka, don't leave me.' What would Alexei do if something happened to me? Then, on the sixth day of the coma, I saw Lev by my bedside. He was so scared."

"Arkady Nikolaevich piled lie upon lie. He counted on me dying and covered up for the other surgeon."

Alisa shook her head in disgust. This type of *vranya* was so much a part of Russian life.

"Alisa, nothing has changed since Soviet times. You wouldn't believe the bribes and threats that Alexei had to pump into the greedy hospital system to get results. We even had to rely on Moscow friends to bring me medicine."

"But, it got worse." She described how Tolya, who had once driven the red Ferrari, provided the muscle. "While Tolya was in a hospital bed dying of cancer, his nephew visited the surgeon's office to inform him that he would cut off his hands if I died. Arkady and the surgeon were conspiring to transfer me to a different hospital so that I would not die on their watch."

Alisa squeezed her friend's hand, sharing her agony, thinking *You can't take life for granted.* Alisa now better understood Alexei's abruptness on the phone. She imagined his vigilant watch over Vera. He would not have let Vera eat a bite of food that wasn't prepared by him.

"After I came home, Alexei continued to watch over me and feed me. He developed rituals. He would not take a bite until I finished. Then he opened a bottle of wine and recited a monologue, the same every night, describing every aspect of the past months, reliving the trauma until I finally said, 'I can't stand it anymore.'"

Still concerned, Alisa asked about her current health. Vera assured her that the final surgery last month was successful. "This was my typical 'Jewish luck' before my final exit from Russia," she said "Perhaps, for the next few years, I will be free of drama."

Before they left the restaurant, Vera presented Alisa with a dark blue, velvet box. Alisa opened it to find earrings and a matching ring gleaming with delicate diamonds. She gasped. She was anxious. *Perhaps Vera was still very ill.* Vera stroked her hand. "This is what I would do if I had a sister, and you are the closest to a sister I have. I bought these pieces to complete a set that RD and Lars gave me. I kept the necklace and bracelet from them, and I want you to have the other half of the set. You see, together, we are complete."

Together with their husbands, Vera and Alisa celebrated the arrival of 2013 in the Caymans. It was the first time they had ever been together for New Year's.

Truthiness(Methodology)

There's method to our madness
—Paraphrased from Shakespeare

Notes on Our Process

No matter how improbable these events may seem to the reader, according to our sources, they all occurred. Like Vladimir Nabokov, we commanded Vera and Alisa: "Speak, Memory." Then the philosophical questions breached the dike, and we were inundated with doubt—how accurate is memory? Is anyone's memoir or autobiography factual?

After much debate among our editor, trusted friends, and the two of us, we arrived at the decision to call our work "memoir." We have done our best to echo the voices and tones of Vera and Alisa.

We interviewed Vera and Alisa weekly for a year, either by Skype, e-mail, phone, or in person. They were beyond generous in opening their lives to us. We interrupted them endlessly with picayune and metaphysical questions and every type of question in between. We sent them a rough draft as soon as we finished a section, and they commented as quickly as they could. As much as possible we verified and augmented their memories through interviews with others. Still, all of the telling depends on perception and memory. Some of the conversations were reconstructed to reflect the emotions reported to us by Vera and Alisa. Whenever possible, we used Vera and Alisa's words as they remember them. Leslie kept a diary during her two summers in the Soviet Union and the accounts of meeting Vera and her family are based on these entries. Isya is a special "character," and we could not possibly have invented him. He exists for Vera, so that's how he is presented.

We also had excellent sources a few miles from our homes. Lars Peterssen and RD Zimmerman have known Vera since the 1970s, hosted her, visited her in Russia, and invested in her projects. They kept us on track throughout our writing process by clarifying and explaining the complexities of Vera's business ventures. They also have superb memories. We had easy access to Vera's son Lev and fact-checked with him and his wife.

The most exciting methodological approach was traveling to St. Petersburg and Stockholm. Early in our research we justified the necessity for this trip. We followed the trails of Vera and Alisa in St. Petersburg (formerly Leningrad) and listened carefully as the city spoke to them. In Stockholm we traipsed around Alisa's new life, enjoying her Östermalm neighborhood. We talked to many people in both cities including the women's older brothers who generously shared their impressions and memories.

We based the historical synopses on compilations from a myriad of sources. Wherever possible, we used information made available after some of the Soviet archives were opened in 1991. We list these sources in the bibliography. We did not provide an endnote for each source, so if you recognize Richard Overy next to Gal Beckerman in conjunction with Hedrick Smith, you are probably correct and well-read. Statistics from the Soviet Union are notoriously inaccurate. We provide statistics that we consider to be the most accurate.

Notes on Our Title

Jewish Luck is an intentionally provocative title. During our early interviews with Vera she would recount a series of misfortunes, click her tongue and say, " It's my Jewish luck." Curiosity led us to a Soviet propaganda film, *Jewish Luck*

(Yiddishe Glickn, directed by Alexis Granowsky, Moscow, USSR: Goskino, 1925), based on a Sholom Aleichem story. The intended message of this film subtitled in Yiddish is that the unfortunate lot of Jews will improve under communism. You probably know how that turned out.

Notes on the Transliteration

We are grateful Swedish is written in Roman characters. Hebrew, Yiddish, and Russian words all presented special problems. For Hebrew, we use *ḥ* to indicate the guttural *ḥet* and *kh* to indicate *khaf.* When the silent *ayin* or *alef* appears at the beginning or end of a word, it is not indicated in the transliteration. When either one appears in the middle of a word, it is indicated by an apostrophe. We make no distinction between *samekh* and *sin.* For *tsadi* we use *ts.* For Yiddish transliterations, *kh* is used for either a *ḥet* or a *khaf.* For Russian, we followed the Library of Congress standards with a few simplifications for readability. Alisa transliterates her father's name as Belenkij, which is different than our transliteration. Rolf Bornstein proofread the Swedish but if there are errors, we claim them.

Bibliography

Tzay ul'mad.
"Go forth and learn."

—Passover Haggadah

Albats, Yevgenia. *The State within a State: The KGB And its Hold on Russia Past, Present, and Future.* New York: Farrar, Straus, Giroux,1994.

Alexander, Robert (pen name for RD Zimmerman). *The Kitchen Boy: A Novel of the Last Tsar.* New York: Viking Press, 2003.

———. *Rasputin's Daughter.* New York: Viking Press, 2006.

———. *The Romanov Bride.* New York: Viking Press, 2008.

Alexeyeva, Ludmilla, and Paul Goldberg. *The Thaw Generation: Coming of Age in the Post Stalin Era.* Boston: Little, Brown and Co. 1990.

Althaus, Frank, and Mark Sutcliffe, eds. *Petersburg Perspectives*. London: Fontanka, 2003.

Altshuler, Mordechai. "Some Statistical Data on the Jews among the Scientific Elite of the Soviet Union." *Jewish Journal of Sociology*, 15 no. 1 (June, 1973): 45–56.

Ålund, Aleksandra, and Carl-Ulrik Schierup. *Paradoxes of Multiculturalism*. Brookfield, VT: Gower Publishing Company, 1996.

Andrew, Christopher, and Oleg Gordievsky. *KGB: The Inside Story*. New York: HarperCollins Publishers, 1990.

Ashwin, Sarah, ed. *Gender, State and Society in Soviet and post Soviet Russia*. London: Routledge, 2000.

Azbel, Mark Ya. *Refusenik: Trapped in the Soviet Union*. Boston: Houghton Mifflin Company, 1981.

Backstein, Joseph, Ekaterina Degot, Boris Groys,and Olga Sviblova.. *Glasnost: Soviet Non-Conformist Art from the 1980s*. London: Haunch of Venison, 2010.

Barnes, Andrew. *Owning Russia. The Struggle over Factories, Farms, and Power*. Ithaca, NY: Cornell University Press, 2006.

Beckerman, Gal. *When They Come for Us We'll be Gone: The Epic Struggle to Save Soviet Jewry*. Boston: Houghton, Mifflin Harcourt, 2010.

Beizer, Mikhail. *The Jews of St. Petersburg. Excursions through a Noble Past*. Translated by Michael Sherbourne. Philadelphia: Jewish Publication Society, 1989.

Berliner, Joseph S. *Factory and Manager in the USSR*. Cambridge, MA: Harvard University Press, 1957.

Bruni, Attila, Silvia Gherardi, and Barbara Poggio. *Gender and Entrepreneurship*. London: Routledge, 2005.

Buckley, Mary, ed. *Perestroika and Soviet Women*. Cambridge: Cambridge University Press, 1992.

Bonnell, Victoria. "Russia's New Entrepreneurs" in Victoria Bonnell and George Breslauer, *Russia in the New Century: Stability or Disorder*. Boulder, CO: Westview Press, 2001.

Bridger, Sue, Rebecca Kay, and Kathryn Pinnick. *No More Heroines? Russia Women and the Market*. London: Routledge, 1996.

Brown, Archie. *The Gorbachev Factor*. Oxford: Oxford University Press, 1996.

Buckley, Mary, ed. *Post Soviet Women from the Baltic to Central Asia*. Cambridge, UK: Cambridge University Press, 1997.

Clowes, Edith W. *Russia on the Edge: Imagined Geographies and Post-Soviet Identity*. Ithaca, NY: Cornell University Press, 2011.

Cohen, Stephen F. *Failed Crusade: America and the Tragedy of Post-Communist Russia*. New York: WW Norton, 2000.

———. *The Victims Return: Survivors of the Gulag after Stalin*. Exeter, NH: Publishing Works, 2010.

Cook, Linda J. "Brezhnev's Social Contract and Gorbachev's Reforms." *Soviet Studies* 44, no. 1 (1992): 37–56.

Eaton, Katherine Bliss. *Daily Life in the Soviet Union*. Westport, CT: Greenwood Press, 2004.

Edmondsom, Linda, ed. *Gender in Russian History and Culture*. Hampshire: Palgrave, 2001.

Engel, Barbara Alpern. *Women in Russia: 1700–2000*. Cambridge, UK: Cambridge University Press, 2004.

Etzioni-Halevy, Eva, and Zvi Halevy,. "The Jewish Ethic and the Spirit of Achievement." *Jewish Journal of Sociology* 19 no. 1 (June, 1977): 49–66.

Field, Mark G., and Judyth L. Twigg. *Russia's Torn Safety Nets*. New York: St. Martin's Press, 2000.

Froese, Paul. *The Plot to Kill God: Findings from the Soviet Experiment in Secularization*. Berkeley: University of California Press, 2008.

Gaidar, Egor. "From Central Planning to Markets: Transformation of the Russian Economy" in *Conversations with History* video series. Berkeley: Institute of International Affairs, University of California. Recorded on November 26, 1996.

Gessen, Masha. *Ester and Ruzya: How My Grandmothers Survived Hitler's War and Stalin's Peace*. New York: Dial Press, 2004.

———. *The Man Without a Face: The Unlikely Rise of Vladimir Putin*. New York: Riverhead Books, 2012.

———, ed. *Half a Revolution: Contemporary Fiction by Russian Women*. Pittsburgh, PA: Cleis, 1995.

Gilbert, Martin. *Atlas of Russian History*. New York: Oxford University Press, 1993.

———. *Jewish History Atlas*. New York: Collier Books, 1969.

———. *The Jews of Hope*. New York: Viking Penguin, 1984.

———. *Russian History Atlas*. London: Weidenfeld and Nicolson, 1972.

Gitelman, Zvi. *A Century of Ambivalence: The Jews of Russia and the Soviet Union.* New York: Yivo Institute, 1988.

Goldman, Marshall. *Petrostate: Putin, Power and the New Russia.* Oxford: Oxford University Press, 2008.

————. *What Went Wrong with Perestoika.* New York: WW Norton, 1991.

Gorokhova, Elena. *A Mountain of Crumbs.* New York: Simon and Schuster, 2009.

Goscilo, Helena, and, Stephen M. Norris. *Preserving Petersburg.* Bloomington: Indiana University Press, 2008.

Grekova, I. (Yelena Sergeyevna Ventsel). "The Hairdresser" in *Russian Women, Two Stories.* San Diego, CA: Harcourt, Brace, Jovanovich, 1983.

Hoffman, David E. *The Oligarchs. Wealth and Power in the New Russia.* New York: Public Affairs, 2002.

Iossel, Mikhail. *Every Hunter Wants to Know: A Leningrad Life.* New York: WW Norton, 1991.

Isham, Heyward, and Natan Shklyar, eds. *Russia's Fate through Russian Eyes: Voices of the New Generation.* Boulder, CO: Westview Press, 2001.

Jacoby, Susan. *Inside Soviet Schools.* New York: Hill and Wang, 1974.

Kamali, Masoud. *Distorted Integration: Clientization of Immigrants in Sweden.* Uppsala: Uppsala Multiethnic Papers, 1997.

Karlovna, Evelina Vasilieva. *The Young People of Leningrad.* White Plains, NY: International Arts and Sciences, 1975.

Keep, John. "Gorbachev Era in Historical Context." *Studies in East European Thought* 49 no. 4 (December 1997): 271–86.

Klier, John D., and Shlomo Lambroza. *Pogroms: Anti-Jewish Violence in Modern Russian History*. Cambridge, UK: Cambridge University Press, 1992.

Klimontovich, Nikolai. *The Road to Rome*. Chicago: Northwestern University Press, 2004 (part of Glas New Russian Writing, #35).

Klugman, Jeffrey. *The New Soviet Elite. How They Think and What They Want*. New York: Praeger Publishers, 1989.

Kochan, Lionel. *The Jews in Soviet Russia Since 1917*. London: Oxford University Press, 1972.

Koval, Vitalina, ed. Women in Contemporary Russia. Providence, RI: Berghahn Books, 1995.

Kotkin, Stephen. *Uncivil Society: 1989 and the Implosion of the Communist Establishment*. New York: Modern Library, 2009.

Lapidus, Gail Warshofsky. *Women in Soviet Society*. Berkeley: University of California Press, 1978.

Ledeneva, Alena V. *How Russia Really Works: The Informal Practices That Shaped Post-Soviet Politics and Business*. Ithaca, NY: Cornell University Press, 2006.

Lovell, Stephen, *Destination in Doubt: Russia since 1989*. London and New York: Zed Books, 2006.

———. *Summerfolk: A History of the Dacha 1710-2000*.Ithaca, New York: Cornell University Press, 2003.

———. *The Soviet Union. A Very Short Introduction*. Oxford: Oxford University Press, 2009.

Mandelbaum, Michael. "Political Reforms Caused the Collapse of the Soviet Union" in *The Break up of the Soviet Union*, William Barbour and Carol Wekesser, eds. San Diego, CA: Greenhaven Press, 1994.

Matisoff, James A. *Blessings, Curses, Hopes, and Fears: Psycho-ostensive Expressions in Yiddish*. Stanford CA: Stanford University Press, 2000.

Matthews, Mervyn. *Education in the Soviet Union. Policies and Institutions since Stalin*. London: George Allen and Unwin, 1982.

Medvedev, Roy. *On Soviet Dissent*. New York: Columbia University Press, 1980.

———. *Post Soviet Russia: A Journey through the Yeltsin Era*. New York: Columbia University Press, 2000.

Miller, Jack, ed. *Jews in Soviet Culture*. London: Transaction Books, 1984.

Montefiore, Simon Sebag. *Stalin: In the Court of the Red Tsar* New York: Knopf, 2004.

Morawska, Ewa. *Insecure Prosperity: Small Town Jews in Industrial America*. Princeton, NJ: Princeton University Press, 1996.

Morozov, Boris. *Documents on Soviet Jewish Emigration*. London: Frank Cass, 1999.

National Intelligence Estimate [CIA] "The Deepening Crisis in the USSR: Prospects for the Next Year." 4: 11-18-90, November 1990. Available from https://www.cia.gov/library/center-for-the-study-of-intelligence/csi-publications/books-and-monographs/at-cold-wars-end-us-intelligence-on-the-soviet-union-and-eastern-europe-1989-1991/16526pdffiles/NIE11-18-90.pdf

Oettingen, Gabriele. "Explanatory Style in the Contest of Culture" in G. M. Buchanan and M. E. P. Seligman, eds. *Explanatory Style*, 209–23. Hillsdale, NJ: Erlbaum, 1995.

Oren, Dan A. *Joining the Club: A History of Jews and Yale.*, 173-214. New Haven,CT: Yale University Press, 1985.

Orttung, Robert. *From Leningrad to St. Petersburg: Democratization in a Russian City.* New York: St. Martin's Press, 1995.

Overy, Richard. *Russia's War.* New York: Penguin Books, 1998.

———. *The Dictators: Hitler's Germany and Stalin's Russia.* New York: WW Norton, 2004.

Penninx, Rinus, and Judith Roosblad. *Trade Unions, Immigration and Immigrants in Europe 1960-1993.* New York: Berghahn Books, 2000.

Petrovsky-Shtern, Yohanan. *Jews in the Russian Army 1827–1917.* New York: Cambridge University Press, 2009.

Pinkus, Benjamin. *The Jews of the Soviet Union.* Cambridge, UK: Cambridge University Press, 1988.

———. *The Soviet Government and the Jews. 1948–1967.* Cambridge, UK: Cambridge University Press, 1984.

Popov, Vladimir. "The State in the New Russia (1992–2004) from *Collapse to Gradual Revival?* PONARS (Program on New Approaches to Russian Security) Policy Memo 342. Washington, DC: Russian and Eurasian Program at the Center for Strategic International Studies, November, 2004.

Pred, Allan. *Even in Sweden.* Berkeley: University of California Press, 2000.

Prozorov, Sergei. *The Ethics of Postcommunism.* London: Palgrave-Macmillan, 2009.

Pryce-Jones, David. *The Strange Death of the Soviet Empire.* New York: Metropolitan Books, 1995.

Pushkareva, Natalia. *Women in Russian History.* Translated by Eve Levin. Armonk, NY: M.E. Sharpe, 1997.

Rabe, Monica. *Living and Working in Sweden.* Göteborg: Tre Böcker Förlag, 1994.

Rai, Shirin, Hilary Pilkington, and Annie Phizacklea, eds. *Women in the Face of Change. The Soviet Union, Eastern Europe and China.* London: Routledge, 1992.

Reid, Anna. *Leningrad: The Epic Siege of World War II, 1941–1944.* New York: Walker, 2011.

Remnick, David. *Resurrection: The Struggle for a New Russia.* New York: Random House, 1997.

Rhodes, Richard. *Arsenals of Folly: The Making of the Nuclear Arms Race.* New York: Alfred A. Knopf, 2007.

Riasanovsky, Nicholas. *A History of Russia*, 6th ed. New York: Oxford University Press, 2000.

Robinson, Christina Johansson, and Lisa Werner Carr. *Modern Day Viking: A Practical Guide to Interacting with Swedes.* Yarmouth, ME: Intercultural Press, 2001.

Robinson, Logan. *An American in Leningrad.* New York: WW Norton, 1982.

Roi, Yaacov, ed. *Jews and Jewish Life in Russia and the Soviet Union.* Essex, UK: Frank Cass, 1995.

Rosenberg, Chanie. *Women and Perestroika.* London: Bookmarks, 1989.

Roxburgh, Angus. *The Strongman: Vladimir Putin and the Struggle for Russia.* London: I.B. Tauris, 2012.

Rusinek, Alla. *Like a Song, Like A Dream: A Soviet Girl's Quest for Freedom.* New York: Charles Scribner and Sons, 1973.

Sachar, Howard Morley. *The Course of Modern Jewish History.* New York: Dell Publishing, 1958.

Salisbury, Harrison E. *The 900 Days: The Siege of Leningrad.* New York: Harper & Row, 1969.

Sawyer, Thomas E. *The Jewish Minority in the Soviet Union.* Boulder, CO: Westview Press, 1979.

Sebestyen, Victor. *Revolution 1989: The Fall of the Soviet Empire.* New York: Pantheon Books, 2009.

Shevtsova, Lilia. *Lonely Power.* Washington, DC: Carnegie Endowment for International Peace, 2010.

Sholom Aleichem. *The Adventures of Menahem Mendl.* Translated by Tamara Kahana. New York: G.P. Putnam and Sons, 1969.

Shtern, Ludmilla. *Leaving Leningrad.* Hanover, NH: Brandeis University Press, 2001.

Shturman, Dora. *The Soviet Secondary School.* Translated by Philippa Shimrat. London: Routledge, 1988.

Silberman, Charles. *A Certain People: American Jews and their Lives Today,* 51-57. New York: Summit Books, 1985.

Simon, Gerhard. *Nationalism and Policy toward the Nationalities in the Soviet Union.* Boulder, CO: Westview Press, 1991.

Smith, Hedrick. *The Russians.* New York: New York Times Books, 1983.

Smith, Hedrick. *The New Russians.* New York: Random House, 1990.

Spufford, Francis. *Red Plenty.* Minneapolis, MN: Graywolf Press, 2010.

Stotland, Ezra. *The Psychology of Hope.* San Francisco: Jossey-Bass, 1969.

Taubman, William. *Khrushchev: The Man and His Era.* New York: W.W. Norton and Company, 2004.

Taylor-Gooby, Peter, ed. *Welfare States under Pressure.* London: Sage Publications, 2001.

Ulitskaya, Ludmila. *Sonechka.* New York: Schocken, 2005.

Varese, Federico. *The Russian Mafia: Private Protection in a New Market Economy.* Oxford: Oxford University Press, 2001.

Veidlinger, Jeffrey. *Moscow State Yiddish Theater: Jewish Culture on the Soviet Stage.* Bloomington: Indiana University Press, 2000.

Volkogonov, Dmitri. *Autopsy for an Empire: The Seven Leaders Who Built the Soviet Regime.* New York: Free Press, 1998.

Volkov, Solomon. *St. Petersburg: A Cultural History.* Translated by Antonina W. Bouis. New York: Free Press, 1995.

Volkov, Vadim. *Violent Entrepreneurs: The Use of Force in the Making of Russian Capitalism.* Ithaca, NY: Cornell University Press, 2002.

Wilmers, Mary-Kay. *The Eitingons: A Twentieth Century Story.* London: Verso, 2010.

Wiseman, Richard. *The Luck Factor: Changing Your Luck, Changing Your Life: The Four Essential Principles.* New York: Hyperion Books, 2003.

Wright, Rochelle. *The Visible Wall: Jews and Other Ethnic Outsiders in Swedish Film.* Carbondale: Southern Illinois University Press, 1998.

Zimmerman, R. D. *Blood Russian.* New York: Ballantine Books, 1987.

————. *The Cross and the Sickle.* New York: Kensington, 1984.

————. *The Red Encounter.* New York: Avon Books, 1986.

Films

12, directed by Nikita Mikhalkov. Moscow: Federal Agency for Culture and Cinematography, Studio Trite, and Three T Productions, 2007.

Brother, directed by Aleksey Balabanov. Moscow: Gorky Film Studios, Kinikompaniya CTB, Roskomkino,1997.

Commisar, directed by Aleksandr Askoidov, Moscow: Gorky Film Studio, 1967.

Harbour of Hope (Hoppets Hamn), directed by Magnus Gertten. Sweden: Magnus Gertten and Lennart Ström for Auto Images, 2011.

The Irony of Fate, directed by Eldar Ryaznov, Moscow: Bazelevs Productions, Channel One Russia, 1975.

Jewish Luck (Yiddishe Glickn), directed by Alexis Granowsky, Moscow: Goskino, 1925.

My Perestroika, directed by Robin Hessman, Red Square Productions, Bungalow Town Productions, 2011.

Nina Resa, directed by Lena Einhorn. Stockholm: East of West Film, Svensk Film Industry, 2005.

Office Romance, directed by Eldar Ryaznov. Moscow: Mosfilm, 1977.

Appendix

Maps

The Jewish Pale of Settlement

Vera and Alisa's grandmothers were born in Gorodok, a shtetl in the province of Vitebsk.

Leslie and Meryll's grandmother was from the town of Ekaterinoslav in the province of the same name. When our grandmothers were born in the early 1900s, 21,000 Jews lived outside the Pale of Settlement in St. Petersburg – the largest enclave of Jewish settlement outside the Pale.

THE PALE 1835–1917

0   200
Miles

St.Petersburg

1891. 2,000 Jews deported, many of them in chains

1855. Open to Jews

Moscow

1891. 20,000 Jews expelled

Baltic Sea

GERMANY

KOVNO

VITEBSK

SUWALKI

VILNA

MOGILEV

PLOCK

LOMZA

GRODNO

MINSK

KALISZ

WARSAW

SYEDLITZ

PIOTRKOW

RADOM

LUBLIN

KIELCE

VOLHYNIA

CHERNIGOV

Brody

Kiev

KIEV

POLTAVA

AUSTRIA

HUNGARY

PODOLIA

EKATERINOSLAV

BESSARABIA

KHERSON
Nikolaev

RUMANIA

TAURIDA

Sebastopol   Yalta

Black Sea

Principal town from which in 1880 began the exodus of over two million Jews from the Pale to the United States, Britain, Europe, South America, and Palestine

In 1882 500,000 Jews living in rural areas of the Pale were forced to leave their homes and live in towns or townlets (shtetls) in the Pale. 250,000 Jews living along the western frontier of Russia were also moved into the Pale. 700,000 Jews living east of the Pale were driven into the Pale by 1891

The Pale of Settlement, Russian Jews confined to this area by laws of 1795 and 1835. By 1885 there were over 4 million Jews living in the Pale

Towns within the Pale barred to Jews without special residence permits

© *Martin Gilbert 2010.*

Figure B. 1978 Map of Leningrad (CIA-Public Domain)

The Soviet Union carefully guarded the distribution of city maps lest they reveal any strategic location. Part of the CIA's task in the Cold War was to create city and regional maps. Alisa's neighborhood was in the area south and west of the Astoria Hotel. Nevsky Prospekt is marked on the map. The Institute of Finance and Economics is just north of Nevsky Prospekt which is Leningrad/St. Petersburg's Fifth Avenue.

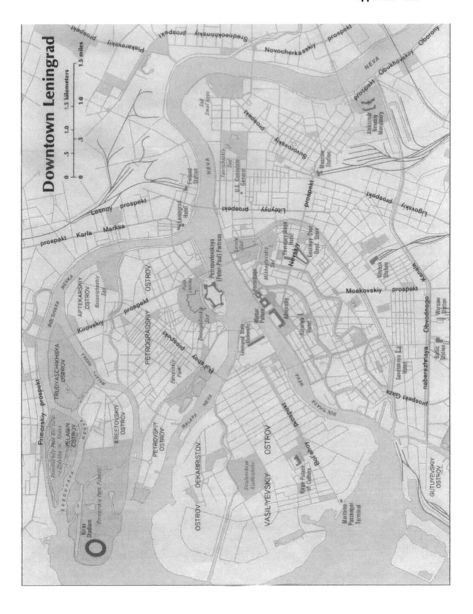

Figure C. Map of the Baltic Region

St. Petersburg (at the extreme right of the map) is at approximately the same latitude as Stockholm. Both cities are defined by their links to the water. The weather and the topography are similar but the feel of the two cities is very different.

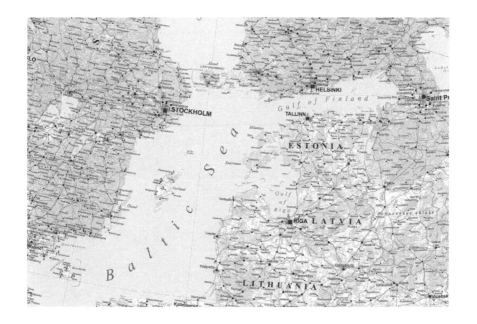

Acknowledgments

Skoro skazka skazyvayestya, da ne skoro delo
delaetsya.
"The tale is told quickly, but the job is done slowly."
—Russian proverb

We were never able to distill *Jewish Luck* into a simple
elevator speech. However, as soon as we launched into the
complicated précis; it was as if we had skipped a stone into the
water to find a never ending ripple effect. Listeners seemed to
extend the words further connecting to a personal insight or
story shared with us. What a delightful, unexpected gift!

First and foremost, thank-you Mom and Dad. You
prophesied that when we grew up, we three siblings would be
best friends. We know Dad is smiling and holding his brother's
hand beyond the grave as he watches us lovingly fight and
write. Mom was one of our first readers and has encouraged
our dream from the start.

Minneapolis is a city that nurtures its writers. We availed
ourselves of free workshops from the Loft and the resources of
the local libraries. Hennepin County Libraries—we couldn't
have done it without you! Pen Pals, MPR's Talking Volumes,
and the St. Paul JCC book talks inspired us.

The OLLI Memoir Writing Group helped Meryll

revise and rewrite monthly. We are deeply grateful to our developmental editor, Patricia Francisco, and our first readers who gave us valuable feedback: Lisa Katz Shimoni, Laurie Bangs, Lynne Ackerberg, and RD Zimmerman. We thank our friends and colleagues for their valuable advice: Dr. Marjorie Bingham, Dr. Riv-Ellen Prell, Dr. Phyllis Deutsch, Soni Cohen, Michael Cohen, and Debbie Orenstein. Thanks to the Twin Cities book groups and the Seacrest community of Encinitas, California who invited us to read before the manuscript was published. We are lucky to have enlisted a team of professionals who moved us seamlessly from manuscript to book: Leslie Rubin, Scott Edelstein, Patti Frazee, and Cathy Spengler.

We are grateful to all those we interviewed in St. Petersburg in 2011. We appreciated our time with Grisha and his family and Vera's friend, Svetlana. Alexei was crucial to driving this project forward. Thanks also to Nadezhda Simonovna as well as extraordinary hosts, Volodya and Sveta Manovich. To Rolf Bornstein, Daniella Bornstein, Gera Belenky, Cantor Maynard Gerber, and Lena in Stockholm— thank-you for your time and insights. We are grateful to have met Bella before her death. Closer to home, we thank Bob Hazen in Portland, Oregon for his memories. Thanks to the Copen brothers of Tupelo, Mississippi for sharing stories and video. To RD and Lars, as ever, we appreciate your generosity, encouragement, and suggestions. Thank-you for the ultimate trust of letting us include you in the story. Thanks to Lev and Lauren for your perspective and enthusiasm and your beautiful wedding, which inspired the idea. Lev and Lauren, along with Daniella, gave deeper purpose to our project. *L'dor vador.*

Leslie: I extend my love and deep appreciation to Vera who started the whole process by adopting me into her family and truly being an open book. In a land of *vranya*, Vera is transparent and remains the most spellbinding storyteller I know.

To my husband, trusted reader, critic and friend, Harry Adler, thank-you for your kindness and tolerance during three years of preoccupation. Thanks to Harry and my children, Isaac and Maya, for being the most important part of my story.

Meryll: Thanks to Alisa for being a friend and teacher

over the course of the book, slowly opening her life and digging into painful memories as well as celebrating joyous ones.

For three years, talk of *Jewish Luck* swirled around our families. In the tradition of Ecclesiastes, my husband, Christopher Page, and my children and grandchildren have understood there was a time to offer help and hugs and a time to withhold advice. Excellent judgment, family!

And, finally, we are forever grateful to be sisters.